The New Griffon 12

ATHENS 2011

HIDDEN TREASURES
AT THE GENNADIUS LIBRARY

THE GENNADIUS LIBRARY
AMERICAN SCHOOL OF CLASSICAL STUDIES AT ATHENS

The New Griffon • 12
«Κρυμμένοι Θησαυροί της Γενναδείου Βιβλιοθήκης»
Περιοδική έκδοση της Γενναδείου Βιβλιοθήκης
Αμερικανική Σχολή Κλασικών Σπουδών
Σουηδίας 61, Αθήνα, 106 76
Τηλ.: + 30 – 210 – 72.10.536 / Fax: + 30 – 210 – 72. 37.767
http: // www.gennadius.gr

Επιμέλεια: Μαρία Γεωργοπούλου, Ειρήνη Σολομωνίδη
Μετάφραση - Διόρθωση: Stefanie Kennell
Επιμέλεια Έκδοσης - Συντονισμός για τη Γεννάδειο Βιβλιοθήκη: Μαρία Σμάλη

Σχεδιασμός, Παραγωγή και Κεντρική Διάθεση: Εκδόσεις Δημ. Ν. Παπαδήμα
Ιπποκράτους 8, 106 79 Αθήνα
Τηλ.: + 30 – 210 – 36.27.318 & 36.42.692
Fax: + 30 – 210 – 36.10.271
http:// www.papadimasbooks.gr

The New Griffon • 12
"Hidden Treasures of the Gennadius Library"
A Gennadius Library Publication
American School of Classical Studies at Athens
61 Souidias Street, Athens, GR 106 76
Tel.: + 30 – 210 – 72.10.536 / Fax: + 30 – 210 – 72. 37.767
http: // www.gennadius.gr

Editing: Maria Georgopoulou, Irini Solomonidi
Translation - Copyediting: Stefanie Kennell
Proofreading - Coordination for the Gennadius Library: Maria Smali

Designed, produced and distributed by D. N. Papadimas Books
8 Ippokratous Street, Athens, GR 106 79
Tel.: + 30 – 210 – 36.27.318 & 36.42.692
Fax: + 30 – 210 – 36.10.271
http:// www.papadimasbooks.gr

ISBN: 978-960-99945-0-7
ISSN: 1107 - 3136

Εικόνα εξωφύλλου: Edward Lear, *Ρέθυμνο*, υδατογραφία (7 Μαΐου 1864). Γεννάδειος Βιβλιοθήκη, Αμερικα- νική Σχολή Κλασικών Σπουδών στην Αθήνα

Cover illustration: Edward Lear, *Rethymnon*, watercolor (May 7, 1864). Courtesy of the Gennadius Library, American School of Classical Studies at Athens

ΠΕΡΙΕΧΟΜΕΝΑ
CONTENTS

1. Arms of Eugene of Savoy, *In Calumniatorem Platonis libri quatuor*, Venice 1516. Gennadius Library B/GC 3050q.

2. Ornamental title page, *Oratione di Bessarione*, Venice 1471. Gennadius Library B/TH 58/B55.

3. Arms of Michael Wodhull on the upper cover of *Oratione di Bessarione*, Venice 1471. Gennadius Library B/TH 58/B55.

4. Upper cover, *Orationes de gravissimis periculis*, Rome 1543. Gennadius Library B/TH/B551.

5. Lower cover, *Orationes de gravissimis periculis*, Rome 1543. Gennadius Library B/TH/B551.

6. Gennadius MSS 4 (14th century), folio 43v, showing a section of the ekphonetic notation used for scriptural passages. The hypokrisis and teleia signs are in red.

7. Gennadius MSS 4 (14th century), fol. 32v, showing a section of the notated chants for the feast of the Annunciation of the Theotokos (March 25).

8. Gennadius MSS 26 (A.D. 1801), folio 12v, with the beginning of the *anastasima*, resurrectional *kekragaria* of Saint John of Damascus, and *stichera* of the New Chrysaphes, as indicated in the title, mode 1.

9. Gennadius MSS Kyriazes 25 (A.D. 1777), folio 106v, written by Joannes of Chios, containing the *Anastasimatarion* of the New Chrysaphes.

10. Gennadius MSS 23 (A.D. 1713), folio 1r, and the beginning of the *protheoria*, ἀρχὴ σὺν Θεῷ ἁγίῳ τῶν σημαδίων τῆς ψαλτικῆς τέχνης.

11. Gennadius MSS 24 (A.D. 1734), folio 5r contains a *protheoria* with ktitoric notes about the manuscript's ownership.

12. Gennadius MSS Kyriazes 25 (A.D. 1777), folio 25r: wheel-shaped *kanonion* of the eight modes of Joannes Koukouzeles. The inscription reads: "ὁ κοπιάσας δι᾽ αὐτοῦ, ταχέος ἀμέριμνος ἔσται (= he who struggles with this will soon be free from care).»

13. Gennadius MSS 23 (A.D. 1713), folio 11v: another parallage diagram, in the form of a tree. The inscription below the branches reads: "ὁ κοπιάσας ἐν αὐτῷ ὀφεληθήσετε (= the one who studies this will receive benefit)."

14. Gennadius MSS 27, folio 45r. This composition by Georgios Rysios, an ekloge of the polyeleos using the text of Psalm 71, is dated October 1840 and dedicated "for Hellas" at the request of his friend Elias Tantalides.

15. Gennadius MSS Kyriazes 31, folio 1r. This collection of doxology compositions and selections for the Divine Liturgy was written before the year 1819.

16. Gennadius MSS Kyriazes 27, folio 129r. The notation used here is of the exegematic type, the text is from Psalm 118, used in memorial services, and the melody is one still used today.

17. Gennadius MSS 25, folio 249v, from the year 1777, with a kalophonic heirmos composed by Petros Bereketes.

5

*Unless otherwise noted all images are published courtesy of the Gennadius Library, American School of Classical Studies at Athens

6

49. Dimitrios Gounaris, the Greek priest, Mrs. Pesmazoglou, Ion Dragoumis, and the village's Greek inhabitants, Αρχείο Ίωνος Δραγούμη, Ενότητα VI, Φάκελος 45, Αρ. 187.

50. The Greek teacher of Cargèse, Mr. Peter Ragatsaki Stephanopoli, Ion Dragoumis, Mrs. Pesmazoglou, Dimitrios Gounaris, and Greek inhabitants, Αρχείο Ίωνος Δραγούμη, Ενότητα VI, Φάκελος 45, Αρ. 167.

51. The Greek priest at Cargèse, Father Kaisaris Kottis, in front of Saint Spyridon, Αρχείο Ίωνος Δραγούμη, Ενότητα VI, Φάκελος 45, Αρ. 193.

52. The shoe-maker, the old man, Dimitrios Gounaris, Mrs. Pesmazoglou, Ion Dragoumis, the teacher Mr. Peter Ragatsaki Stephanopoli, and some of the village children, Αρχείο Ίωνος Δραγούμη, Ενότητα VI, Φάκελος 45, Αρ. 176.

INTRODUCTION

MARIA GEORGOPOULOU,
Director

AND IRINI SOLOMONIDI,
Senior Librarian

On October 18, 1922, Joannes Gennadius signed the deed of gift that presented his extraordinary collection of 30,000 volumes "relating to the history and civilization of Greece from the time of Homer to the present day" to the American School of Classical Studies at Athens, "in the confident hope that the American School may be enabled to become a world centre for the study of Greek history, literature, and art both ancient, Byzantine, and modern and for the better understanding of the history and constitution of the Greek Church…"[1] The thoroughness and breadth of the collection reflect the genius of their collector's mind, as these books have been an unparalleled scholarly foundation for the study of post-classical Greece.

A passionate collector and wise bibliographer, Joannes Gennadius assembled the best private collection of Greek imprints, including first and rare editions, precious bindings, and manuscripts, together with an almost complete collection of early European books about travel to Greece and the Eastern Mediterranean. The donation of his library to the American School was accompanied by a detailed typewritten catalogue bound in 13 thick volumes and his wish that the Library's holdings be published. The careful account of his acquisitions provided a wise bibliographic basis for the current Gennadeion catalogue, showing the founder's intimate knowledge of early printed books, his fascination with the history of the book, and his will to disseminate the erudition he had amassed. For, in addition to safeguarding and preserving his collections, Gennadius had always been interested in making the treasures he had managed to acquire known to the world.

In the 85 years since the Gennadius Library's foundation, its holdings have grown to 120,000 volumes, and the Library has become one of the most significant institutions of its kind. Building on the strengths of the incomparable collection of Joannes Gennadius since 1926, when it opened its doors to the public, the Library has acquired tens of thousands of scholarly publications and academic journals, while generous donations of manuscripts, works of art, and important archival collections have supplemented and invigorated the original gift.

In fulfilling Gennadius' mandate to create a library that would preserve and disseminate knowledge about Hellenism, we believe it is our duty to preserve and share the wonderful riches of the Gennadius Library with the world. Since 1995, the

---

1. Gennadius Library, American School of Classical Studies, Gennadius Library Records, Deed of Gift; cf. "Deed of Gift," New Griffon N.S. 4 (2001), pp. 9–14.

Gennadius Library Board has provided funds and counsel to modernize the Library and to protect its treasures with state-of-the-art fire fighting systems, climate control, and new shelving and archives facilities. The union catalogue of the Gennadius and Blegen Libraries of the American School in cooperation with the Library of the British School at Athens has been available online since 2004. The immediacy and flexibility of the electronic catalogue system has been all the more important for the Gennadeion, a library distinguished by its holdings of rare books, prints, and manuscripts, so that the retrospective cataloguing of our most valuable treasures has been a priority. Several grants have funded the cataloguing of our Greek manuscripts, engravings, maps, scrapbooks, scholarly journals, and archival collections. Librarians, archivists, bibliographers, and historians have paid meticulous attention to documenting these unique treasures in detail in order to showcase the riches of the Gennadius collections.

At times, an anniversary triggers the re-examination of a particular collection. For instance, several new editions of musical works by the composer and conductor Dimitri Mitropoulos (1896–1960), whose papers belong to the Gennadius Archives, appeared in 2010 to mark the passage of 50 years since his death. As well, the 200th anniversary this year of Lord Byron's poem "The Maid of Athens" has given library staff the opportunity to explore anew the impressive collection of Byroniana that Gennadius assembled more than a century ago.

For it is only when such treasures are uncovered by attentive readers that they take on life. The essays assembled in this volume can be multiplied infinitely, and we hope that many more such treasures will see the light of publication very soon. As part of the prestigious institution of higher education that is the American School, the Gennadius Library is committed to bringing similar materials to life through research, exhibitions, and publication. As a rare book library, the Library seeks to share its treasures online with an ever broader audience through the use of innovative educational technologies. These two objectives — scholarship leading to publication, and dissemination of knowledge of the treasures among a wider public — are inextricably connected, requiring both a critical eye to decipher, contemplate, and interpret their form and content, and a storyteller's gift to make their discovery and significance come alive. For this, we are indebted to the scholars who make the study of the Gennadius treasures their own.

The Reading Room of the Gennadeion attracts researchers from Greece, the United States, and around the world. Whether they are fellows who have come from afar, occasional readers who pop in to study a particular item, or our beloved "regulars," the scholars who ponder on the materials held by the Library invariably share one experience: the joy of discovery when they stumble upon an unknown treasure. Some of the most memorable moments associated with working in the Library are when enthusiastic patrons call out, eager to show off what they have discovered: a previously unnoticed autograph letter attached to a volume, original drawings interleaved among the pages of a printed album, the only extant copy of a published book, the discovery of a rare yet modest pamphlet, or a long sought after essay in an obscure 19th-century publication. The excitement of discovery is what makes scholarly work rewarding, and it is this enthusiasm that we would like to share with you in the following pages.

The present volume of the New Griffon seeks to highlight several discoveries in a variety of areas and time periods: Maria-Christina Chatziioannou explores the personal archive of Joannes Gennadius to paint a portrait of the Gennadeion's founder in the context of British society; Leonora Navari presents the published works of Cardinal Bessarion, one of the heroes of Joannes Gennadius because of his active role in promoting the study of Hellenism in Italy; Father Konstantinos Terzopoulos explores 16 manuscripts of Byzantine chant; Cristina Pallini dissects an early hand-drawn map of Smyrna; Massimo Pinto considers the works of the 19th-century forger Constantinos Simonidis, a complete set of which was eagerly sought by Gennadius; Stephen Duckworth follows Edward Lear's wanderings on Crete through a careful study of his watercolors; Aliki Asvesta presents a wealth of information from the archive of cartographer Barbié du Bocage; American School Director Jack Davis analyzes topographical drawings connected with the presence of the French in the Peloponnesus in the early 19th century; and Eleftheria Daleziou examines the archives of Greek politician Ion Dragoumis, focusing on his exile on Corsica in the early 20th century. The volume is not all-inclusive, as the unique holdings of the Gennadeion could not possibly fit within the pages of a single issue of a journal. Our hope is that readers will be tempted to browse the Library's catalogue in person or online (www.gennadius.gr) in order to find their very own hidden treasures.

BETWEEN TRADITION AND MODERNITY: JOANNES GENNADIUS AT THE END OF THE 19TH CENTURY

MARIA CHRISTINA CHATZIIOANNOU

As I was researching the papers and books of Joannes Gennadius for a presentation on him for the 2010 "Day for Remembering Joannes Gennadius" organized by the Association of Friends of the Gennadius Library in Greece (the "Philoi") together with the Director of the Gennadius Library, I became conscious of the parallels presented by his age and the situation today. 1878 and 2011 — what do these two years in the history of the Greek state have in common? Then and now, we have the weakness of the Greek state's ability to borrow and the presence of international evaluators. Gennadius was an innovative diplomat who contributed to the solution of the most important national problem of his time, the restoration of the country's creditworthiness within a framework of national irredentism. Today economists and politicians negotiate proposals and solutions, constantly rearranging the context of public history in order to legitimize their views. History is called upon once again to show not only its usefulness but also its scholarly skill.

In this essay in reading the history of Joannes Gennadius, I will make use of especially rich archival and historiographical source material for his life and work (I refer to Gennadius's own archives as well as the edition of his correspondence with Trikoupis published by Lydia Tricha) and will endeavor to draw it into a new methodological framework. Taking the ideas worked out by Eric Hobsbawm in his book *The Age of Empire: 1875–1914* as my point of departure along with more recent approaches, I shall inscribe the case of Gennadius within the historical context of the British Empire and the Greek state. In the age of empires, the world of Europe would give rise to different rates of development and would form cohesive bonds with the other continents through the movement of goods, people, capital, and ideas. It is the period that exemplifies the development of globalization.[1]

In the 19th century, modernity was identified with the Industrial Revolution and the new social, economic, and political changes connected with it. Conceptually, modernity is related to a complex assemblage of institutions, with each of these

1. The Gennadius Library holds his archives and has published a considerable number of small volumes devoted to his life and work while maintaining a well-documented website. As an indication of this activity, I cite Nicol 1990 and Tricha 1991. For the general historical framework, see Hobsbawm 1989, 2000. G. Daudin, M. Morys and Kevin H. O'Rourke "Globalization 1870-1914", in: St. Broadberry, K.H. O'Rourke, *The Cambridge Economic History of Modern Europe*, v. 2 1870 to the Present, Cambridge University Press, 2010, 5-29.

institutions undergoing a variety of changes and modifications in the course of time. In this particular presentation, we are interested mainly in the political, economic, and cultural processes that determine the establishment of the civil state and the development of the capitalist world economy.[2] This theoretical proposition can be historicized through the paradigm of Joannes Gennadius. In this period, Joannes Gennadius was an agent who moved between the modern Greek state, a modern form of political organization — the traditional version is characterized by a society loosely organized in communal, guild, or kinship social networks — and the Greek diaspora, a heterogeneous community which is distinguished by an "imagined solidarity" with the modern Greek nation-state. Here, the idea of "imagined community" is being elaborated in the sense in which Benedict Anderson introduced it in 1983 when he published his homonymous study of the phenomenon of nationalism.[3]

Joannes Gennadius was a diplomatic representative of the modern Greek state in the last quarter of the 19th century. In this capacity he lived, observed, and dealt with the potent processes of national organization of the political, economic, and cultural life in the modern Greek state within the framework of global economic developments. On the economic level, this period is associated with international lending, global trade, and the development of big business. Anthony Giddens, taking as a given that the central institutions of western modernism were capitalism and the nation-state, has maintained that globalization is one of the most visible consequences of modernity.[4] Joannes Gennadius was very active during the period in which the globalization of Europe was developing. He had grasped the rules of the economic game of globalization, recommending that the nation-state be strengthened not only by means of the Greek example — Greek state, Greek diaspora, Greeks of the East (the Ottoman Empire) — but also through the Armenian demand for the creation of an independent Armenian state.

In the 19th century, globalization meant intensive trade in commodities, ideas, and capital between continents. Essentially, it had to do with the development of international trade through the increasing integration of international markets at the end of the 19th century. This period, a time in which Europe was without military conflicts (1871–1914), was favorable to financial aggrandizement and international lending. At the same time in the East, the period of the Sultan Abdul Hamid's reign (1876–1909) and the Young Turk movement (1906–1908) were distinguished by conflicting ethni-

2. Hall, Held, and McGrew 2003, Introduction, pp. 16–20.
3. Anderson (2006, pp. 6–7) defines the nation as "an imagined political community" that is imaginatively conceived as "inherently limited and sovereign." He explains that the nation is an "imagined" community because its members do not know most of the people of whom the nation is composed; it is never a matter of them meeting or of hearing about them, "yet in the minds of each lives the image of their communion." According to Anderson, communities must be distinguished not according to their falsity or genuineness, but by the style in which they are imagined. See also Kitromilides 1989.
4. Giddens's thesis is discussed by McGrew (2003).

cist claims, with Armenians and Greeks as the principal groups inside the Ottoman Empire, that culminate in the Balkan Wars as well as in the Armenian genocide of 1915. After the Congress of Berlin in 1878, the Greek and Armenian diaspora in Britain, united in their common involvement with international commercial transactions, would meet with Joannes Gennadius as principal agent in the negotiations.[5]

The story of Joannes Gennadius's role in Greek diplomacy has been the object of a fair amount of scholarship; Joannes Gennadius indisputably constitutes one of the most significant figures in the world of 19th-century Greek diplomacy, as he combined wide-ranging erudition with an aptitude for negotiating and the British paradigm of the culture of collecting. If the reception of technological innovation represents a sample for measuring the spread of modernity, then it is worth dwelling on the fact that, in 1896, Gennadius paid for 10 lessons in riding a bicycle in traffic in London, a small personal detail, yet one of substance, that associates him with his age's most modern means of transport, according to Hobsbawm.[6]

Most contemporary scholarship revolves around the collections of Joannes Gennadius, which constituted the core of his gift to the American School in 1922 for the creation of the library in Athens which bears his name. It is a gift that might have been dictated by strong political claims since, as has recently been maintained, with this gift he sought American recognition of the Greek campaign in Asia Minor, the American Protestant philhellenic standpoint at a crucial point in Greek irredentist policy.[7] Gennadius's posthumous fame has been based to a great degree upon the superb brilliance of his creation, the Gennadius Library; it is the collections themselves that have conferred value on their creator. We lack a biography that can come to terms with this diplomat and collector, who was shaped by the interweaving of modern

5. The relevant material relates especially to 1896. See Gennadius Library, American School of Classical Studies, Joannes Gennadius Archive, Scrapbook 014, vol. 2, : 1) letter of Edward Atkin, who on behalf of the Duke of Westminster asked Gennadius to participate in a demonstration (October 19, 1896) of protest against the acts of violence that were being perpetrated in Turkey; 2) Ticket of participation in the demonstration of protest against the acts of violence in Turkey on October 19, 1896; 3) Invitation from the Anglo-Armenian Association to a dinner and anniversary sermon on October 26, 1896; 4) Information leaflet from the Anglo-Armenian Association about the anniversary sermon of the Armenian priest Canon Charles Gore at St. Andrew's Church in London on October 26, 1896; 5) Announcement by the Byron Society that it would welcome all Armenians from the surrounding areas who wanted to participate in the annual celebration organized by the Anglo-Armenian Association October 26, 1896, and had no place to stay, from the Daily News, October 21, 1896; 6) "The Public Feeling. Peace and Dishonour," a report on the annual celebration of the foundation of the Anglo-Armenian Association, and on the acts of violence by Turks against Armenians, from the Daily Chronicle, October 27, 1896; 7) "ORDER OF PROCEEDINGS (subject to alteration) and DRAFT RESOLUTIONS to be Submitted to the St. James's Hall Meeting Monday, October 19th, 1896, at 8 p.m.," regarding a series of acts and proposed statement connected with the meeting to protest the acts of violence that were being committed against various ethnic groups in the Ottoman Empire, and especially about the slaughter of the Armenians.
6. Hobsbawm 1989, p. 52.
7. Papadopoulos 2008, pp. 455–456.

Greek history with British liberalism from the last quarter of the 19th century down to the period between the two World Wars.

The archival corpus of the correspondence constitutes a valuable source for the history of Joannes Gennadius. Correspondence constitutes a social practice which displays relationships with others, signifies exchange and reciprocity, pursues some goal, and refers to old and new relationships. Correspondence is at once impersonal and personal: it combines stereotypical expressions with the expression of sentiments.[8] Gennadius's incoming correspondence contains a mixture of letters of a public nature that have to do with his official position in the diplomatic sphere with many private letters from the world of the Greek diaspora. As a whole, the correspondence shows him as a mediator between the modern Greek state and the world of the Greek diaspora.

From the wealth of material in the Joannes Gennadius archive, I would just like to emphasize the significance of the well-known scrapbooks, the albums that contain clippings and photographs. Albums, which were a particularly widespread social phenomenon in the Victorian period, contain material that allows one to approach the identity of the person who compiled them. These albums became popular not only with women and children in 19th-century England, but also with men from different socio-political spheres.[9] Joannes Gennadius's compilation of scrapbooks (116 volumes) connects him with new models of social behavior. A new method of organization is evident from the study of the totality of his archive, which refers to the formation of a private archive with a personal entrepreneurial strategy.

Gennadius signifies the archetype of the social agent, who participates in the social life of Victorian England, in the circles of the Greek diaspora and of international diplomacy. Gennadius himself constituted the principal representative of diplomatic mediation in Greek-British relations during the last quarter of the 19th century through to the First World War. Of particular importance was his participation in the Congress of Berlin (1878), since he had been involved in the diplomatic negotiations concerning the admission of Greece to the conference. This congress was a stage in the advance of nationhood of different religion-based ethnic groups from the Ottoman Empire.[10] Greece's main demand in this period was still the expansion of its borders and consequently the issue of national irredentism that constituted the main characteristic of Gennadius's politics.

Joannes Gennadius handled two crucial issues connected with Greece's position in the international markets during the last quarter of the 19th century: the settlement

---

8. Moullas 1992.

9. Hunt 2006. For example, the politician and businessman Lynch Davidson (1873–1952), who lived in the American state of Texas at the same time as Gennadius, left a series of 21 political scrapbooks that he compiled between 1920 and 1931; see the Dolph Briscoe Center for American History, The University of Texas at Austin: http://www.lib.utexas.edu/taro/utcah/02079/cah-02079.html (accessed May 16, 2011).

10. Kofos 2001, p. 181.

of the debt resulting from the first loan to Greece in 1824–1825 and the problem of the import tax on currants levied by the Americans and the British, at a crucial stage of the "currant crisis" at the end of the 19th century. At the same time, he played a significant role in the world of the Greek trade diaspora in Britain from the last quarter of the 19th century all the way to the period between the two World Wars.

Already at the time of the Dilessi Murders (1870) and the unjust accusations made against Greece because of an unfortunate isolated incident, Gennadius had indicted Britain's anti-Greece stance together with the loans of 1824-1825. He held back on making Greece's unjust exclusion from international money markets public, accusing the British of Turcophilia and imperialism. In the period of preparations for the Congress of Berlin, Gennadius's handling of the problem of Greece's borrowing at the time when the nation rose up against the Turks intensified. He recounted the case of the loans for Greek independence, which had shut Greece out of borrowing in the international money markets as well as the assertion of its political claims, according to his testimony.[11]

In 1878, the law "Concerning the settlement of the old loans of the years 1824 and 1825," an arrangement for administering the debt between the Greek government on the one hand, represented by Joannes Gennadius, secretary at the Greek Embassy in London, Themistokles Malikiopoulos, and N. A. Nazos, and on the other the representatives of the holders of foreign securities and especially of Greek bonds. After many months of negotiations with the Corporation of Foreign Bondholders and the Committee of Greek Bondholders, Gennadius concluded an agreement on September 4, 1878; after being approved by the bondholders, it was debated and approved by the Greek Parliament, with Theodoros Deligiannis as Prime Minister. The main points of the agreement were 1) instead of the total demanded amount of £10,000,000, which included the initial principal and the unpaid interest, it was agreed the sum of £1,200,000 would be paid; 2) the debt would be paid off in 33 years with a grace period; 3) new bonds equal in value to the reduced sum and bearing 5% interest were to be issued for the liquidation of the loans. Every £100 bond issued in 1824 was to be exchanged for £31,12. Every £100 bond issued in 1825 was to be exchanged for £30,10. The detached coupons were to be funded at the rate £11,12% in bonds of the same issue; 4) the Greek's government's mortgaging of the proceeds from the stamp duties (£4,400) together with the income from the Customs office on Corfu constituted a guarantee for the annual payment of £75,000.[12]

Here we are interested in Gennadius's activity as intermediary with a newfangled institution of his time, the Corporation of Foreign Bondholders, an association of British investors that had been set up in 1868 and was licensed by the Board of Trade

---

11. Gennadius 1870, pp. 160, 164, 172.

12. Mauro and Yafeh 2003. For the administration of loans, see the Greek government official gazette (ΦΕΚ) 82 for December 28, 1878, Law ΨΛΔ; the same text was also published as a leaflet in 1879. For a full analysis, see Levandis 1944, pp. 27–28.

in 1873.[13] This organization laid claim to the smooth coordination of foreign loans by the debtor countries in the international securities market for bonds, particularly in the period 1870–1913. It was precisely at this period that Britain and other countries lent enormous capital sums to emerging markets. The Corporation of Foreign Bondholders managed to attain successful settlements with highly indebted countries such as the Ottoman Empire, Spain, Greece, Portugal, Mexico, Argentina, and Brazil. The involvement of Joannes Gennadius in this settlement acted as a catalyst for the Greek state.

Within the sphere of international financial markets, international trade in agricultural products was the other sector which interested the Greek state's foreign economic policy. In 1888, a new tariff on the import of currants had been debated in the U.S.A. and the Greek government sent Joannes Gennadius from London to avert its impact. A little while later Gennadius sent a copy of Antoine Pecquet's *Discours sur l'art de négocier* (1737) to the U.S. State Department, obviously as an act of courtesy.[14] It is known that at the end of the 1880s, the most dynamic sector of the 19th-century Greek agricultural economy had fallen under the wheels of the currant crisis. The demand for a reduction in the import tax on Corinthian currants, according to Gennadius, was above all concerned with the increase in the consumption of the product in the American market, and not with the reduction in the product's transport cost or in the increased profits to Greek producers. At any rate, independent of the justification for his goal, Gennadius's intervention was instrumental in this case as well.

From early on, Joannes Gennadius had developed close ties with Anglophone Protestant education as a result of his association with John Henry Hill, founder of the well-known school in Athens, as well as his studies at the British Protestant College in Malta. The study of Protestantism was one of the topics that excited Gennadius's interest. He chose to settle in England and to work at the merchant firm of Ralli Brothers, with the mercantilist conviction that commerce contributed to general progress: "I was desirous of gaining commercial experience, in the belief that I would be able to use it later on for the advancement and development of the country."[15]

The social relationships which Gennadius systematically cultivated in Britain permitted him to develop a personal network of diplomats, politicians, intellectuals, and businessmen. The social life of the London clubs allowed him to mingle on familiar terms with Greek and British entrepreneurs such as the Rallis and the Rothschilds. And so it was in 1890 that he wrote to Charilaos Trikoupis to say that he could act

13. Mauro and Yafeh 2003, pp. 6–14.
14. See his "Autobiographical Notes" (Gennadius Library, American School of Classical Studies, Joannes Gennadius Archive, Series III, Box 11, Folder 11.1) and the thank-you letter he received from A. W. Dulles in Washington, August 24, 1922 (Series I, Box 5, Folder 5.4).
15. Quoted from Gennadius's letter to S. Parasyrakis, December 18/30, 1897, Gennadius Library, American School of Classical Studies, Joannes Gennadius Archive, Series III, Box 11, Folder 11.1.

as an intermediary with Nathaniel M. Rothschild (1840–1915) in connection with the loans of that period: "when an opportune moment presents itself, I will repeat my exhortations to Lord Rothschild, whom I meet frequently in society". Furthermore, at a time of personal financial difficulties, Gennadius was able to seek employment at the mighty branch of the Rothschild firm in Vienna, and had the social ease and facility to apply to Stephanos Rallis and to the British royal court for the sale of books from his library.[16] His experience on the international diplomatic stage and in the world of international business allowed him to handle major economic issues pertaining to the Greek state's foreign borrowing and the export trade (in currants), as mentioned above.

Joannes Gennadius developed a personal strategy, entering the sphere of diplomacy and taking up leading positions in the Greek state's diplomatic corps from the last quarter of the 19th century on, with the spread of panhellenism as his aim, analogous to comparable ideological currents of the period. Many texts from his pen articulate the quest for the unity of Hellenes in the Greek state, in the East (the Ottoman Empire), and in the diaspora. An "imagined solidarity" interwoven with personal relationships is recorded in his correspondence and a large number of published texts[17]. Diplomacy, not commerce, offered Gennadius the opportunity to play a significant role in Greek-British relations, developing liberal political models during the period when Britain's global political and economic power increased. In his capacity as an employee of Ralli Brothers, and as a high-placed member of Greece's diplomatic service, he was not permitted to publish his views freely, so that much of what he wrote was unsigned or circulated under a pseudonym. Yet both of those posts were what allowed him to be at the center of information and to associate with businessmen, politicians, intellectuals, and religious leaders.

Joannes Gennadius's personal archive shows off his activities as a systematic social intermediary in providing services to a circle of his compatriots. Gennadius maintained a very wide circle of personal contacts and favors through an abundance of letters. For instance, a member of the prominent Vallianos family firm had asked that Gennadius have a young relative appointed to the Greek embassy in London. After this request was fulfilled, a check for FF 5,000 was offered to Venizelos by Gennadius in 1917.[18] This testifies that positions at embassies and consulates were much sought-after because they conferred the value of social capital and above all functioned as access points to an information network. Gennadius's services as a personal go-between, however, seem to have supported a network for funding political activity as well, especially that of Eleftherios Venizelos.

---

16. Tricha 1991, pp. 142, 340, 19, 237, 257.

17. Gennadius's personal papers and documents offer a rich source for his relations with Diaspora Greeks. For Gennadius and the Eastern question, see Ailianos 2007.

18. Athanasios S. Vallianos (Paris), letter to Gennadius in London, May 16/29, 1917, Gennadius Library, American School of Classical Studies, Joannes Gennadius Archive, Series I, Box 6, Folder 6.6.

A diplomat's position could become an object of public criticism, or of adulation. Gennadius became a principal figure in patronage relationships not only with the Greek and British bourgeoisie, but also with his fellow-countrymen, who would mobilize flattery, complaints, and emotional blackmail with patriotic outbursts.

A typical instance of this is represented by Gennadius's relationship in 1918 with an employee of the Bank of Athens in London. Nicolas Milo Vlassis came from Cheimara and boasted of the Epirote ancestry he and Gennadius shared; he regarded the latter's success and/or failure in the diplomatic service as a mutual concern. Vlassis defended Gennadius's public image in London: the emigrant from Cheimara in London wrote to Gennadius in Greek, at the same time also made remarks and rhetorical phrases in Greek and Albanian in the Greek alphabet, such as "They will throw our fez in the mud," emphasizing the value of their manly honor. Again, in public debates among gatherings of Greeks in London, where Gennadius was accused of giving preference to a Jewish supplier to the Greek public sector, Vlassis responded rather threateningly to the accuser, "Surely you've become bored with living to speak thus about Gennadius, because the Ambassador is an Epirote and does not deign to do what you are saying." This relationship of devotion and mutual support was apparently reciprocated, because Gennadius interceded so that the emigrant from Cheimara in London would be hired by the shipowner Antonis A. Empeirikos (1870–1931) as secretary on his estate in England at a higher wage than the Bank of Athens paid, and with housing and food provided free. Vlassis, who had been located in London as an employee of the Bank of Athens, obviously could not communicate well with the group of Greek businessmen in Britain who had already become Anglicized by the end of the First World War. Rather, he came from the world of the Mediterranean, which has been described in terms of the gender-based behavioral code of honor and shame, a code linked to the client-patron system. The lack of understanding between Vlassis and Empeirikos, the clash of different codes of behavior in Victorian England, led to the annulment of their collaboration, an event that was publicized in the British press.[19]

The post of Greece's diplomatic representative in a foreign country served, smoothed, and facilitated the affairs of Greek subjects. A group of commercial entrepreneurs of Greek origin had dealings with Gennadius that reveal their international identity and dealings with the Greek state. For example, the international firm Paterson, Zochonis & Co., Ltd., which was founded at the end of the 19th century by the Scot George Henry Paterson and Georgios V. Zochonis from the Peloponnesus, had branches in Manchester, Liverpool, Marseille, and much of West Africa, including Conakry (Guinea), Sierra Leone, Monrovia (Liberia), and Lagos and Calabar

20

19. N. M. Vlassis, letters to J. Gennadius, April 23/May 6, 1918; May 8/21, 1918; January 26/ February 8, 1918 (Gennadius Library, American School of Classical Studies, Joannes Gennadius Archive, Series I, Box 2, Folder 2.9); newspaper clipping, "A Greek Secretary and his Employer" (Series I, Box 5, Folder 5.5). On the subject of honor in the Mediterranean, see Campbell 1964; Pitt-Rivers 1965.

(Nigeria). From the firm's second generation, Vasilis G. Zochonis requested that a passport be issued for his niece so that she could travel to Switzerland. The niece was a British subject, but her father was a Greek subject. Many people of Greek descent in the business world of international transactions would acquire British citizenship in the course of the 19th century; for them, the official services provided by Greek diplomatic authorities were superfluous.[20]

As has already been mentioned, Joannes Gennadius from the beginning combined the life of an emigrant in London with working together with the commercial house of Ralli Brothers in 1862. He remained in this position for a period of time for which we have little information despite the fact that during this interval he evidently made his acquaintance with the Greek world of international commerce. He left Ralli Brothers because of issues of political behavior. Gennadius's relationship with the Ralli family, or to be more precise with certain members of the family, nevertheless remained close to the end of his life in England.[21]

Gennadius managed a network of intermediations between the Greek state and Greeks of the diaspora connected with the Ralli family. Since the mid-19th century, the family network that was the Ralli Brothers' multinational company extended from Britain to Europe, America, Asia (Turkey, Iran, and India), and Africa. Their network of informants and the development of their enterprises was extensive, following the routes taken by the spread of British colonialism and international business deals.[22]

The Rallis could provide capital and/or jobs in the offices of their commercial establishment. The position of broker at one of the most important firms in England conferred a high degree of authority to Joannes Gennadius as well. Thus did the University of Athens professor Neokles Kazazis thank Gennadius, via a mutual acquaintance, for the role he played in having Kazazis's son hired by the house of Ralli Brothers. Another instance was when the dire financial situation of a diaspora Greek was communicated to Gennadius by the man's sister so that Gennadius would intervene for him with Ralli Brothers.[23] Business-related introductions by means of a network of friends represented a supportive prerequisite for establishing oneself as a professional, but at the same time were an authoritative advertisement for services provided with success and effectiveness.

Gennadius's position in the Greek community in London as well as in British soci-

---

20. V. Zochonis (Manchester), letters of July 5, 1917, and July 23, 1910, to J. Gennadius, Gennadius Library, American School of Classical Studies, Joannes Gennadius Archive, Series I, Box 2, Folder 2.9.

21. In 1897, for example, Stephanos Rallis invited Gennadius to attend a show put on by the students at Bedford College: Gennadius Library, American School of Classical Studies, Joannes Gennadius Archive, Scrapbook 014, vol. 2. J. Gennadius, *Stephen A. Ralli: a biographical memoir*, 1902.

22. Vourkatioti 2006.

23. See the letters from N. Argyriades in Istanbul (June 12/25, 1910) and Marietta Kephala (February 28, 1921) to Gennadius in London: Gennadius Library, American School of Classical Studies, Joannes Gennadius Archive, Series I, Box 2, Folder 2.9 and Box I, Folder 1.11.

ety more generally, especially after his marriage to Florence Laing in 1902 established him as a receiver of announcements for consumer products, either for his personal use or to advertise and promote them commercially.[24] His relations with the world of learning in England are as evident from his ties to universities (King's College, London, as a member of the committee for the Koraes Chair), institutions (the Anglo-Hellenic League, the Classical Association, the University of Reading), and learned journals (Revue des Études Grecques), as from the requests that his compatriots directed to him. Greeks who wanted to study in Britain asked Gennadius for letters of recommendation, or for contributions toward financial help in their studies. The requests he received were both direct and indirect, for example, a thank-you letter from a Greek in London to Gennadius for his intercession to obtain his election to a research center (the Institution of Mining and Metallurgy, since 2002 The Institute of Materials, Minerals and Mining), and a request for financial aid from a Greek studying at the London School of Economics. Requests also came from individuals in Gennadius's personal network. A businessman from Ithaki associated with the company Drakoulis Ltd., which was a steamship broker and trader in charcoal, asked Gennadius in his quality as a noted intellectual to write a letter of introduction for the son of the ship owner I. Matsoukis, also from Ithaki, in order for him to enroll at an Oxford college.[25] In London's Greek community, finding employment could be facilitated by means of a favorable introduction from Gennadius.

22   Gennadius's connections with the commercial and political world of the Greek community in Britain, as well as in the eastern Mediterranean, developed during his residence in London through his identity as a diplomat and his involvement with the book trade. It was a result of meticulous organization, which is also mirrored in the arrangement of his personal archive. Within his correspondence, Gennadius classified one bundle of letters as "English, socially, 1917–1925," and another "Requests from various persons and thanks regarding their affairs." He himself archived various thank-you letters from the governors of the Bank of England, Englishmen of the highest bourgeois social class, in the set "Congratulatory letters to various persons," while a comparable set bore the title "Letters of condolence to various persons," containing letters mainly from the world of the Greek community of London.[26]

In the course of his career, Gennadius acquired great authority, and his views

---

24. Accordingly, among Gennadius's preserved papers are circulars advertising pens from a British firm, along with an offer to have them photographed by Elliott & Fry, a famous photographic studio of Victorian England: Gennadius Library, American School of Classical Studies, Joannes Gennadius Archive, Series I, Box 2, Folder 2.8, dating from 1930, 1931, and 1932.

25. Gennadius Library, American School of Classical Studies, Joannes Gennadius Archive, Series III, Box II, Folder II.7; see also Series I, Box 2, Folder 2.9, containing letters to Gennadius from N. Mavrokordatos (November 12/24, 1898) and V. Akylas (April 29, 1917), L. Tzikaliotis (May 29, 1919), and Drakoulis (May 27, 1921).

26. Gennadius Library, American School of Classical Studies, Joannes Gennadius Archive, Series I, Box 2, Folder 2.9.

on the Eastern Question were welcomed in more extended English social circles and among the Greeks of the diaspora. I. L. Chalkokondylis, managing editor of the newspaper *Νέα Ἡμέρα* (*New Day*) of Trieste, asked him for books and opinion pieces on Greece and the Eastern Question. Gennadius's interest in the "Greek East" was intense; he had become known throughout a wide circle of Greek intellectuals such as Alexandros Pallis and Angelos Simiriotis.[27]

In addition, Gennadius acted as an intermediary in connection with monetary support for the publication of books, as in the case of Z. D. Ferriman's *Some English Philhellenes* (1917). For this book, he had drawn a check for £150 from Athanasios Vallianos, with whom he had already openly had social and financial dealings. The British writer Percy F. Martin asked leave to publish as portrait of Gennadius in his book *Greece of the Twentieth Century*, with a foreword by Andreas Andreades and a dedication to King George I.[28] From the plethora of letters, it becomes understandable that social exchanges with Gennadius ranged from desirable to necessary in English and Greek diaspora intellectual circles that maintained a variety of interests in regard to Greece and the Levant.

The promotion of certain titles and copies of books created a self-renewing chain of relationships and readings, as well as of advertisement for those books. Gennadius sent copies of an edition of Korais's letters — supposed to have been privately published by Pandelis Rallis — to a Chian businessman of the diaspora.[29] This act can also be interpreted as an effort to emphasize the connection "Chios– Greek diaspora–Chian entrepreneurs." Years earlier, in 1881, Gennadius himself had advanced this connection by publishing *Loukis Laras: Reminiscences of a Chiote Merchant during the War of Independence*, his own translation into English of Demetrius Vikelas's *Λουκῆς Λάρας* (1879). The story of Loukis Laras from Chios, written in the 1870s, created the moral exemplar of a victim of the Revolution of 1821 who survived and immigrated to England. The book is the story of a self-made man, a member of a particular local group, with an international financial network and success in business. The choice to become involved in the buying and selling of books became Gennadius's characteristic attribute in England. Equipped with the cultural tools of an intellectual, he distinguished himself within the community of Greek businessmen in

23

27. Letters to Gennadius in London from Chalkokondylis in Trieste, June 15, 1900, and Simiriotis in Athens, February 26, 1923: Gennadius Library, American School of Classical Studies, Joannes Gennadius Archive, Series I, Box 5, Folder 5.3, and Box 6, Folder 6.5. Simiriotis's letter indicates that the a copy of the polyglot Constantinople Pentateuch printed in 1547 by Eliezer (Albert) Soncino for ex-Greek Jews of the Karaite persuasion was on sale in Athens for £300.

28. Gennadius Library, American School of Classical Studies, Joannes Gennadius Archive, Series I, Box 5, Folder 5.3, and Series III, Box 11, Folder 11.1: letters to Gennadius in London from John Mavrogordato, February 25, 1918, and Percy F. Martin, May 11, 1912. Martin's book was published by T. F. Unwin of London in 1913.

29. Gennadius to Philip Chrysovelonis, January 18, 1928, Gennadius Library, American School of Classical Studies, Joannes Gennadius Archive, Series I, Box 6, Folder 6.3. The work in question is probably Korais [1898] 2011. Gennadius had been engaged with Korais's works as well: see Gennadius 1903.

Britain. Through his copious letter-writing, he exchanged views on various issues — publications, education, the Eastern Question — which renewed his great authority and leading position in Greek Diaspora circles as well as among the philhellenes in London society at the dawn of the 20th century.

The departure of a Greek diplomat from his post usually meant a series of ceremonious farewell meetings that Greek communities in England would organize. In Gennadius's case, we can speak of a farewell period (1918–1919) after the end of the First World War. Greek politicians, with Eleftherios Venizelos at their head, and the members of the Greek communities in Britain publicly expressed their gratitude to Gennadius after roughly a half-century of service in the Greek diplomatic corps. Loukas E. Rallis in London took a leading part in the organization of farewell banquets, farewell speeches, and farewell gifts.[30]

Georgios V. Zochonis from Manchester, as president of the Greek community there, invited Gennadius to such a dinner, leaving the date open. At the same time, he took advantage of the opportunity by requesting that Gennadius intercede on behalf of his nephew so that the latter, who was in Switzerland, could serve in the Greek rather than the British army. The dinner was in fact arranged for the end of 1918. The Greek communities of Manchester and Liverpool provided both the organizing committee and the 58 guests, as well as speeches and an assurance on Gennadius's part that the matter of Zochonis's nephew was progressing well. The detailed description of the reception, the assembled diners, and the speeches for Gennadius was circulated in print, and it gave the opportunity for strong Venizelist sentiments to be expressed, for Gennadius's anti-Turkish and anti-Bulgarian politics to be praised, for the dimensions of the Megali Idea to be set forth by Gennadius himself, and for the Greek ancestry of the assembled diners to be noted. The main accounts refer to the public praise of Gennadius, with political references, while no mention is made of financial questions.[31]

Joannes Gennadius was a descendant of the urban middle class that took part in the Greek Revolution of 1821, of a world that was shaped by Greek education and Orthodox religion as much on the part of his father George Gennadius as on his mother Artemis Benizelou's side. Gennadius entered British life during the period when the British Empire was growing and when Europe was rising as a modern economic and cultural entity. This was the time at which his personal social network was assembled. The 1860s represented a preparatory stage when he was becom-

24

30 N. Giannakopoulos to Gennadius, December 31, 1918, and June 25, 1919: Gennadius Library, American School of Classical Studies, Joannes Gennadius Archive, Series III, Box 11, Folder 11.5. Even Venizelos himself was present at an official farewell dinner.

31. Zochonis to Gennadius, November 29, 1918, and December 12, 1918, Gennadius Library, American School of Classical Studies, Joannes Gennadius Archive, Series III, Box 11, Folder 11.5. See also the pamphlet "Το εν Μαγκεστρία Συμπόσιον της 29/12 Δεκ. 1918 εις τιμήν της Α.Ε. του κ. Ι. Γενναδίου αποχωρούντος της ενεργού υπηρεσίας. Οι εκφωνηθέντες λόγοι," published in Manchester in 1919.

ing acclimatized to England through contact with Greek diaspora circles and trade networks. After 1875, from his post as a diplomatic representative of the Greek state, he would make his way into the world of British liberal politics. After 1902 and his English marriage, the philo-European cultural tendencies of Edwardian society would open up opportunities that even today have not been recognized or viewed in combination with the period of Venizelism in Greece.

Gennadius created a personal network — a result of careful management — that surpassed the bonds of family and local kinship. At a time when capital and markets were becoming globalized, he maintained a multifaceted relationship between the Greek diaspora and the Greek state. The interconnections between where he was brought up and where he settled highlight the question of the political nationality and cultural identity of Greek emigrants in England. Joannes Gennadius understood that in this discussion the nation-state complex constituted an institutional cause of the end of the diaspora, as it would lead to assimilation by the social and political environment of the place of residence or, less often, to repatriation back to the nation-state.[32]

Joannes Gennadius, by virtue of his position at key nodal points in European centers and in the international networks of the Greek diaspora, represents a version of the "globalization" of his time, which was not limited to the economic level but rather forged on the level of social relationships. He managed client-patron networks that had their roots in traditional forms of power and that continued to function uninterruptedly even in the modern period. Gennadius's story reveals a course that intersects with economic power, state authority, and cultural values.

BIBLIOGRAPHY

Ailianos, K. I. 2007. *Ο Ιωάννης Γεννάδιος και το Ανατολικό ζήτημα* (όγδοη ετήσια διάλεξη, ημέρα μνήμης Ι. Γενναδίου, 5/4/2006) Athens.

Anderson, B. 2006. *Φαντασιακές κοινότητες*, trans. P. Chantzaroula, Athens (orig. ed. *Imagined Communities: Reflections on the Origin and Spread of Nationalism*, 1983).

Campbell, J. K. 1964. *Honour, Family and Patronage: A Study of Institutions and Moral Values in a Greek Mountain Community*, Oxford.

Gennadius, I. 1870. *Notes on the Recent Murders by Brigands in Greece*, London.

Gennadius, I. 1878. *The Greek Loans of 1824 & 1825: How They Were Handled, and What the World Thought of It. Opinions of the Day, without Comment*, London.

Gennadius, I. 1903. *Κρίσεις και σκέψεις περί των επιστολών του αοιδίμου Κοραή, μελέτημα*, Trieste.

Gilroy, P. [1994] 1999. "Diaspora," in *Migration, Diasporas and Transnationalism*, ed. S. Vertovec, R. Cohen (International Library of Studies on Migration 9), Cheltenham, pp. 293–298 [= *Paragraph* 17.1 (1994), pp. 207–212].

---

32. Gilroy [1994] 1999.

Hall, S., D. Held, and A. McGrew. 2003. *Η Νεωτερικότητα σήμερα: οικονομία, κοινωνία, πολιτική, πολιτισμός*, Athens (orig. ed. *Modernity and its Futures*, 1992).

Hobsbawm, E. J. 1989. *The Age of Empire, 1875–1914*, New York.

Hobsbawm, E. J. 2000. *Η εποχή των αυτοκρατοριών (1875–1914)*, trans. K. Sklaveniti, Athens.

Hunt, L. I. 2006. "Victorian Passion to Modern Phenomenon: A Literary and Rhetorical Analysis of Two Hundred Years of Scrapbooks and Scrapbook Making" (Diss. Univ. of Texas at Austin).

Kitromilides, P. M. 1989. "'Imagined Communities' and the Origins of the National Question in the Balkans," *European History Quarterly* 19, pp. 149–192.

Kofos, E. 2001. *Η Ελλάδα και το Ανατολικό Ζήτημα 1875–1881*, Athens.

Korais, A. I. [1898] 2011. *Koray's Letters written from Paris, 1788–92. Translated from the original Greek, and edited by P. Ralli*, repr. London.

Levandis, J. A. 1944. *The Greek Foreign Debt 1821–1898*, New York.

Mauro, P., and Y. Yafeh. 2003. "The Corporation of Foreign Bondholders," *IMF Working Paper* WP/03/107, Washington, D.C.

McGrew, A. 2003. "A Global Society?", in Hall, Held, and McGrew 2003, pp. 103–116.

Moullas, P. 1992. *Ο Λόγος της Απουσίας. Δοκίμιο για την επιστολογραφία με σαράντα ανέκδοτα γράμματα του Φώτου Πολίτη (1908–1910)*, Athens.

Nicol, D. M. 1990. *Joannes Gennadios – The Man. A Biographical Sketch*, Athens.

Papadopoulos, G. 2008. "Η μετανάστευση από την οθωμανική αυτοκρατορία στην Αμερική (19ος αιώνας–1923): οι ελληνικές κοινότητες της Αμερικής και η αλυτρωτική πολιτική της Ελλάδας" (Diss. Panteion Univ. of Social and Political Sciences, Athens).

Pitt-Rivers, J. 1965. "Honour and Social Status," in *Honour and Shame: The Values of Mediterranean Society*, ed. J. G. Peristiany, London and Athens, pp. 19–78.

Tricha, L., ed. 1991. *Διπλωματία και πολιτική. Χαρίλαος Τρικούπης–Ιωάννης Γεννάδιος: Αλληλογραφία 1863–1894*, Athens.

Vourkatioti, K. 2006. "The house of Ralli Brothers (c. 1818–1961)," in *Following the Nereids: Sea Routes and Maritime Business, 16th– 20th centuries*, ed. M.-C. Chatziioannou and G. Harlaftis, Athens, pp. 99–110.

CARDINAL BESSARION AND THE GENNADIUS LIBRARY

LEONORA NAVARI

This article was inspired by the paper on the Council of Ferrara-Florence given by Judith Herrin at the Gennadius Library in May 2010.[1] She highlighted the role played by Bessarion during the Council, his activities as a collector of manuscripts, and his importance in the transmission of ancient Greek texts to the West. While listening to her, I asked myself what works by Bessarion were to be found in the Gennadius. Joannes Gennadius would almost certainly have collected material by Bessarion, that ambivalent figure in the cultural history of Greece, Greek and yet not Greek, because of his conversion from Orthodoxy to Catholicism.

Much has been written on Bessarion (1403–1472).[2] Born in Trebizond, he was sent to Constantinople to study around 1415; he became a monk in 1423 and was ordained as a priest in 1431. Sometime after 1423 he studied with George Gemisthos Plethon at Mistra. In 1436 he was named abbot of the monastery of St. Basil in Constantinople and soon afterward was appointed Bishop of Nicaea. He never visited his see, but was immediately chosen to accompany the Emperor John VIII Palaeologus and the Patriarch Joseph II to Ferrara, to a council which was to discuss the possibility of union between the Eastern and Western churches.

Bessarion's presence at the Council of Ferrara marked a turning point in his life. As an intellectual of the Orthodox Church, known for his philosophical and theological studies, he was one of several bishops who represented the Eastern Church in the theological discussions during the Council. The Greek contingent left Constantinople in November 1437 and reached Ferrara in February 1438. Serious theological discussions started in October, 1438, with the main issue being the *filioque*, in other words the procession of the Holy Spirit.[3] According to Gill, Bessarion began by opposing the Latin position on the *filioque* vigorously but was gradually swayed by the arguments of the Latin Church. In Florence (to which the council was transferred when cases of plague were identified in the neighborhood of Ferrara) he ended by being

---

1. "The West meets Byzantium: Unexpected Consequences of the Council of Ferrara-Florence 1428–1439," delivered May 25, 2010 in Cotsen Hall.
2. See Labowsky 1967. The basic account of Bessarion's life and works is Mohler 1967. An extremely useful list of contemporary sources, articles, and a bibliography of Bessarion is given in Coccia 1973.
3. See Gill 1973 for an account of the role played by Bessarion during the Council.

convinced that the Latin viewpoint was correct and pressed for unity on that basis.[4] Many and various reasons have been attributed to Bessarion for committing himself to the Latin position on the *filioque*, but whatever the truth of the matter, this decision was critical to his future. He returned to Constantinople with the Byzantine delegates in late 1439. In December of that year, while still at sea, he was named cardinal by Pope Eugenius IV. Although the union of the churches was accepted by the Byzantine delegation at Florence, it was rejected in Constantinople. Bessarion's reception at Constantinople by the Orthodox clergy was hostile; he returned to Italy where he converted to Roman Catholicism, enjoying preferment and a life of study. He settled in Rome in 1440 and was given the cure of the church of the Holy Apostles. His tomb and a memorial plaque are to be found in the church. He amassed an important library of Greek manuscripts which he presented to the Venetian Senate four years before his death. Bessarion's bequest became the nucleus of the Library of St. Mark's (Biblioteca Marciana) and was his lasting achievement.[5]

The Gennadius Library is fortunate in possessing most of Bessarion's works. We are concerned here with those published during his lifetime or during the following two centuries. Only two of Bessarion's works were printed during his lifetime: his work on Plato and his oration on the Turks. Some of his theological works, the writings devoted to the Council, and his translations of Xenophon and Aristotle, were printed in the 16th century. However, a number of his works were not published until the 19th century, and several still remain only in manuscript.[6]

The first of Bessarion's works to be printed during his lifetime, and perhaps his most important, was his defense of Plato, *In Calumniatorem Platonis*, a reply to the accusations of George of Trebizond, who believed that all Christian heresy was rooted in Platonism; it has been called "the most important platonic text in the Renaissance before the work of Marsilio Ficino."[7] It circulated in manuscript from about 1459 for ten years before its publication in 1469; the printed edition is extremely rare and known in only a few copies. However, the Gennadius Library possesses both the second and third editions. The second, corrected, edition was printed by Aldus in Venice in 1503 as *Quae hoc in volumine tractantur: Bessarionis... in calumniatorem*

4. Gill 1973, p. 120. A Jesuit, Gill was concerned to present Bessarion's support for the union of the churches as genuine, not as a means of satisfying his ambitions.

5. Much work has been done on Bessarion's library: see Labowsky 1979; Miscellanea marciana 1976; Mioni 1991.

6. A word about the bibliography of Bessarion: It is difficult to establish a complete bibliography of the first editions of his printed works, as they were published during the first three centuries after his death. Most bibliographical references to them are to the texts published mainly in Migne's *Patrologia Graeca*, vol. 161, some of which were edited directly from the manuscripts, or to individual editions by various scholars such as Mohler. Émile Legrand's *Bibliographie Hellénique* (see the Bibliography) gives the most complete listing of editions of Bessarion's works as they were first printed, but it is organized chronologically, not by author. See the entries for individual books below.

7. See Monfasani 2007. For a bibliographical notice, see Legrand 15–16th c. III, no. 1.

Platonis libri quatuor... (GC 3049q).[8] This volume contains the *In calumniatorem* and two other works, Bessarion's corrections to George of Trebizond's translation of Plato's *Laws* and his criticisms of George's tract *De natura*.[9] This copy was bound for Gennadius in brown morocco in the early 20th century.

The third edition was published by Aldus in 1516 under the same title, *Bessarionis... in calumniatorem Platonis libri quatuor...* (B/GC 3050 q)[10], but with an important difference. The work now also includes Bessarion's translation of Aristotle's *Metaphysics* (see below), as well as a translation of Theophrastus's *Metaphysics*. The Gennadius Library copy is of particular interest for its binding and its associations. Firstly, on a preliminary blank leaf, it bears the signature of the German Catholic humanist, poet laureate, and professor at the University of Tübingen Johann Alexander Brassicanus (1500–1539). Brassicanus owned an extensive library and may have been the first owner of this copy. It was later acquired by François de Carignan, better known as Prince Eugene of Savoy (1663–1736), and bound for him in the late 17th century in French red morocco: triple gilt filets on both sides enclose his large central gilt arms (Fig. 1), and the back is gilt with his smaller coat of arms. Prince Eugene left his books to the Emperor Charles VI and they eventually formed part of the Imperial Library of Vienna. When the library was reorganized, some duplicates were sold, including this copy.[11] These associations would have been of particular interest to Joannes Gennadius for two reasons. Firstly, Brassicanus was the editor of Gennadius Scholarius's *De sinceritate christianae fidei dialogus seu de via salutis humanae* (Vienna, 1530). Moreover, Prince Eugene fought against the Turks during the siege of Vienna in 1683 and won a serious victory at the Battle of Zenta in 1697; he also took part in the third Austrian campaign against the Turks in 1716–1718, during which Corfu was under Turkish siege.

Bessarion's actions at the council of Ferrara-Florence are perhaps best illuminated by another of his works, his orations against the Turks. Bessarion believed that only through an alliance with the West could Byzantium be saved from conquest by the Turks, and it has been suggested that he was willing to pay the price of such an alliance with a union of the churches.[12] Thus, the only other work printed during his lifetime was a plea for the undertaking of a new crusade against the Turks, his *Epistolae et orationes de bello Turcis inferendo*. Written soon after the fall of Negroponte (Chalcis in Euboea) to the Turks, it was first printed at Paris in 1471 by Ulricus Gering, Martinus Crantz and Michael Friburger. It is of the utmost rarity.[13] The Gennadius

---

8. Legrand 15th–16th c. III, no. 121.

9. For the relationship between Bessarion and George of Trebizond, see Monfasani 2007 and 1976.

10. Legrand 15th–16th c. III, no. 176.

11. Guigard 1890, p. 84.

12. See Gill (1973, pp. 119, 121–122), who discusses the divergent views of Bessarion held by various scholars.

13. See Legrand 15th–16th c. III, no. 5. Bessarion sent a manuscript copy of the oration to his friend Guillaume Fichet, professor of theology at the Sorbonne, asking for to arrange for its publication. The speech is

Holy League of Spain, Venice, and the Pope was created to fight against the Turks; the Austrians were fighting the Turks in Hungary; and the victory at Lepanto in October 1571 demonstrated that the Turks were not invincible at sea. In 1668, the city of Candia (Herakleion) capitulated to the Turks, and the whole of Crete came under Turkish rule.

Not only was the Council of Ferrara-Florence pivotal to Bessarion's future life, but it was the focus of many of his writings. A number of his works are connected not only with its theological disputes, but with the history of the Council itself. The Gennadius Library possesses two editions of the proceedings of the Council of Ferrara, one in Latin, the other in Greek, which include discussions of theological questions by Bessarion.

The earlier is a Latin edition of the *Practica* or *Acta* of the Council, translated from the Greek by Abrahamus Cretensis: *Que in hoc volumine continentur Acta generalis octave synodi sub Eugenio quarto Ferrarie...*, published in Rome by Antonio Blado in 1526 (B/T 882.8).[21] This edition contains not only the proceedings of the Council, but also George of Trebizond's translation of St. Basil's third book against Eunomius on the Holy Spirit, and two works by Bessarion: his *Oratio ad Grecos habita, que inscribitur dogmatica vel de coniunctione*, in which he presents his arguments for union with the Church of Rome, and his letter to Alexis Lascaris Philanthropinos concerning the procession of the Holy Spirit, an important text which illuminates Bessarion's arguments on the question of the *filioque*. The Gen- **31** nadius copy is finely bound in 17th-century French black morocco, with triple gilt filets on both sides, and the spine gilt with composite-tooled ornaments, including fleurons, stars, and circles. There are several pages of very interesting notes by a later French owner on the final blank leaves concerning the significance of the use of the word "eighth" in describing the Council of Ferrara-Florence. This copy later came into the hands of Sir David Dundas (1799–1877) of Ochtertyre in Perthshire, Scotland. He was Solicitor-General in England and Judge-Advocate General, a member of the Privy Council, and one of the trustees of the British Museum. He is described by William Carew Hazlitt in *The Book Collector* as a fastidious collector who purchased a book as he might a picture or a fine piece of porcelain.[22] Dundas left many of his books to Charles Wentworth George Howard, son of the Earl of Carlisle and Member of Parliament for Cumberland for over 40 years, whose bookplate is mounted on the inner pastedown.

The Greek edition was published in Rome about 50 years later, in 1577, by Francesco Zanetti with the title Αγία και οικουμενική εν Φλωρεντία γενομένη Σύνοδος (T 883 QS).[23] It contains the *Practica* of the Council and two works by George Gennadius Scholarius, Patriarch of Constantinople. According to Legrand, the information on

---

21. Legrand 15th–16th c. III, no. 280.
22. Hazlitt [1904] 2009, p. 45.
23. Legrand 15th–16th c. II, no. 156.

the Council was written by Bessarion.[24] The work was edited by Matthieu Devaris.[25] The Gennadius copy is in contemporary vellum, with two ownership signatures on a preliminary blank leaf, the first of which connects us immediately with the period in which this book was published. It is the ownership signature of Paolo del Grasso, Roman Catholic bishop of Zakynthos and Cephalonia from 1574 to 1587. He was most likely the first owner of this book, and he probably purchased it to be able to deal with the theological questions he would encounter in confronting the Orthodox clergy in his see. The ownership signature of Andrew Fletcher (1655–1716) of Saltoun is also present on the same leaf. Writer and political theorist, he was forced to leave Scotland for the Continent in the late 17th century. While living in Amsterdam, he purchased many rare books. Andrew Fletcher was reputed to have the best library in Scotland. It approximated 6,000 volumes and was not dispersed until the 1960s.[26]

Although Bessarion translated several ancient Greek texts into Latin, only two were printed close to his lifetime. The earliest is the *Metaphysics* of Aristotle, first published in 1515 at Paris by Henri Estienne.[27] It was reprinted in the third edition of Bessarion's works published by Aldus in 1516, *Bessarionis... in calumniatorem Platonis libri quatuor...* (B/GC 3050q, see description above). The Gennadius Library also possesses a late edition printed in 1593 at Venice by Domenico Nicolini. The work is actually an edition of St. Thomas Aquinas's exposition of the *Metaphysics*, with Bessarion's translation used for the text of Aristotle: *Divi Thomae Aquinitatis... expositionem in duodecim libros Metaphysices Aristotelis* (GC 3154.4Q). The Gennadeion copy is bound in contemporary vellum, with the title in red and black within a large woodcut border.

The other translation by Bessarion published within half a century of his lifetime is of Xenophon's memoir of Socrates: *Xenophontis de factis & dictis Socratis memoratu dignis Bessarione Cardinale Niceno interprete.* (GC 2319.2).[28] It was published by Giovanni Mazzocchi and printed in 1521 at Rome by Ariotto da Trino. The Gennadius copy is in contemporary vellum, with the ownership signature of Vincentius Armannus on the title page. This Armannus may be identified with Vincenzo Armanno, a Flemish landscape painter who worked in Rome in the early part of the 17th century and died at Venice in 1649. This copy also contains a long note in a contemporary hand on a preliminary leaf, a poem to the emperor Charles V, signed "Pie Petrus." The title is framed by a beautiful woodcut border with a coat of arms in the center of the lower section, possibly that of Egidio da Viterbo, the dedicatee.

Bessarion's position as a cardinal in Rome, close to the Pope, made him a mag-

---

24. Legrand (15th–16th c. II, p. 25) cites as his authority Vast 1878, pp. 437–449.
25. Gill 1947. Devaris was a Greek from Corfu who was brought as a youth to Rome by Janus Lascaris in about 1516.
26. See Willems 1999.
27. Legrand 15th–16th c. III, no. 170.
28. Legrand 15th–16th c. III, no. 241.

net for all Greeks arriving in Italy, and he helped them as much as he could. When Thomas Palaeologus, despot of the Morea, sought refuge in Italy after the Turkish conquest of the Peloponnesus, he turned to Bessarion, who persuaded the Pope to grant him an allowance. After Thomas's death in 1465, Bessarion continued to look after his children, who were settled near Ancona. A letter from Bessarion to the tutor of Thomas's children has been preserved. The original manuscript has disappeared, but its text was first published in a collection of Greek texts edited and translated by Jacobus Pontanus (the main work was Theophylact Simocatta's history of Tiberius II Constantine) printed at Ingolstadt in 1604 by Adam Sartorius (BL 1526)[29]. Bessarion's letter is on pages 309–311, at the end of George Phranztes's *Chronicon*. It was reprinted by Jan Meurs in his edition of Hesychius of Miletus, printed in Leiden in 1613 by Godfrey Basson (GC 2796B).[30] The Gennadeion has copies of both works. But the Gennadius Library copy of the Leiden edition has a special association for students of Byzantium, for it was owned by Charles du Fresne, Sieur du Cange (1610–1688), the great scholar of medieval Greek and Byzantine history. His ownership signature is found on a preliminary leaf dated 1623, while at the end stands the note "ανεγνωκα" and the date 1634. The Gennadius copy is in a fine 17th-century calf binding, with both upper and lower covers framed by a border of fleurs-de-lys separated by the initial "S," enclosing a central medallion with a fleur-de-lys, and with the S and the fleur-de-lys in the corners as well.

Despite that fact that Bessarion converted to Catholicism after the Council of Ferrara-Florence and lived in Italy for the rest of his life, he remained a Greek. His greatest concern was to preserve the cultural heritage of the Greek and Byzantine civilizations, and his home became the focal point of a wide circle of intellectuals who met regularly, the so-called "Academy of Bessarion." This "Academy," the intellectual ferment it generated, and the library which Bessarion left to the Venetian Senate are the lasting monuments of this great personality, a personality reflected in all its richness by the books he wrote that are preserved in the Gennadius Library.

BIBLIOGRAPHY

Coates, A., et al. 2005. *A Catalogue of Books Printed in the Fifteenth Century, now in the Bodleian Library*, Oxford I, Oxford.

Coccia, A. 1973. "*Vita e Opere del Bessarione*," in *Il Cardinale Bessarione nel V centenario del suo morte (Miscellanea Franciscana* 73) Rome, pp. 265–293.

Gill, J. 1947. "The printed editions of the *Practica* of the Council of Florence," *Orientalia Christiana Periodica* 13, pp. 486–494.

29. Legrand 17th c. I, no. 13.
30. Legrand 17th c. V, no. 32.

Gill, J. 1973. "The sincerity of Bessarion the Unionist," in *Il Cardinale Bessarione nel V centenario del suo morte* (*Miscellanea Franciscana* 73) Rome, pp. 119–136.

Guigard, J. 1890. *Nouvel Armorial du Bibliophile* I, Paris.

Hazlitt, W. C. [1904] 2009. *The Book Collector*, Teddington, Middx.

Labowsky, L. 1967. "Bessarione," in *Dizionario degli Italiani* 9, Rome, pp. 686–696.

Labowsky, L. 1979. *Bessarion's library and the Biblioteca Marciana*, Rome.

Legrand 15th–16th c. = Legrand, É. *Bibliographie hellénique, ou Description raisonnée des ouvrages publiés en grec par des Grecs aux XVe et XVIe siècles*, 4 vols., Paris 1885–1906.

Legrand 17th c. = Legrand, É. *Bibliographie hellénique, ou Description raisonnée des ouvrages publiés par des Grecs au XVIIe siècle*, 5 vols., Paris 1894–1903.

Mioni, E. 1991. "Vita del Cardinale Bessarione," in *Miscellanea marciana* 6, Venice, pp. 11–219.

Miscellanea marciana 1976. *Miscellanea marciana di studi Bessarionei*, Padua.

Mohler, L. 1967. *Kardinal Bessarion als Theologe, Humanist, und Staatsmann*, Aalen.

Monfasani, J. 1976. *George of Trebizond: A Biography*, Leiden.

Monfasani, J. 2007. "A Tale of Two Books: Bessarion's *In Calumniatorem Platonis* and George of Trebizond's *Comparatio Philosophorum Platonis et Aristotelis*," *Renaissance Studies* 22, pp. 1–15.

Ricci, S. de. [1930] 1960. *English Collectors of Books and Manuscripts (1530–1930) and their Marks of Ownership*, Bloomington.

Vast, H. 1878. *Cardinal Bessarion*, Paris.

Willems, P. J. M. 1999. *Bibliotheca Fletcheriana, or, The Extraordinary Library of Andrew Fletcher of Saltoun*, Wassenaar.

34

HIDDEN IN PLAIN SIGHT: MUSICAL TREASURES IN THE GENNADIUS LIBRARY BYZANTINE REPERTOIRES AND A SNIPPET OF MODERN GREEK HISTORY

KONSTANTINOS TERZOPOULOS

The driving force behind manuscript research is perhaps the capacity for new discovery. Although it can take years of painstaking, tedious, and patient examination of manuscript catalogues, followed by the even more strenuous folio-by-folio study of codices long forgotten, uncovering remnants of an ancient musical culture gives the researcher a reward: the opportunity for a deep breath of satisfaction. Piecing together Byzantine and post-Byzantine musical repertoires and making them accessible to modern scholars strengthens musical ties with a rich artistic and liturgical culture that offers even greater potential for exploring new connections.

This article highlights some of the riches of the hidden musical treasures that have been the subject of two years of careful and detailed examination by the author. Sixteen Greek manuscripts housed in the Gennadius Library of the American School of Classical Studies at Athens contain Byzantine chant notation. Most have never received any scholarly attention, and no attempt to compile a detailed catalogue of the entire corpus has been made for musicological purposes.[1] Although few in number, these manuscripts turn out to be a rich source of Byzantine and post-Byzantine musicological, hymnographical, and liturgical data.

1. GENERAL OVERVIEW

In the table presented here, the 16 Gennadius manuscripts that contain chant notation are listed in chronological order with the chant repertoire they contain.

Table 1

MSS No.	Date	Hymnbook
4	14th century	Menaion, Pentekostarion
23	1713	Anastasimatarion of the New Chrysaphes
24	1734 & 1758	Anastasimatarion of the New Chrysaphes
K25	August 14, 1777	Anastasimatarion of the New Chrysaphes
26	June 8, 1801	Anastasimatarion of the New Chrysaphes
27.1	April 1, 1817	Heirmologion of Petros Lampadarios

---

1. A full discussion of existing descriptions of the Gennadius manuscripts can be found in Kontogiannes and Terzopoulos (forthcoming a and b); see also Terzopoulos (forthcoming); Chatzegiakoumes 1975, 1980, 1999. Cf. Gennadius 1922; Walton, Gregory, and Papageorgiou 1981; *John Gennadius* 1986; Gennadius Library 2001.

K31	1818 (?)	Anthology of the Papadike
25.2	19th century	Anthology of the New Papadike
K30	May 23, 1820	Kalophonic heirmologion
K26	August 1827	New Anastasimatarion of Petros Lampadarios
K29	19th century	Kalophonic heirmologion
K32	19th century	Kalophonic heirmologion
K28	19th century	Kalophonic heirmologion
K27	19th century	Anthology of the Papadike
27	19th century	Anthology of the Papadike
25	19th century	(i) Argon heirmologion; (ii, iii) Anthology of the Papadike; (iv, v) Kalophonic heirmologion

K = Kyriazes collection

As has been noted, there is one manuscript from the Byzantine era — the 14th-century *Menaion* and *Pentekostarion* fragment — and the rest are from the 18th–19th centuries. The most efficient means to give a quick overview of the information hidden in these musical treasures is to proceed according to their repertoire.

2. A 14TH-CENTURY *MENAION* AND *PENTEKOSTARION* FRAGMENT (MSS 4)

Hymnbooks for the propers (hymns "proper" to a specific feast day, as opposed to the "ordinary" hymns belonging to the daily cycle of offices) of the Byzantine Rite for the monthly and Paschal liturgical cycles are called the *Menaion* and the *Pentekostarion* respectively. The *Menaion*[2] (Book of the Months) contains hymns for the morning and evening services of the daily office of prayer. The morning service is called the *Orthros* and the evening service is known as the *Hesperinos*, corresponding to the services known as Matins and Vespers in the West. The *Menaion* contains the stationary feasts, those feasts that are celebrated each year on the same date. In contrast, the *Pentekostarion* is a companion to another book known as the *Triodion*; together, they cover the movable feasts whose commemorations are dependent on the date of Pascha (Easter), which is celebrated on a different date each year.[3] *The Pentekostarion* contains the services from the Sunday of Pascha to the Sunday of All Saints, the Sunday after the feast of Pentecost, celebrated 50 days after Christ's Resurrection.

MSS 4, a 14th-century fragment of these two hymn books, is particularly rich in hymnographic and chant notations, while also preserving unique rubrics pertaining to the important Byzantine hymn type known as the *kontakion*, a long metrical ser-

---

2. Noret 1968, pp. 338, 349.

3. Cappuyns 1935; Gedeon 1899; Tillyard 1960.

mon in the style of a poetic narrative that was sung in both simple and florid chant forms.[4] The manuscript bears witness to an older practice, no longer followed, which places one of the most famous of Byzantine hymns, the "Akathistos", on the feast of the Annunciation (March 25).[5] The Kontakion was made famous by the preeminent Byzantine *melodos*, Romanus the Melodist, known as "the Pindar of Byzantine hymnography," who was active in Constantinople during the 6th century.[6]

Showing signs of extensive use, this parchment manuscript contains two types of chant notation: ekphonetic notation[7] (Fig. 6), used for the recitation of scriptural lections (Old Testament prophecies and New Testament Epistle and Gospel readings), and Middle Byzantine diastematic chant notation proper (Fig. 7), used for the repertoire of poetic hymns, known generally as *troparia*.[8]

The careful study of the hymnic content of this manuscript resulted in the discovery of 25 unpublished hymns, 12 of which are *idiomela stichera* (independent melodies)[9] written in chant notation. The metrical analysis of some of these hymns also allowed the detection of *prosomoia stichera*[10] attributed to another important 8th-century Byzantine hymnographer, Cosmas of Maiuma,[11] the foster-brother of St. John of Damascus.

3. *ANASTASIMATARIA* (MSS 23, 24, K25, 26, K26) AND *ANTHOLOGIES OF THE PAPADIKE OR NEW PAPADIKE* (MSS K31, 25.2, K27, 27, 25II, 25III)

The bulk of the Gennadius manuscripts containing Byzantine chant notation contain repertoires of the *Papadike*[12] and the *Anastasimatarion*, which contains the Sunday

---

4. For a general discussion of the *kontakion* genre, see Mitsakes [1971] 1985, pp. 171–193; Maas and Trypanis 1963, xi; Wellesz 1961, pp 179–197.

5. Mitsakes [1971] 1985; Peltomaa 2001; Tomadakes 1964.

6. Romanus Melodus has been the focus of much scholarship. A basic bibliography can be gathered from Mitsakes [1971] 1985, pp. 483–509; Romanus 1970, pp. xxvii–xxxviii; Tomadakes 1964, [1965] 1993, pp. 153–172.

7. See Engberg 1982; Floros 1998, 2005; Høeg 1935; Høeg and Zuntz 1937; Martani 2001, 2003; Thibaut [1913] 1976.

8. A generic term used in the Eastern Church for almost any hymn chanted with or without a psalmic verse; cf. Conomos 2008; Paschos 1999, p. 29; Tomadakes [1965] 1993, pp. 51–53; Wellesz 1961, 171–178.

9. *Sticheron* and *stichera* (plural) denote *troparia* that are chanted with verses (*stichoi* in Greek). The term *idiomelon* means that the hymn has no melodic model, but is chanted to its own particular melody. This type of hymn has no exact Western parallel, although similarities have been observed; see Troelsgård 1991. For a basic bibliography, see Floros 1970; Raasted 1958; Stathes 1979, pp. 37–47; Wellesz 1961, pp. 243, 358.

10. The term *pros-homoion* means "to the same (sc. melody);" *prosomoia* are therefore hymns chanted to a model melody: Wellesz 1961, p. 275.

11. Follieri and Strunk 1975, pp. 62–63. For a full bibliography of Cosmas, see Szövérffy and Topping 1978, vol. 2, pp. 14–16.

12. The Papadike, one of the most important hymnbooks, contains the chant repertoires for the psalmic repertoire of the offices of Vespers and Orthros and for the Divine Liturgy; cf. Jeffery 2001, pp. 183-184. Editions of it are often prefaced with theories of the chant notation and mode system. See Stathes 1975, pp. λε΄–λϛ΄, 44–45 (on the codex), and 34, 39–40, 44–47, 59–62 (on the genre); Wellesz 1961, pp. 284–287.

hymns whose subject is the Resurrection. These repertoires historically are directly related to the work of St. John of Damascus, the 8th-century saint from the St. Sabas monastery in the Palestinian desert who created the *Oktoechos*.[13] This name refers both to the system of eight musical modes and to the book of the *Oktoechos*, which set up the framework for subsequent Byzantine chant composition. From the end of the 8th century onward, this system would also leave its mark on the organization of chants in the Latin West.[14] The hymns (troparia) in this book are called *stichera*, after the Greek word for verse (*stichos*), since these hymns are always chanted after a Psalm verse.

The *Anastasimatarion* is a hymnbook containing the *stichera* chants for the Sunday Divine Liturgy each week. Every Sunday the chief commemoration is that of the Resurrection (*Anastasis* in Greek). Hence, the name for the book containing these chants is the *Anastasimatarion*. The melic tradition for these hymns to the Resurrection evolved during the Byzantine era, culminating with compositions of these hymns by a certain Manuel Chrysaphes, the Lampadarios of the royal clergy (ca. 1410–ca. 1475).[15] It is this work of composition that Panagiotes the Protopsaltes would take up and build upon in the 17th century so that he received the epithet "The New Chrysaphes" (Fig. 8).[16] This chant repertoire of Resurrection hymns for the Sunday services would also be disseminated beyond the Greek Church in the form of adaptations in the Slavonic dialect for the various Churches of the Balkans.[17]

38

The New Chrysaphes' *Anastasimatarion* compositions would continue to be used until a new, shorter, quicker style of rendering the *stichera troparia* became the norm. The representative of that new Ecclesiastical, *syntomon* ("concise," i.e. "fast")[18] style of chant is another Lampadarios of the Patriarchate of Constantinople, Petros the Peloponnesian (d. 1777).[19] His *Anastasimatarion* is referred to as the *New Anastasimatarion*.

The *Anastasimataria* in the Gennadius collection contain examples of chant notation from the late Byzantine period, making the each one of them a worthy representative of the Byzantine chant heritage. MSS Kyriazes 25 (Fig. 9), dated August 14, 1777, written by one Joannes of Chios, contains a note from a past librarian mentioning one of the fathers of modern musicology. It reads, "Examined by O. Strunk[20] July 20,

---

13. For a recent discussion with bibliography, see Jeffery 2001.

14. Floros 2005, pp. 8–10; Atkinson 2001. See also Mathiesen (1999, chapter 7, pp. 609-668) on the survival and transmission of Greek music theory in the Middle Ages.

15. He is also the author of an important Byzantine theoretical treatise on chant; see Chrysaphes and Conomos 1985.

16. Χρυσάφης ὁ νέος. See Stathes 1996.

17. See Velimirović and Stefanović 1966.

18. Jung 1996; Stathes 1979, pp. 41, 43, 61.

19. Patrinelis 1973, pp. 162–163, 166.

20. Born in 1901, William Oliver Strunk was the first editor of the *Journal of the American Musicological Society* and also served as director of the *Monumenta musicae Byzantinae* with C. Høeg. His publications remain fundamental to the study of Byzantine chant; for a representative selection of his work, see Strunk 1977.

1955. He says this presents more interest than the other music MSS of the Kyriazes gift" (between fols. 2 and 3).

In contrast to the *stichera* hymns, the *Papadike* hymnbook contains compositions for the chanting of the Psalms of David, as well as some other hymns from the Ordinary of the Divine Liturgy such as the Alleluia, the Trisagion, the Hagios (Sanctus) and the Cherubic and Communion Hymns. In the Middle Byzantine era, the chant repertoires were distributed between two main books, the *Asmatikon*[21] and the *Psaltikon*.[22] The *Asmatikon* contained choral compositions and the *Psaltikon* contained parts for the soloists. However, after the Latin occupation of 1214–1261, the order of service was modified, turning away from the Constantinopolitan "Cathedral Rite" toward the "Monastic Rite";[23] in reality, a dynamic combination of both would result in the production of a new type of hymnbook called the *Akolouthia*. In the post-Byzantine era, these books would be termed the *Anthologia* (Anthologies) of the *Papadike*. This type of hymnbook seems to have appeared around the end of the 13th century and contains the basic chants used in the daily services of the Church — the Vespers, the Orthros, and the Divine Liturgy. The person who is probably most representative of this era in Byzantine musical culture is the 13th-century saint and *Maïstor* (meaning "Master" or "Teacher," Master Musician) Joannes Papadopoulos Koukouzeles.[24]

In its fullest form, the *Papadike* begins with a series of short treatises on music theory and *Methodoi*,[25] or song-lessons, summarizing the nature and effects of the notational signs and the relationships between the modes (Figs. 10 and 11). Some take quite interesting graphic form, such as a *Kanonion* or *Parallage* of Koukouzeles in the shape of a wheel (Fig. 12) and a diagram of modal transformations (*Heteron Parallage*) that resembles a tree (Fig. 13). The Gennadius collection has preserved at least nine such *Methodoi*.

In the same way as there are Old *Sticherarion* and New *Sticherarion* chant traditions, the same holds true with the melodies of the *Papadike*, which is why some versions of the *Papadike* are termed "New" or, more properly, "of the New Teachers." The notational styles of the *Papadike* in the Gennadius collection run the gamut from Late Byzantine (MSS 25.2) through the exegematic notation (MSS 25 and 25.2) to the New Method (MSS K31) still used today in Greek Orthodox worship.

MSS Kyriazes 27, an *Anthologia of the Papadike*, contains an interesting piece of modern Greek history within its five original compositions by the Rev. Fr. Georgios

---

21. Floros 1970, vol. 2, pp. 259–261, 265–272; Floros 2009, pp. 18–33; Stathes 1975, p. λζ΄; Wellesz 1961, p. 144.

22. Floros 1970, vol. 2, pp. 259–261; Stathes 1975, p. λς΄; Stathes 1979, pp. 44–45; Wellesz 1961, p. 143.

23. Robert Taft, *The Byzantine Rite: A Short History* (Collegeville, MN: Liturgical Press, 1992) at 78-84.

24. Stathes 1994; Wellesz 1961, pp. 238, 261; Williams 1968.

25. Alygizakes 1997; Stathes 1997; Troelsgård 1997b.

Rysios (d. 1865).[26] One of these compositions is of special historical interest because of the dedication by its composer, "1840: Κατὰ ὀκτώβριον, διὰ τὴν Ἑλλάδα" (fol. 45 recto) at a time when modern Greece was not even 20 years old! The rendition in mode IV plagal of Psalm 71 according to the Greek numbering, Ὁ Θεός, τὸ κρῖμά σου τῷ βασιλεῖ (= Ps. 72: "Give the king thy judgments, O God"), came at a time when Otho was on the throne of Greece and would have been used liturgically in a morning service (Orthros), perhaps commemorating some royal or national event as an ekloge in the *polyeleos*. The composition is also recorded as having been specially requested by Fr. Rysios' friend, the Constantinopolitan poet and scholar Elias Tantalides (Fig. 14).[27]

Another manuscript, this one written in 1818 (MSS K31), may bear witness to the inertia of the Third Patriarchal School and its sphere of influence. Internal evidence seems to point to a student from the city of Prusa (Bursa) (Fig. 15).[28]

4. THE *HEIRMOLOGION* (MSS 251, 27.1) AND THE *KALOPHONIC HEIRMOLOGION* (MSS K29, K32, K28, 25IV, 25V)

After the *Sticherarion* and the *Papadike*, the last genre of Byzantine chant composition is that of the *Heirmologion*.[29] The troparia known as *Heirmoi* are the defining melodies for the Byzantine poetic form of the *Kanon*, which is thematically attached to of the eight Old Testament canticles (or Odes) and the New Testament canticle of the *Magnificat*, together with the *Song of Zacharias* (Ode 9 in the Byzantine reckoning). These troparia are chanted with the verses of these Biblical canticles. The hymnbooks containing them are thus called *Heirmologia*. The Gennadius collection contains two in the "exegematic" chant notation (Fig. 16).

The *Kalophonic Heirmologion* is a unique creation of post-Byzantine musical culture. The term "kalophonic," literally "beautiful voice," refers to a style of embellished chant. While the kalophonic tradition[30] can be studied in manuscripts reaching as far back as the 14th century — a kind of *Ars Nova* of this period — as a natural progression from the *Psaltikon* style reaching as far back as the 10th century, the *Kalophonic Heirmologion* is mostly represented from the 17th century onward by post-Byzantine composers like Petros Bereketes the Melodist, Germanos of New Patras, and Balasis the Priest, continuing through to the teachers of the 19th century (Fig. 17). These virtuosic compositions were meant to be performed by accomplished cantors in a

---

26. Papadopoulos [1890] 1977.
27. Blind from the age of 27, Tantalides had graduated from the Great School of the Nation in Constantinople and the Evangelical School in Smyrna, then continued his studies in Athens. He returned to Constantinople in 1845, where he taught rhetoric, ancient Greek literature, and chant at the Theological School of Halki.
28. Papadopoulos [1904] 1990, p. 232; Romanou 1990, pp. 98–100.
29. Wellesz 1961, pp. 141–142.
30. Stathes 1979 may be the most comprehensive publication to date.

highly embellished style, usually on festive occasions and in vigil settings. With the exception of sections IV and V of MSS 25, all the Gennadius Library's *Kalophonic Heirmologia* use the New Method of chant notation; MSS K30 is an especially beautiful specimen (Figs. 18 and 19).

The 16 manuscripts containing chant notation held in the Gennadius Library of the American School of Classical Studies in Athens prove upon examination to be a rich source of period musicological and liturgical information, both Byzantine and post-Byzantine. It is hoped that the careful and detailed description will be a worthy contribution to the specialized fields of Byzantine musicology and liturgy.

BIBLIOGRAPHY

Alygizakes, A. E. 1997. "Interpretation of Tones and Modes in Theoretical Handbooks of the 15th century," in Troelsgård 1997a, pp. 143–150.

Atkinson, C. M. 2001. "The other *modus*: on the theory and practice of intervals in the eleventh and twelfth centuries," in *The Study of Medieval Chant: Paths and Bridges, East and West*, ed. P. Jeffery, Woodbridge, Suffolk and Rochester, New York, pp. 233–256.

Cappuyns, N. 1935. "Le Triodion. Étude historique sur sa constitution et sa formation" (diss. Pontifical Oriental Institute, Rome).

Chatzegiakoumes, M. K. 1975. *Μουσικὰ χειρόγραφα τουρκοκρατίας (1453–1832)* I, Athens.

Chatzegiakoumes, M. K. 1980. *Χειρόγραφα Ἐκκλησιαστικῆς Μουσικῆς 1453–1820*, Athens.

Chatzegiakoumes. M. K. 1999. *Ἡ Ἐκκλησιαστικὴ Μουσικὴ τοῦ Ἑλληνισμοῦ μετὰ τὴν Ἅλωση (1453–1820)* Athens.

Chrysaphes, M., and D. E. Conomos. 1985. *The treatise of Manuel Chrysaphes, the lampadarios: On the theory of the art of chanting and on certain erroneous views that some hold about it (Mount Athos, Iviron Monastery MS 1120, July 1458)* (Monumenta musicae Byzantinae. Corpus scriptorum de re musica 2) Vienna.

Conomos, D. E. 2008. "What is a Troparion?" *Sobornost* 30. 2, pp. 59–81.

Engberg, S. G. 1982. "The Ekphonetic Chant — The Oral Tradition and the Manuscripts," *Jahrbuch der Österreichischen Byzantinistik* 32.7, pp. 41–47.

Floros, C. 1970. *Universale Neumenkunde*. 3 vols., Kassel.

Floros, C. 1998. *Η ελληνική παράδοση στις μουσικές γραφές του μεσαίωνα· Εισαγωγή στη νευματική επιστήμη. Συγκριτική παρουσίαση της ιστορικής και τεχνικής εξέλιξης των βυζαντινών, των παλαιοσλαβικών και των λατινικών μουσικών νευματογραφιών*, trans. K. Kakavelakis, Thessaloniki [orig. ed. *Einführung in die Neumenkunde*, Wilhelmshaven, 1980].

Floros, C. 2005. *Introduction to Early Medieval Notation*, trans. N. K. Moran, Warren, Mich.

Floros, C. 2009. *The Origins of Russian Music: Introduction to the Kondakarian Notation*, Frankfurt.

Follieri, E., and W. O. Strunk. 1975. *Triodium Athoum: codex Monasterii Vatopedii 1488 phototypice depictus. Pars principalis.* Copenhagen.

Gedeon, M. I., ed. 1899. *Βυζαντινὸν ἑορτολόγιον*, Constantinople.

Gennadius, J. 1922. "Catalogue of Manuscripts in the Gennadius Library..." (unpublished typescript, London).

Gennadius Library. 2001. *The Gennadius Library: 75 Years. Catalogue of the Exhibition. Γεννάδειος Βιβλιοθήκη 75 χρόνια. Κατάλογος Έκθεσης*, Athens.

Høeg, C. 1935. *La Notation Ekphonétique* I (Monumenta Byzantinae Musicae, Subsidia I.2), Copenhagen.

Høeg, C., and G. Zuntz. 1937. "Remarks on the Prophetologion," in *Quantulacumque: Studies Presented to Kirsopp Lake by Pupils, Colleagues and Friends*, ed. R. P. Casey, S. Lake, and A. K. Lake, London, pp. 189–226.

Jeffery, P. 2001. "The Earliest Oktōēchoi: The Role of Jerusalem and Palestine in the Beginnings of Modal Ordering," in *The Study of Medieval Chant: Paths and Bridges, East and West*, ed. P. Jeffery, Woodbridge, Suffolk and Rochester, New York, pp. 147–210.

John Gennadius. 1986. *John Gennadius and his Collection: An Exhibition organized by the Gennadius Library of the American School of Classical Studies*, Athens.

Jung, A. 1996. "Syntomon, A musical Genre from Around AD 800." *Cahiers de l'Institut du Moyen-Âge grec et latin* 66, pp. 25–34.

Kontogiannes, S. D., and K. Terzopoulos. Forthcoming-a. "Ἀνέκδοτα τροπάρια στὸ χειρόγραφο ἀρ. 4 τῆς Γενναδείου βιβλιοθήκης τῆς Ἀμερικανικῆς Σχολῆς Κλασσικῶν Σπουδῶν, Ἀθήνα," *Ἐπιστημονικὴ ἐπετηρὶς τῆς Θεολογικῆς Σχολῆς Ἀθηνῶν*.

Kontogiannes, S. D., and K. Terzopoulos. Forthcoming-b. "Athens, Gennadius MS 4: observations on the hymnography, chant notation and *ordo* in a Pentekostarion and Menaion Fragment from the 14th century," *Cahiers de L'Institut du Moyen-Âge Grec et Latin*.

Maas, P., and C. A. Trypanis, eds. 1963. *Sancti Romani Melodi Cantica: Cantica Genuina*, Oxford.

Martani, S. 2001. "Neume Combinations in the Ekphonetic Notation of the MS Vienna Suppl. gr. 128," in *Pravoslavna Monodija: 2 bohoslovisïka, liturgichna ta estetychna suthistï do 2000-littia khristyiansïkoi doby* (Naukovij visnik 15), Kiev, pp. 178–193.

Martani, S. 2003. "The theory and practice of ekphonetic notation: the manuscript Sinait. gr. 213," *Plainsong and Medieval Music* 12.1, pp. 15–42.

Mathiesen, T. J. 1999. *Apollo's Lyre: Greek Music and Music Theory in Antiquity and the Middle Ages*, Lincoln, Neb., and London.

Mitsakes, K. [1971] 1985. *Βυζαντινὴ ὑμνογραφία*. Athens.

Noret, J. 1968. "Ménologes, synaxaires, ménées: Essai de clarification d'une terminologie," *Analecta Bollandiana* 86, pp. 21–24.

Papadopoulos, G. I. [1890] 1977. *Συμβολαὶ εἰς τὴν ἱστορίαν τῆς παρ' ἡμῖν ἐκκλησιαστικῆς μουσικῆς*. Athens.

Papadopoulos, G. I. [1904] 1990. *Ἱστορικὴ ἐπισκόπησις τῆς βυζαντινῆς ἐκκλησιαστικῆς μουσικῆς*, repr. Katerini.

Paschos, P. V. 1999. *Λόγος καὶ μέλος. Εἰσαγωγὴ στὴ βυζαντινή-λειτουργικὴ ὑμνογραφία τῆς Ὀρθοδόξου Ἐκκλησίας: Προεισαγωγικά*, Athens.

Patrinelis, C. 1973. "Protopsaltæ, Lampadarii, and Domestikoi of the Great Church during the post-Byzantine Period (1453–1821)," in *Studies In Eastern Chant* 3, ed. M. Velimirović, London, pp. 141–170.

Peltomaa, L. M. 2001. *The Image of the Virgin Mary in the Akathistos Hymn*, Leiden.

Raasted, J. 1958. "Some Observations on the Structure of the Stichera in the Byzantine Rite," *Byzantion* 28, pp. 529–541.

Romanou, K. 1990. "A New Approach to the Work of Chrsyanthos of Madytos: the new method of musical notation in the Greek Church," in *Studies in Eastern Chant* 5, ed. D. Conomos, Crestwood, NY, pp. 89–100.

Romanus. 1970. *Kontakia of Romanos, Byzantine melodist*. 2 vols., trans. M. Carpenter, Columbia, Missouri.

Stathes, G. Th. 1975. *Τὰ χειρόγραφα βυζαντινῆς μουσικῆς: Ἅγιον Ὄρος* I, Athens.

Stathes, G. Th. 1979. *Οἱ ἀναγραμματισμοὶ καὶ τὰ μαθήματα τῆς βυζαντινῆς μελοποιίας*, Athens.

Stathes, G. Th. 1994. "Ἰωάννης Κουκουζέλης ὁ βυζαντινὸς μαῖστωρ," in *Κύκλος Ἑλληνικῆς Μουσικῆς· Βυζαντινοὶ Μελουργοί*, Athens , pp. 62–66.

Stathes, G. Th. 1996. "Παναγιώτης Χρυσάφης ὁ νέος καὶ πρωτοψάλτης" in *Μελουργοὶ τοῦ IZ´ αἰῶνα* (Megaron Mousikes music program guide, 1995–1996), Athens, pp. 7–16.

Stathes, G. Th. 1997. "Ἡ μέθοδος τῶν θέσεων τοῦ Ἰωάννου Κουκουζέλη καὶ ἡ ἐφαρμογή της," in Troelsgård 1997a, pp. 189–204.

Strunk, W. O. 1977. *Essays on Music in the Byzantine World*. New York.

Szövérffy, J., and E. C. Topping. 1978. *A Guide to Byzantine Hymnography: A Classified Bibliography of Texts and Studies*, 2 vols., Brookline, Mass.

Taft, R. 1992. *The Byzantine Rite: A Short History*, Collegeville, Minn.

Terzopoulos, K. Forthcoming-a. "Athens, Gennadius MS 4: observations on the hymnography, chant notation and *ordo* in a Pentekostarion and Menaion Fragment from the 14th century." *Cahiers de L'Institut du Moyen-Âge Grec et Latin*.

Terzopoulos, K. Forthcoming-b. "A Checklist of Manuscripts Containing Byzantine Chant Notation in the Gennadius Library of the American School of Classical Studies in Athens, Greece," *Manuscripta*.

Thibaut, J. B. [1913] 1976. *Monuments de la notation ekphonétique et hagiopolite de l'Église Grecque*, repr. Hildesheim and New York.

Tillyard, H. J. W., ed. 1960. *The Hymns of the Pentecostarium* (Monumenta musicae Byzantinae, Transcripta 7), Copenhagen.

Tomadakes, N. B. 1964. *Ἡ Ἀκάθιστος ἑορτὴ καὶ ἡ ὑμνολογία της*, Athens.

Tomadakes, N. B. [1965] 1993. *Ἡ βυζαντινὴ ὑμνογραφία καὶ ποίησις*, repr. Thessaloniki.

Troelsgård, C. 1991. "The musical structure of five Byzantine stichera and their parallels among Western antiphons." *Cahiers de l'Institut du Moyen-Age grec et latin* 61, pp. 3–48.

Troelsgård, C., ed. 1997a. *Byzantine Chant: Tradition and Reform: Acts of a Meeting held at the Danish Institute at Athens, 1993* (Monographs of the Danish Institute at Athens 2), Athens.

Troelsgård, C. 1997b. "The Development of a Didactic Poem. Some remarks on the Ison, oligon, oxeia by Ioannes Glykys," in Troelsgård 1997a, pp. 69–86.

Velimirović, M., and D. Stefanović. 1966. "Peter Lampadarios and Metropolitan Serafim of Bosnia," in *Studies in Eastern Chant* I, ed. M. Velimirović, New York and London, pp. 67–88.

Walton, F. R., T. E. Gregory, and S. Papageorgiou. 1981. *The Gennadius Library: a survey of the collections*, Athens.

Wellesz, E. 1961. *A History of Byzantine Music and Hymnography*, 2nd ed., Oxford.

Williams, E. V. 1968. "John Koukouzeles' Reform of Byzantine Chanting for Great Vespers in the Fourteenth Century" (diss., Yale Univ.).

BARBIÉ DU BOCAGE IN THE GENNADIUS LIBRARY: A PRELIMINARY INVESTIGATION

ALIKI ASVESTA

A hoard filled with information of manifold interest — antiquarian, topographic, cultural, diplomatic, commercial, and so on — is held in the remnants of the archive of the renowned French hellenist and cartographer Jean Denis Barbié du Bocage (1760–1825) that are deposited in the Gennadius Library (MSS 124–145), an archive which Joannes Gennadius purchased in 1889.[1]

As is well known, the French hellenist and cartographer Barbié du Bocage lived and took an active part in an age when the map of his country changed radically and repeatedly on all levels — territorial, political/constitutional, diplomatic, social, and ideological — as it passed from the *Ancien Régime* to the Revolution, the empire of Napoleon, and the restoration of the monarchy. These changes had reverberations in Greek affairs as well, leaving their echo and rhythm in the remains of Barbié's archive.

These remains in the Gennadius Library are composed of notes about and ex- cerpts of passages from ancient writers, sketches and drawings for maps, and notes based on travelers' texts, as well as Barbié's correspondence with a wide network of French officers scattered across the territory of the Ottoman Empire that channeled information to him. All these items represent tangible evidence of his profound knowledge of the ancient world, his tireless talent for drawing, his constant gathering of information, and his skill in coordinating projects. The impressions of his long-term progress — the routes taken, their ramifications, and the decisive moments in Barbié du Bocage's life from his beginnings to the height of his enterprises — have been left in these remnants of his writings and drawings. They display not only the stages of his solitary labors but also his talent for managing collaborative projects, his distinctively methodical and determined nature, and the alertness or even haste with

---

1. Reference to this archive and its purchase by Gennadius was made by Lowe (1936, p. 206). To be indicated here is that the material in the Gennadius Library includes, as a sort of supplement, the catalogue of the Parisian antiquarian bookseller Dufossé featuring the items for sale, directed mainly to a select clientele in Paris and London (MSS 124). This bookseller specialized in unpublished material and letters as well as manuscripts, as is noted in the catalogue, which provides descriptions of the items and lists their prices. Furthermore to be noted is that the remains of Barbié du Bocage did not initially represent a unified corpus; rather, as the catalogue shows, certain of them were sold separately and Gennadius bought them since Barbié du Bocage was the central figure. Part of this archive is also mentioned by Koumarianou (1966, pp. 128, 132), whose comments present Barbié's scientific activity as well as the scholarly and social relationships that united him with a learned circle of colleagues.

which he roughed out the sketches of his journeys so that they could be elaborated later on. The material under discussion in many respects represents the preliminary stages of development that led to the emergence of his more important works, but at the same time a part of this material can constitute an object of study on its own.

The bulk of this multifarious material cannot be exhausted by a single introductory investigation, nor can mention be made of all the files that the archive contains. Furthermore, in this article I do not claim to promote and present the work of Barbié du Bocage that is already in print; instead, I seek to identify part of the material that was used as a constituent element of his published work, from the time of its conception to its final realization, and is preserved in the Gennadius Library.

In order to understand and to evaluate the value and significance of this archive, it should suffice to recall the following points: 1) the significant role played by Barbié du Bocage as a cartographer both in the monumental publications of the time when (1785–1792) he was working alongside the Abbé Barthélemy in the Cabinet des Médailles of the Bibliothèque Nationale of France and in his public position as a geographer in the Foreign Ministry from 1803 onward; 2) the historical context in which he moved, was engaged in various activities, and distinguished himself.[2] References to his published works will be connected and combined with the corresponding preliminary works. Starting from the maps that he created for the Abbé Barthélemy's *Voyage du jeune Anacharsis*, I shall refer to the new augmented editions of these maps as well as to the drawing of other maps in relation to new political demands, and to new scientific data. In addition, I shall dwell briefly on the felicitous translation of Chandler's travel book and Barbié's contribution to the work of Choiseul-Gouffier.

A student of the geographer D'Anville, Barbié du Bocage provided the maps to accompany the Abbé Barthélemy's *Voyage du jeune Anacharsis en Grèce*, an imaginary antiquarian journey through 4th-century B.C. Greece in seven volumes which were published on the eve of the French Revolution.[3] Barthélemy was responsible for the structure and narrative of the work, but our cartographer played a very important role in the whole enterprise, for his maps, as documents, succeed in transporting the book's readers in this journey of the imagination.[4] Going beyond simple technical expertise and requirements, Barbié defines regions in his maps, picks out the passes of strategic significance where memorable events have occurred, extols regions often featuring in political thought and debate that lead to aesthetically pleasing monuments

---

2. For Barbié du Bocage's work in general, as well as for all stages of research on his archive at the Gennadeion, see Tolias (1993), an invaluable article that contains detailed information about his life and work, including its critical reception and an extensive bibliography; it also notes the libraries and government departments where Barbié du Bocage's massive *oeuvre* is kept and presents the complete catalogue of his works, which are in the Bibliothèque Nationale. See also Tolias 1996, pp. 69–72, 113–125.

3. Barthélemy 1788; in English, *Travels of Anacharsis the younger in Greece during the middle of the fourth century before the Christian era.* See Guilmet 2007, pp. 149–151.

4. Barbié du Bocage 1788.

and shrines associated with rituals, services, and habitual acts performed there. In this way he throws light on aesthetic, ideological, and political values and features of ancient Greece, educating, activating, and inscribing in memory the messages and values of the Enlightenment.

In his notes, recorded in his personal notebooks (MSS 124), Barbié methodically treasures the antiquarian material that he assimilates and uses for drawing the maps for the *Voyage du jeune Anacharsis*. Fragments of sources from the corpus of ancient Greek literature are organized according to author, geographical region, and/or monument, displaying the extent of the sources which he has collated to identify places, monuments, distances, and routes, and making evident the sense of curiosity and love that led him to this object of the mapping of antiquity, as he transforms these pieces of information into signs on a map. Examples of this in the notebooks are the references to passages from Pausanias, Strabo, Herodotus, and other writers (Figs. 20 and 21). In addition, scattered notes by Barbié derived from the works of significant 17th-century antiquarian writers such as Meursius and Gronovius can be found in MSS 140 from page 17 on, as well as in the first part of MSS 141, which contains an abundance of remarks on the topography of Attica.

Thanks to Barbié's artistic talent, details are clearly indicated on his maps. Preserved in the remains of his archive at the Gennadeion are sketches and plans of areas that helped him to calculate distances. MSS 145, under the title "A Collection of manuscript maps and plans from the archive of cartographer Barbié du Bocage," contains many of them. What is being discussed here are the drawings and plans of which he constantly writes, particularly in the foreword to his *Recueil des cartes géographiques, plans, vues et médailles*, and which show the stages in his work and the system he used before each map took final form. An example of his working methods can be gleaned from page XI of the *Recueil des cartes*, with its combination of elements, organization of material, and use of the observations made by the traveler George Wheler from the summits of Hymettus and Acrocorinth in order to determine the latitude and longitude of those regions (Fig. 22).[5]

The cartographer's enumeration of his sources and indebtednesses makes it easier for us to identify his borrowings. In addition, we encounter notes drawn from portolans for reckoning the longitude and latitude of islands (MSS 140), remarks by travelers that cover a wide range of archaeological manifestations, and descriptions of regions that are also found on his maps, certain of which contain the handwriting of his teachers D'Anville and the Abbé Barthélemy. As well, there are descriptions by the Abbé Fourmont, excerpts of testimonia by travelers (some, for example, are taken from the work of the architect Le Roy), descriptions of regions whose coinages he draws, for example from the numismatist La Motraye's *Voyages*, while his notes taken from Greek geographical writers of the 18th century — Meletios Mitrou,

---

5. MSS 145, p. 59. See also Wheler 1682, pp. 410, 443.

Anthimos Gazis, and Daniel Philippides — occupy a special place.[6] As George Tolias has observed, calling it "a triumph of critical reasoning," the cartographic work *Recueil des cartes* notably advanced the career of Barbié du Bocage.

Barbié du Bocage enriched his translation of Richard Chandler's *Travels in Asia Minor* (1775) and *Travels in Greece* (1776) with notes from Fourmont's writings and the journals of Foucherot and Fauvel, which Barbié had taken care to acquire.[7] These notes, which originated from the recent explorations in Greece by the French engineer Jacques Foucherot (1780–1781) and the connoisseur of ancient world, dealer in antiquities, and later vice-consul in Athens Louis François Sébastien Fauvel (1780–1781, 1787–1800), are linked with the identification, description, and drawing of ancient monuments and sites. As a result of Barbié's information-gathering, the French translation of Chandler's work that went into circulation embodied the progress made in the study of antiquity up to the end of the 18th century.

Significant as well was Barbié du Bocage's involvement in Choiseul-Gouffier's travel book, an ambitious archaeological undertaking that entailed the drawing of ancient monuments, the transport of ancient remains, and excavation.[8] For this project, the antiquities-loving collector and ambassador to Constantinople (1784–1792) dispatched the members of his scientific and artistic team to Asia Minor, the Cyclades, and Attica with the aim of carrying out excavations and gathering together the finds to be studied in order to shed light on aspects of ancient history and art.[9] The contribution of Barbié du Bocage to this monumental work consists mainly of the mapping of regions of Asia Minor and has left its mark in Gennadius Library MSS 125–127.

In the whirlpool of the Napoleonic Wars and the new political and ideological state of affairs that emerged, the creation of new strategic alliances, and the new, fragile spheres of influence and diplomatic alliances that formed are mirrored in Barbié du Bocage's archive. A revised edition of the *Voyage du jeune Anacharsis* was undertaken in 1798, at a time when Napoleon's armies were making their triumphant progress through Europe, in an age when new ideological messages were being hammered out in France.[10] This new edition included a map of ancient Greece, as did the previous printings, but now its geographical boundaries were extended toward Asia Minor and the Balkans, and even took in the region of Magna Graecia

---

6. Gennadius Library MSS 129, a typewritten copy of Fourmont's notes; MSS 140 (La Motraye); MSS 145 (Greek geographers). See Tolias 1993, p. 364.

7. Chandler 1806. For Fourmont, see Gennadius Library MSS 129 (typewritten transcription); Foucherot and Fauvel, "Journal de voyage fait en Grèce (1780) par les ordres de comte de Choiseul Gouffier par Foucherot et Fauvel;" MSS 132; Fauvel, "deuxième voyage de Fauvel," MSS 133. Fauvel's incoming correspondence has been published by Clairmont (2007) with a detailed cumulative bibliography.

8. Choiseul-Gouffier 1809.

9. For the research and artistic activities of Choiseul-Gouffier's staff and the transport of archaeological finds, recent studies and a comprehensive bibliography have been brought together in the catalogue of the 2007 exhibition in Avignon (Cavalier 2007).

10. Barthélemy 1799.

in Italy; the drawings were completed in 1809 and published in 1811 at the zenith of Napoleon's domination.[11] This territorially expanded map contains added evidence from direct observations made by French consuls and other officers operating in various parts of the Ottoman Empire whose letters are in Barbié du Bocage's archive. It should be noted here that after the end of the French-Turkish war in Egypt and the restoration of diplomatic relations between the two countries in 1802, France guaranteed certain favorable terms of alliance which permitted the reopening of commercial relations. The founding of new consulates in Black Sea regions and the re-establishment of operations at previously existing consulates at which activity had declined led to the presence of consuls in these regions who were acquaintances of Barbié du Bocage, and to their letters ending up in his archive.[12] These letters are referred to in the topographical and archaeological information for the areas in which their authors were serving. They came from Jean-Baptiste Martin, French consul at the Dardanelles, the consul in Bithynia Louis Allier de Hauteroche, and Fauvel, the vice-consul in Athens.[13] In addition, it contains Barbié du Bocage's correspondence with François Pouqueville, consul general in Epirus (1805–1814). This part of the dossier is important, among other things, for the topographical observations for the drawing of maps of the wider region of Ioannina, letters which the French officer Jean-Jacques Tromelin sent him from the Dalmatian coast (held by the French at that time) about his efforts to trace the footpaths of Macedonia and Epirus.[14] Aside from the testimonia provided by consular officials, we also find organized notes with detailed references to the visits by European travelers to the Greek islands down to the end of the 18th century (MSS 140), an additional indication of Barbié's steadfast alertness and gathering of information (Fig. 23).

49

One example from Barbié du Bocage's archive that is interesting for numerous reasons and deserves to be mentioned, an example partly inscribed on the materials used to make the map, is a set of notes in the form of a report with information about the area of eastern Macedonia.[15] These notes came to Barbié prior to April 1807 from the report's author, Charles François Guillaume de Chanaleilles, who compiled them in 1791; they are concerned with economic and mercantile data from

11. *Carte générale* 1811.

12. Consulates: Deherain 1924. See also Clairmont (2007, pp. 266, 272) for biographical data.

13. Martin: Gennadius Library MSS 136, "Martin consul de France aux Dardanelles. Six a.[utograph] l.[etters] to B.[arbié] du B.[ocage], an V to 1806." Allier de Hauteroche: Gennadius Library MSS 142, "Notes données par M. Allier… sur son voyage du tour de la Propontide de l'an XI (1803)," pp. 17–19. Fauvel: Gennadius Library MSS 134.

14. Pouqueville letters: Gennadius Library MSS 128; see Koumarianou 1966, p. 132. Autograph letters from Tromelin: Gennadius Library MSS 139, "Deux lettres autographes signées de J. J. de Tromelin, avec mémoires et cartes itinéraires à Barbié du Bocage, Zara, 4 Juin, 4 Juillet 1808," pp. 12–20.

15. Gennadius Library MSS 140, pp. 74–80, "Notes de Chanaleilles sur la Macedoine et Thrace ;" the full title is "Extrait de quelques papiers qui m'a confié M. de Chanaleille (*sic*) et qui sont relatifs à la levée qu'il a faite d'une partie des côtes de la Thrace et de la Macedoine."

the wider region of Macedonia, with their main emphasis on the fertile plain of the Strymon and the river of the same name that watered it.[16]

The early years of the 19th century were a crucial period for the political situation (1807), when strong ethnic liberation movements had been ignited in Macedonia in the wake of the Serbian uprising. The fertile plain of the Strymon and its river were not only a space for the production and interchange of people, goods, and ideas that connected Macedonia from the port of Thessaloniki to the wider area of the Balkans and the commercial hubs of central Europe; the region was also a place for the passage of revolutionary armies.[17] Finally, let us note that with the outbreak of the Russo-Turkish War (1806–1812), France ranged itself diplomatically on the side of Turkey, a fact which would allow it economic, commercial, and diplomatic penetration into the wider territory of the Balkans. The notes of Chanaleilles are a response to the tracing of Macedonia, this land of crossroads and prospects, and their objective is to highlight ways to exploit it.

The report projects a contoured image of the organization of the productive land combined with the productive activities of its inhabitants. The marked industrial development of the region, the techniques of cultivating cotton (and other useful species), and the trade routes which the harvest follows, the trade fairs and the working relationships present evidence for administrative structures and show aspects of the region's economic development and traffic patterns. The compiler offers statistical data and material relating to the demographic makeup of the inhabitants of the region, giving detailed information about the Koutsovlachs that is unprecedented for the period. This information extends over one route leading from Kavala to the Chalkidiki; in addition, it contains data about the fortifications, as well as scattered mentions of the antiquity of the cities along the way (Fig. 24). This wider region of eastern Macedonia is included on the *Carte générale* of 1811, whereas it is absent from the previous editions of the *Voyage du jeune Anacharsis*. Nevertheless, Barbié du Bocage did not note many of the toponyms for which he had information, perhaps because he was not completely familiar with the relevant ancient sources. Symptomatic of this practice is that the city of Serres is marked on the map: Choiseul-Gouffier had published an inscription for it at that time which provided historical evidence for the ancient city.[18]

The information supplied by Chanaleilles possesses independent interest for the local history of Macedonia and enriches the corpus of travel writing with new details,

---

16. See Clairmont 2007, pp. 112, 115: Barbié gave this data to Fauvel in two letters that also informed his correspondent of Chanaleilles' cartographic advice for the publication of the second volume of Choiseul-Gouffier's *Voyage pittoresque* (then in press); contained in this work is the map of the isthmus of Mt. Athos that Chanaleilles drew in 1791, as well as a statement that the information had been supplied by a French naval officer, namely Chanaleilles: Choiseul-Gouffier 1809, pp. 148, 115. For Chanaleilles, see Koutzakiotis 2005.
17. Objective data and other information are derived mainly from Vakalopoulos 1988, pp. 518–527.
18. Choiseul-Gouffier 1809, p. 161.

showing the efforts made by the French to strengthen their position in the region by renewing the commercial ties that had atrophied after the French Revolution.[19] It should furthermore be remarked that this report was supplemented with new details by Barbié in 1813, as shown by the events to which references are made.[20] Lingering in the wider region, we find another report which has Barbié's style of handwriting and is based on evidence provided to him by Pascal-Thomas Fourcade, the consul in Thessaloniki at the time (1813); it illuminates aspects of the energetic personality of the powerful local official Ismail Bey of Serres, as well as of the bloody internecine conflicts among local strongmen.[21] In addition, the efforts by the European powers to reconcile these local officials are evident. The gifts that Ismail Bey demands from the French are indicative of his up-to-date knowledge of the scientific progress being made in their homeland: books which could, with the learning they provided, turn out to be useful for the development of local industry, as well as the translation of Sonnini's work, originally in French, on the cultivation of cotton.[22] Even if these pieces of information are unconnected with the topic of the preparation of Barbié's map, they show other aspects of this archive that ought to be studied.

The compilation of the map of the Peloponnesus, which possesses strategic and productive interest, began in 1807 and was completed in 1808, but for political reasons that had to do with the will of the emperor Napoleon was not published until 1814. This is a regional map that gives an overview of the physical and strategic space of the Peloponnesus and other regions of central Greece as well as the islands of the Ionian and the Aegean Seas, in which the natural resources and terrain of the region are surveyed and presented, and ways of developing and exploiting it are moreover discernible; place-names, strategic locations, and fortifications are recorded in detail, reflecting the wider-ranging aims and aspirations of the French for the region, a region known and much-loved by Barbié also by way of the routes in the *Voyage du jeune Anacharsis*.

Before concerning ourselves with the preliminary materials for the map, which we can identify among the remains of Barbié's archive, we should recollect the political situation which played a part in the drafting of this map, in a period of brilliant and invigorating accomplishments by the empire of France, with the victorious expansionist progress of Napoleon's armies and other plans. This map was drawn in the period when the Ionian Islands were re-occupied by the French (1807–1813). From the position of strength they occupied there, the French had unhindered opportunities for watching, making sorties into, and generally accessing the nerve centers of the northwest and southern Peloponnesus that could be utilized for broader aims

---

19. For the economic and commercial traffic in the Thessaloniki region as attested in travelers' accounts and consular reports, see Vakalopoulos 1988, pp. 476–487; Svoronos 1956.

20. Recent events in the Balkans: Gennadius Library MSS 140, p. 78.

21. Gennadius Library MSS 139, leaf 54.

22. Sonnini 1801.

connected with strategy and conquest. These aims, and the infiltration activities by the French in the Peloponnesus during the reign of Napoleon, date from the first period of French domination in the Ionian Islands (1797–1799), when Napoleon's emissaries disembarked in the Peloponnesus, particularly the Mani, for the purpose of mobilizing and encouraging the revolutionary inclinations of the region's inhabitants at the moment when the ideas of the French Revolution were continuously gaining ground there. In Barbié's papers are found notes and sketches which show that, despite never having traveled to Greece himself, he had material about the Mani in his possession and drew detailed maps based on journeys in this region. This material consists of notes made by Tzanetakis Bey and excerpts from the work of Demetrius Comnène concerning the character and way of life of the Maniotes.[23]

The manuscript entitled "A Collection of manuscript maps and plans from the cartographer's (sic) Jean Denis Barbié du Bocage archive" (MSS 145) contains handsome regional maps which appear to have been created at the time by Barbié himself, relying on the travel statements of Guilletière, Foucherot, and others. The approaches to and routes through Laconia are depicted; the natural terrain and agricultural/resource-rich areas in the region are delineated, with comments noted above each map; modern toponyms, statistical data, natural passes, and footpaths are marked, in this way demonstrating the way in which Barbié prioritized these constituent elements of the area. The same methodology is observable in other maps as well: those of Arcadia and Boeotia provide comparable information and suggest the means of observation which a cartographer of Barbié's consequence used as he walked in the footsteps of other travelers. The map of Barbié du Bocage that shows the route from Tripolitsa (modern Tripoli) to Karytaina is based on the description of Pouqueville, which is contained in this manuscript (Fig. 25).

In these maps, Barbié's artistic talent is expressed and unfolds, a talent which might be said to have been constricted and sacrificed to cartography for reasons that had mainly do with making a living. At the same time, we observe the new priorities which his work has taken on, with its direction also guided by new criteria of political and especially strategic significance, and the remains of it in the Gennadeion are illuminating for this turn of mind.

The exceptionally good topographical map of Tripoli (Tripolitsa), capital city and headquarters of the Pasha of the Peloponnesus, is of particular interest. In this map, which was published in black-and-white at a small scale in Pouqueville's three-volume work about his travels in various parts of the Ottoman Empire, the social web of the city is displayed in all its contours, with public buildings, passageways, meeting-places, bazaars, and the like.[24] The cartographer follows the description that Pouqueville, who had been a prisoner there in 1801, has in his publication.

23. Gennadius Library MSS 139 (Tzanetakis Bey's notes); Comnène 1784.
24. Pouqueville 1805.

These maps seem to have been created at the beginning of the 19th century and are incorporated into Barbié's *Carte de la Morée* (Map of the Morea).[25] For the drawing up of this regional map, a significant analytical catalogue containing all the toponyms of each area placed in a series has been identified among Barbié's literary remains; here, we can follow the entire route inch by inch through the southern Peloponnesus and central Greece, including the Ionian Islands and certain of the Cyclades. All the toponyms that fill and comprise the map are listed in this catalogue.[26] In addition to the source material from French consular officials and missionaries, I surmise that for the toponyms the map has also been enriched by details from Venetian archives, which at that time were under imperial French control, since the areas featured on the map had in the past come under Venetian domination. Even if this map is not distinguished by its accuracy, the fact that it contains so many place-names, some albeit positioned only approximately, gives it a certain *gravitas*. Besides, we know that this map was not going to end up being useful for strategic reasons at that time, since the breakup of Napoleon's regime swept away all the Emperor's plans.

We should observe that in the annotations contained in the map, the cartographer indicated the sources which he used, something which helps to locate certain of them in his literary remains: detailed statistical data and calculations of distances are given by the consul Félix Beaujour, who traced the region in the 1790s, especially during the years 1797–1799. [27] The testimonia of Fourmont, Foucherot, and Fauvel open new roads and contribute to the identification of ancient cities; they are frequently accompanied by sketches of Attica, Boeotia, and Messenia, which we encounter among Barbié's papers.[28] In these notes (MSS 140) appear items of information interwoven with the productive activities of the inhabitants of the region, with its lucrative tax income and administrative structure.

The literary and artistic remains of Barbié du Bocage at the Gennadeion are revealing both of the foundation on which his work rested and of the cartographer's human side, the methodical, clear, and persevering way in which he worked, on the basis of which he would control his material and put together his works. They offer a sample of his activity and his work involving the geography of ancient and modern Greece. As becomes evident in his papers, every location that was to be drawn on the map was a product of calculation, organization, and cross-checking of many pieces of information, and even of the direct observation of his collaborators. Using his graphic skills, Barbié transformed his information and expertise into an easily readable map. From the calculations, which combine data and parameters — the morphology of the terrain, the proximity, access, or distance of places and passes in the natural

25. Barbié du Bocage 1814.
26. Gennadius Library MSS 140, pp. 117–128.
27. Information from Beaujour: Gennadius Library MSS 139, leaves 4–10.
28. Gennadius Library MSS 140, p. 136; MSS 145; MSS 134, p. 10. Letter to Barbié: Fauvel 1806.

and built-up space — the recipient is called upon to observe and to comprehend the mechanisms and causes of events, and to look for ways of developing and making the most of new ideas, data, and goals. In his papers is charted the progress of his activity and the transition he made from edifying antiquarian maps with observations to regional maps for the period in which he himself lived, when the map became a vehicle for accessing, overseeing, and acting in productive and strategic space.

Beyond showing the stages that entailed working by himself, Barbié's correspondence — which is present in the archive, but which can be mentioned only briefly — lets pieces of information be shown that were written candidly and even confidentially on certain occasions, and have carefully been preserved in his papers. And certainly beyond the articulation of questions to a particular collaborator of his, who was usually some consul charged with personally inspecting places in the region where he was serving, the replies, usually associated with topographical or archaeological content, do possess interest. Thus, items of information have been preserved which display aspects of the local history of regions of the Ottoman Empire. Otherwise, over and above its convergence with and integration into large-scale works and enterprises, Barbié's material frequently constitutes an object of study in its own right, or even can even supply information relevant to other subject areas: history, geography, biography, travel literature, and diplomatic correspondence.

Many scholars have made much of one part of the archive of Barbié du Bocage in the Gennadius Library but, as this study shows, the material which the archive contains has far more to offer to researchers. A great part of the material remains unexplored. I am working on a finding aid that will provide assistance in this direction and contain subjects such as 1) written notes and sketches of ancient and modern geographical features, including place-names, which cover a wide area of the Ottoman Empire; 2) persons whom Barbié mentions or with whom he works; and 3) topics of archaeological, topographical, commercial, and diplomatic interest, as well as historically significant events.

This archive illuminates many facets of the history of pre-revolutionary Greece, as well as the viewpoint and aspirations of the French with regard to the ancient and modern history of Greece. What is more, it bears witness to the constant engagement, the discernment, and the farsightedness of Joannes Gennadius, who purchased these remains — a part of which, as we have seen, comprises the basis for Barbié's drawing up of the maps for Barthélemy's work — in the year 1889, a century after the first edition of the *Voyage du jeune Anacharsis*.

BIBLIOGRAPHY

Barbié du Bocage, J. D. 1788. *Recueil des cartes géographiques, plans, vues et médailles de l'ancienne Grèce, relatifs au voyage du jeune Anacharsis: précédé d'une analyse critique des cartes*, Paris.

Barbié du Bocage, J. D. 1814. *Carte de la Morée: dressée et gravée au Dépôt de la Guerre par ordre du Gouvernment en 1807*, Paris.

Barthélemy, J.-J. 1788. *Voyage du jeune Anacharsis en Grèce, vers le milieu du quatrième siècle avant l'ère vulgaire*, 7 vols., Paris.

Barthélemy, J.-J. 1799. *Recueil de cartes géographiques, plans, vues et medailles de l'ancienne Grèce relatifs au voyage du jeune Anacharsis: précédé d'une analyse critique des cartes*, Paris.

Carte générale. 1811. *Carte générale de la Grèce et d'une grande partie de ses colonies, tant en Europe qu'en Asie, pour le* Voyage du jeune Anacharsis, *commencée en 1798, et terminée en 1809*, Paris.

Cavalier, O. 2007. *Le Voyage en Grèce du Comte de Choiseul-Gouffier*, Avignon.

Chandler, R. 1806. *Voyages dans l'Asie Mineure et en Grèce*, trans. and comm. J.-P. Servois and J. D. Barbié du Bocage, Paris.

Choiseul-Gouffier, M. G. A. F., Comte de. 1809. *Voyage pittoresque de la Grèce 2*, Paris.

Clairmont, C. W. 2007. *Fauvel: The First Archaeologist in Athens and his Philhellenic Correspondents*, Kilchberg-Zurich.

Comnène, D. 1784. *Précis historique de la maison impériale des Comnènes, où l'on trouve l'origine, les mœurs et les usages des Maniotes*, Amsterdam.

Deherain, H. 1924. "Les premiers consuls de France sur la côte septentrionale de l'Anatolie," *Revue de l'histoire des colonies françaises* 17, pp. 301–380.

Fauvel, L. F. S. 1806. "Copie d'une lettre écrite d'Athènes, le 20 frimaire an XIV," *Magasin Encyclopédique* 3 (May 1806), pp. 116–122.

Guilmet, C., 2007. "Concerning Anacharsis, 1789–1820," in *Following Pausanias: the Quest for Greek Antiquity*, ed. M. Georgopoulou, C. Guilmet, Y. A. Pikoulas, K. S. Staikos, and G. Tolias, Athens and New Castle, Del., pp. 139–154.

Koumarianou, K., ed. 1966. *Αλληλογραφία Δανιήλ Φιλιππίδης, Barbié du Bocage, Ανθιμος Γαζής (1794–1819)*, Athens.

Koutzakiotis, G. 2005. "À la recherche du royaume antique – Les investigations de Choiseul Gouffier et ses collaborateurs en Macédoine (1787–1792)," *Ο Ερανιστής* 25, pp. 119–155.

Lowe, C. G. 1936. "Fauvel's First Trip through Greece," *Hesperia* 5, pp. 206–224.

Pouqueville, F. C. H. L. 1805. *Voyage en Morée, à Constantinople, en Albanie et dans plusieurs autres parties de l'Empire othoman pendant les années 1798, 1799, 1800 et 1801*, 3 vols., Paris.

Sonnini, C. S. 1801. *Voyage en Grèce et en Turquie: fait par ordre de Louis XVI et avec l'autorisation de la cour ottomane*, 2 vols., Paris.

Svoronos, N. G. 1956. *Le commerce de Salonique au XVIIIe siècle*, Paris [= *Το εμπόριο της Θεσσαλονίκης τον 18o αιώνα*, Athens 1996].

Tolias, G. 1993. "Στη σκιά των περιηγητών: Το ελληνικό γεωγραφικό και χαρτογραφικό έργο του Jean-Denis Barbié du Bocage," in *Περιηγητικά Θέματα: Τετραδία Εργασίας* 17 (K.N.E./E.I.E.), Athens, pp. 321–423.

Tolias, G. 1996. *La medaille et la rouille: l'image de la Grèce moderne dans la presse littéraire parisienne (1794–1815)*, Athens.

Vakalopoulos, A. 1988. *Η ιστορία της Μακεδονίας 1354–1833*, Thessaloniki.

Wheler, G. 1682. *A journey into Greece. . . . in company of Dr. Spon of Lyons, with variety of sculptures*, London.

PROSPER BACCUET AND THE FRENCH
EXPÉDITION SCIENTIFIQUE DE MORÉE:
IMAGES OF NAVARINO IN THE GENNADIUS LIBRARY

JACK L. DAVIS

On August 27, 1828, a young French landscape artist and cavalry officer, Prosper Baccuet (1798–1854), submitted his application to join the greatest Western European scientific mission to Greece.[1] He spoke English and Italian, and was only 30 years old. Later, in 1839, Baccuet would join another French scientific team, this time in Algeria. But he remained best known for his work in Greece, his landscapes popularized at the Salon in Paris between 1831 and 1851 through the exhibition of tableaux inspired by his travels.[2]

The "scientific expedition" in which Baccuet enlisted followed in the wake of a military campaign, the so-called *Expédition de Morée*, that left Toulon in late August, 1828.[3] Thus began a four-year military intervention that laid the infrastructure on which a stable modern Greek state could be established. On August 30, Lieutenant General Nicolas Joseph Maison landed with ca. 14,000 troops at Petalidi in Messenia, preferring not to expose himself to cannon fire from the fortress of Neokastro.[4] On October 1, the French troops were reviewed in their camp at Yialova near Paleokastro, in the presence of Ibrahim Pasha. Ibrahim's Egyptian troops began to be evacuated on September 16, 1828, under the terms of a treaty brokered in Cairo by Admiral Sir Edward Codrington, and the fortress of Neokastro was occupied by the French on October 6. The last Ottoman stronghold, the Castle of the Morea near Patras, surrendered on October 30. French troops began to depart Greece

---

1. Peltre 1997, p. 91. I am grateful to many friends for help offered in the course of preparation of this contribution to *The New Griffon*. Thanks first of all to Maria Georgopoulou, who suggested that I write it; next, to Achilleas Costantacopoulos and Shari Stocker, who share my obsession with the geography of Navarino and accompanied me in the field. I am no less grateful to Ioli Vingopoulou for discussions about Baccuet and his work, and to Jennifer and Arthur Stephens for their superb photographs. Melanie Oelgeschläger kindly provided an image of Smyth's map (after Eleftheria Daleziou pointed me to her). Robert Bridges and Irini Solomonidi were trusted advisors in all instances where my own French failed me. Shari Stocker and John Bennet read the text and rescued me from some of the most embarrassing errors. Nikos Kontogiannis and Sophia Sakkari generously shared their knowledge of Medieval and post-Byzantine archaeology in the Pylos area. Finally, Karen Bohrer helped me to locate electronic resources.
2. Peltre 1997, pp. 106, 194.
3. See Musset-Pathay 1829, pp. 195–206, for the historical context of the military mission.
4. In this paper, the name Neokastro refers to the fortress of New Navarino, at the southeast side of the Bay of Navarino, while Paleokastro is the fortress of Old Navarino at its northwest side. Navarino more generally denotes the entire area around the bay, while the town of Navarino is modern Pylos. See Wolpert 2005 and Bennet, Davis, and Harlan 2005.

on December 29, although a military presence in the Peloponnese was maintained until August 1833.

The fighting complete, the remaining troops turned their energies to reconstruction. Among their many projects were a bridge over the Pamisos river, a road to link Neokastro and Modon, and repairs to the fortress of Neokastro itself.

It had been proposed that this military force would be accompanied by a group of scholars and scientists, as had Napoleon's army in Egypt. On November 22, a commission was created officially to establish the scientific program and on December 4 its leaders were chosen. The members of the *Expédition Scientifique de Morée* were organized in three sections: "Archéologie"; "Histoire Naturelle" (later called "Sciences Physiques"); and "Architecture et Sculpture."[5]

Baccuet was to be in charge of the preparation of drawings for the "Histoire naturelle" section and thus found himself in the employ of Jean Baptiste Bory de St. Vincent, one of the greatest naturalists of his day and later also commander of the French mission to Algeria.[6] Some twenty of his drawings were chosen by Bory de St. Vincent to be engraved for lithographic reproduction in the *Atlas* of the Expédition Scientifique de Morée.[7]

JOHN GENNADIUS AND THE EXPÉDITION SCIENTIFIQUE DE MORÉE

A collection of original drawings and vignettes by Baccuet, now in the Gennadius Library, was purchased at auction in Paris by John Gennadius in 1905.[8]

These works of art, many of them never engraved and published, were bound in luxurious red leather to match Gennadius's own copy of publications of the Expédition scientifique de Morée. On a blank front endpaper he pasted a clipping from the sale catalogue beneath a note in pencil:

"THE ORIGINAL DRAWINGS FROM THE "EXPÉDITION SCIENTIFIQUE DANS LA MORÉE."[9]
Gennadius further annotated in pencil: "Bought at P.S. in Paris XI' 05 through E. Paul et fils et Guillimen, nice hf. band volume. The drawings are in a dirty and delapidated

---

5. See Saitas, forthcoming.

6. Bory de St. Vincent, a former cavalry officer himself, spoke of Baccuet with considerable affection and appreciation (1836b, p. viii): "M.M. de Martignac et Siméon, dis-je, m'adjoignirent, en qualité de peintre, M. Baccuet, qui, tout officier de cavalerie qu'il est, comme je l'ai été moi-méme, n'en est pas moins un paysagiste distingué, dont il sera souvent parlé dans une relation à la clarté de laquelle contribue principalement la fidélité des ses dessins."

7. *Atlas*.

8. A catalogue of these drawings was published in 1999 by Ioli Vingopoulou of the National Hellenic Research Center in Athens. Several are illustrated there.

9. The auction catalogue described the lot as follows: RECUEIL DE CINQUANTE QUATRE DESSINS ORIGINAUX AU CRAYON ET A LA PLUME représentant des vues, des monuments et des costumes de la Grèce, faits en 1829 par S. Baccüet, avec des annotations de Bory St-Vincent.

condition. I have cleaned, inlaid them neatly, but have kept them in the same order. They are an invaluable addition to my copy of the Expédition Scientifique. J.G."

The volume came from the collection of Pierre François Lèon Duchesne de la Sicotière. La Sicotière (1812–1895) was a bibliophile and collector, renowned for his passion for history and service both to the "Société des antiquaires de Normandie" and to the "Société française d'Archéologie."

Gennadius was particularly interested in the French expedition, as is clear from another clipping from an auction house catalogue pasted inside the same volume: the one that got away![10]

Folio. Sold at Southeby's. 27/1/21 for £16.

259. Expédition de Morée par Bory de St. Vincent dessins originaux, 73 original drawings for this work by Oufart, Pretre, Meunier and Delile, the drawings of zoology very finely coloured, those of botany plain as in the published work, half cloth. n.d.

BACCUET'S DRAWINGS OF NAVARINO

My purpose in this paper is to consider fourteen drawings and one vignette from the collection acquired by Gennadius, those depicting the town of Navarino, the fortresses of Paleokastro and Neokastro, and other scenes around the Bay of Navarino. These illustrations are among the few contemporary representations of the French military presence in the Morea, and would be valuable for that reason alone since the fortress of Neokastro and the town of Navarino became headquarters for the expeditionary force. They are, however, of interest for many other reasons. The illustrations suggest, for example, how the French viewed their presence in Greece and how they wanted it to be perceived in Western Europe.

Baccuet's drawings were produced so that Bory de St. Vincent could convey information in a particular, interpretive way. I will show how this is so in reference to the final drawing of Navarino in Gennadius's collection, an elaborate, pastoral representation of an unlikely subject — a military hospital. This work, and others produced by Baccuet, can only be understood in reference to the text of Bory de St. Vincent's *Relation*.[11] Although the drawing in question was never published, it was designed to accompany this text and it will be clear that Baccuet was not working independently of Bory de St. Vincent.

Half of the drawings of Navarino in the collection consist of repetitive views of Paleokastro, the old Frankish fortress built by Nicolas St. Omer in the 13th century.[12]

10. Gennadius's disappointment is palpable: "This lot was bought by Anoritch. I missed by giving to the auctioneer a lower limit by a pound or two."
11. 1836a; 1836b.
12. Wolpert 2005, pp. 232–233.

The remainder, however, illustrate the deplorable conditions that existed in the Peloponnese in the aftermath of the Battle of Navarino in 1827 and the departure of Ibrahim Pasha the following year. Although such matters were often treated in the published memoirs of French scholars and military officers, they were rarely represented in the visual arts during the initial years of an independent Greece.

Of the illustrations of Navarino in the Gennadius Library, only three were published in the *Atlas*. The drawings of Navarino are here numbered as they appear in Gennadius's bound volume of originals.[13]

7. VIEW FROM PALEOKASTRO OF TURKISH AND EGYPTIAN VESSELS SUNK IN THE BATTLE OF NAVARINO.

All notes in pencil. Caption, lower right: "(ancienne Pylos) Vue prise de Zonchio, où vieux Navarrin [...] turc et les vaisseaux Egyptiennes apres la Bataille de Navarrin. P. Baccuët, Grèce 1829." Labels: "S. Nicolo"; "Grèce – Navarrin 1829"; "L'île de Sphactérie; Navarrin"; "Batimens Egyptiens coulés [?bas]; Débris de la flotte Egyptienne".

12. BAY OF NAVARINO WITH LOCATION OF FRENCH CAMP AT YIALOVA.

Caption and legend in ink, lower left: "No. I. Navarin au déboucher du col où passe la route de Modon. A. Base du St.-Nicolo. B. Sphactérie. C. D'antique Pylos ou Paleokastro. D. fin de marais. Grèce. P. Baccuët 1829." Upper left, in ink: "(Notes de Bory St. Vincent). Labels: "B. Sphactérie; C. Pylos que avait autrefois [...]; Camp de Yalowa." Others *in rasura*.[14]

19. WOMAN AND CHILD.

Caption in ink, bottom right: "Scene et bataille de Navarin." In pencil, bottom right: "Navarin — Grèce 1829. P. Baccuët."[15]

21. PALEOKASTRO WITH FRENCH BIVOUAC.

Caption in ink, top left: "No. 10. Antique Pylos. La Sphactérie aujourd'hui Sphagia. (Notes de Bory St. Vincent)."

Legend in ink, bottom: "No. 10. Paléo-castro, ou l'antique Pylos. Prise de Sphactérie. A. L'acropole. B. L'ancienne ville des croisés. C. Notre camp. D. Côté [...] ou l'île est coupé à pic. P. Baccuët E. [...] la Baie de Navarin communique avec les détroits de Sphactérie. F. Grande lagune intériéure. G. Isthme." Labels in pencil by Baccuët: "Notre bivouac; Navarrin ou Pylos; L'acropole Navarin vénitienne; Grotte dite de Nestore." Truncated legend in ink, lower right: "marais."[16]

---

13. I provide transcriptions of captions, legends, and labels. All were handwritten on the drawings, in pencil by Baccuet, in ink by Bory; [...] indicates an illegible section. The English titles are my own.

14. Engraved and published as *Atlas*, pl. VII.

15. See Bory de St. Vincent 1836a, p. 159 (description of the "femme sans langue").

16. *Atlas*, pl. x.

22. SHANTYTOWN AT NAVARINO.

"A Navarrin. 1829. Barraques. P. Baccuët. Grèce." Note in upper left: "Route condui-sant à l'hôpital de la marine."[17]

23. EASTERN PART OF THE INTERIOR OF THE FORTRESS OF NEOKASTRO.

Caption in pencil, lower left: "Intérieur de la citadelle ou la ville de Navarin. Grèce. P. Baccuët." Labels in pencil: "Citadelle; Mosquée turc."[18]

24. WESTERN PART OF THE INTERIOR OF THE FORTRESS OF NEOKASTRO.

Caption and legend in ink, lower left: "No. 2. Navarin, vu de la maison qui fut le sérail d'Ibrahim avec Sphactérie. A. L'antique Pylos; B. Sphactérie; C. Tombeau de l'amiral turc tué a la Bataille de Navarin (d'autres disaient d'un saint turc); Grèce Baccuët 1829; D. Point d'où est prise la vue No. 3 [= No. 23 in the Gennadius Collection] autour nous la dos à la mer." Labels in ink: "C. Tombeaux turc; Batteries d'Ibrahim; Sphactérie; La passe; Pylos; Mosquée turc." Label in pencil: "Tombeau Sta. Rosa." Upper left in ink: ("notes de Bory").[19]

30. PALEOKASTRO WITH CAVE OF NESTOR MARKED; VIEW FROM VOIDOKOILIA BAY.

Legends lower left in ink: "Notes de Bory St. Vincent. Paleokastro ou l'antique Pylos, prise de la plage du golphe de Βοϊδοκοιλία. […] indiqué sur aucune carte. L'acropole. B. La grotte dite de Nestor." Labels in pencil on drawing: "Pylos. Tour venitienne. 6." [vacat at location of Cave of Nestor]. In pencil, lower left: "Baccuët Grèce 1829." **61**

33. PALEOKASTRO FROM VOIDOKOILIA BAY.

Caption in pencil, bottom right: "P. Baccuët (Grèce) Zonchio ou vieux Navarin." Labels in pencil: "Vieux Navarin. Ancienne Pylos."[20]

47. VIEW OF NEOKASTRO AND BAY.

Caption in pencil, bottom left: "Navarin en venant de Modon. 1829. Baccuët." Labels in pencil: "L'île Sphacterie. Pylos."

48. FISHERMEN SCAVENGING WRECKS FROM BATTLE OF NAVARINO.

Caption in pencil, bottom left: "(Vieux Navarrin) à Zonchio ancienne Pylos. Pecheurs de Zante à la recherche dans débris du combat du Navarin. (Grèce) 1829. P. Bac-cuët." Label in pencil: "Rade."

49. SHANTYTOWN AT NAVARINO, VIEWED FROM HELONAKI.

Label in pencil, lower left: "Navarin. Baccuët 1829 (Grèce) Navarrin. […] fort.)."[21]

---

17. Vingopoulou 1999, p. 338, fig. 1.
18. Bennet, Davis, and Harlan 2005, p. 253, fig. III.15.
19. Bennet, Davis, and Harlan 2005, p. 253, fig. III.16.
20. *Atlas*, pl. xi.
21. Bennet, Davis, and Harlan 2005, p. 253, fig. III.16.

50. PALEOKASTRO AND FRENCH TENTS.

Legends in ink: "P. Baccuët (Grèce) Ancien Navarin, ou (Pylos), grotte du Nestor. 1829." Labels in pencil: Ancienne Pylos; forteresse vénitienne Navarrin; grotte de Nestor."

51. ENTRANCE TO BAY OF NAVARINO.

Caption in pencil, bottom left: "No. 40. Entrée de la rade de Navarin 1829. En venant de Sicile. P. Baccuët. Grèce 1829."

52. FRENCH MILITARY HOSPITAL NEAR YIALOVA.

Legends in ink: "De le hôpital de la marine. Vue du camp de Yalovva, à Navarin. (Grèce 1829). P. Baccuët." Labels in pencil: "Route de Navarrin; Sphactérie; Pylos; Camp de Yialovva; hôpital de la marine."

THE BACCUET DRAWINGS OF PYLOS AND THE ART OF WAR

Baccuet's role as a painter has been considered by Christine Peltre in the context of contemporary French landscape artists in Greece. Most of a chapter in her book, *Retour en Arcadie*, is in fact devoted to the Expédition Scientifique de Morée and much of the discussion there concerns Baccuet.[22] Peltre describes Baccuet's style in reference to fashions in landscape painting that had recently been established by his teacher, Louis-Étienne Watelet (1780–1866):

> L'oeuvre grecque de Baccuet se souvient des ces leçons, qui recueille avec un intérêt particulier des ravinements, les anfractuosités, le remous d'une terre tourmentée, amplifiant un peu à vrai dire la réalité du pays.[23]

She correctly notes a tendency toward hyperbole that cannot be explained by the scientific purpose of the drawings alone. Relief is exaggerated, giving the land a "physionomie extraordinaire":

> On remarque parfois chez Baccuet une tendance à l'emphase. L'attention géologique n'explique pas tout. Les reliefs sont accentués à l'excès, comme s'il s'agissait de curiosités uniques.[24]

Peltre's particular examples are engravings of Mt. Taygetos and Mistras, although the same tendencies are present in his drawings of landscapes of Navarino.[25] These instances display an amplified reality that contrasts sharply with attempts to repro-

22. Peltre 1997, pp. 73–112.
23. Peltre 1997, p. 97.
24. Peltre 1997, pp. 103–104.
25. The tendency is obvious in at least some, but not all, of the drawings in the Gennadius Library. I thank Ioli Vingopoulou for discussing this point with me. It is also worth noting here that we know nothing about Baccuet's oil paintings of Greek landscapes. See Vingoropoulou, forthcoming.

duce landscapes and monuments with photographic fidelity by predecessors like Edward Dodwell, or successors like Caruelle d'Aligny.

Peltre also argues that the artists of the Expédition did not feel comfortable in conveying back to France a view of a desolated land.[26] She suggests that the goal of these artists was to promote a positive image of Greece, to show readers the genius of the Greek people, and offer a glimpse of the bright future that lay ahead. If this is so, however, an improbable conclusion follows: that Baccuet and other artists did not understand that their art would be published along with texts that described the horrors of war at its worst.

Bory de St. Vincent provided descriptions of the cruelty of Greeks toward Turks as well as that of Turks and Egyptians toward Greeks. One of his most graphic passages introduced pl. ix in the *Atlas*, although, as Peltre notes, there was employed a "caractère bonhomme propre à la lithographie pittoresque" with two living figures masking the more macabre part of the scene.[27] I return to an analysis of this lithograph below, which in any case is not the work of Baccuet.[28]

The pain of war was widespread and witnessed even by the simplest of French soldiers. I quote from a letter sent from Koroni by a young infantryman to his parents more than a year after the arrival of Maison's troops: "Et je vous dirais que le pays a boucoup prospéré depuis que nous y sommes car était affreux de voir de la manière que les villes et villages étaient dévastés et ravagés par les turqs ou les arabes."[29] The devastation was more eloquently documented in the works of several French officers who published accounts of their participation in the military expedition.[30] Three years later, in 1833, one of them could still comment on the destruction in the countryside, although by then the town of Navarino was itself thriving:

> Presque partout des traces d'anciennes habitations; partout des monumens, plus tristes encore, de la barbarie musulmane, dans les énormes troncs d'oliviers brûlés à un pied du sol, de mûriers et de figuiers mutilés par le fer ou la flamme.[31]

THE FRENCH NAVAL HOSPITAL AT NAVARINO

The army suffered most of its casualties from disease. Guillaume Gaspard Roux, the doctor in charge of providing medical care during the first months of the occupation

---

26. Peltre 1997, p. 103.

27. Peltre 1997, p. 103.

28. Peltre is mistaken in believing pl. ix to be Baccuet's work. It is signed "Bory del." and credited to Bory de St. Vincent in the list of plates in the *Atlas*. She considers it to be the only published drawing by Baccuet that shows the horrors of war, whereas there is, in fact, none that does.

29. Letter to Monsieur et Madame Espèrey Brun in Camaret-sur-Aigues, written October 28, 1829. Unpublished; in my own collection. The French is here transcribed precisely; the spellings follow the original.

30. Amaury-Duval 1885; Bessan 1833; Duheaume 1833; Mangeart 1830; Schlumberger 1910, pp. 205–210, 231–283; Pellion 1855; Roux 1829.

31. Lacour 1834, p. 27.

of the Morea, described the deplorable conditions that had existed — particularly in the camp at Yialova, where much of the French army was based before Navarino was evacuated by Ibrahim. In the first seven months of the campaign nearly 5,000 patients were treated, and there were nearly 1,000 casualties, most of them lost to "maladies fiévreux."[32]

After the departure of Ibrahim, conditions were more settled. Roux established a hospital complex at the port of Navarino, east of the modern town square.[33] Two existing buildings were adapted for reuse: one that could hold 160–180 patients in a single room; another, 14 officers and 100 patients separately.

Other medical facilities were built in the wider Navarino area. Halfway between Navarino and Methoni a convalescent facility was established.[34] Lacour describes it thus : "... sur la hauteur à gauche trois corps de bâtimens de construction française, que le général Schneider destinait à une maison de convalesence pour nos soldats." It did not last long. Lacour continues: "L'éloignement des deux villes, l'ennui inséparable de l'isolement des camarades, j'allais ajouter l'absence des vendeurs de crassi, eurent bientôt fait abandonner un établissement où de tristes convalescences ne pouvaient être immédiatement suivies que des plus tristes nostalgies."[35]

A third, probably even more transitory, installation was the "hôpital de la marine," built near the main road leading north from Navarino. It was mentioned by various members of the Expédition Scientifique de Morée and was the focus of Baccuet's unpublished drawing no. 52 in Gennadius's collection (Fig. 26).[36] There can be no doubt that the hospital was situated somewhere near the area called Miden, where, until last year, the road leading north from Pylos forked, one branch continuing along the coast to Gargaliani, the other east to Kalamata.[37] Its location can be more precisely determined from three published itineraries that report its distance from Yialova and from the port of Navarino.

In the case of the first route "d'Arcadia à l'ancienne route de Navarin à Modon," Abel Blouet, author of the archaeological report of the Expédition Scientifique, describes a journey to Navarino from the spring of Kanalos ("Canala") near Marathopo-

---

32. Roux 1829, pp. 165–168.

33. The location is marked on an unpublished draft map produced for the Expédition scientifique, a copy of which is in the National Historical Museum of Greece (acc. no. 1870).

34. There was also a French hospital at Methoni itself; e.g., Schlumberger 1910, p. 237.

35. Lacour 1834, p. 11. This "maison de santé" must have been situated between the modern hamlet of Varakes and the village of Mesochori, probably near the church of Ayios Theodoros; its location is marked on the same map.

36. It is unclear when the hospital was built. Members of the three sections of the scientifique mission reached Navarino on March 2, 1829. The hospital is not mentioned by Roux, whose account stops after February 1829.

37. The Gargaliani branch was recently closed and the road relocated as part of the overall plan for construction of the "Costa Navarino" resort, whose first phase opened in May 2010.

lis, the scala of Gargaliani.[38] At Yialova, Blouet mentions "... à gauche, des moulins." These elsewhere are called the mills of Ayios Spyridon.[39] After passing the mills he notes three minutes later "... des cabanes sur les rive de la rade, " then 31 minutes later "... une grande montée paveé; à droite, un petit bâtiment en bois." It is clear that Blouet here is approaching the "hôpital de la marine." In the text accompanying the itinerary he describes how "une demi-heure de marche nous amena au bas d'une grande montée pavée, à la droite de laquelle était construit un petit bâtiment en bois, destiné à la marine française, qui venait y faire de l'eau à l'époque de notre voyage. À gauche était établi l'hôpital militaire de l'armée française."

On his way to Paleokastro, Bory de St. Vincent also passed the "hôpital de la marine." He relates in an itinerary and in an accompanying narrative how in leaving Navarino "... nous passâmes devant le débarcadaire, tout près de l'hôpital militaire, construit un peu au-dessus du niveau de la mer, à la base des monts calcaires qui dominent la baie par ce côté ...".[40] He then followed the road to Tripolitza (modern Tripolis), that is, the road leading north from Pylos toward Gargaliani and Kalamata. The road "s'élève sur des pentes où circule l'aqueduc, que nous trouvâmes la plupart du temps à fleur de terre et très dégradé." After crossing a narrow ravine by means of a stone bridge, he followed a Venetian paved road in bad condition, with the sea on his left, and "presque sous nos pas ... à pic des montagnes un peu plus loin à droite." He then noted regarding the road that "... il avait traversé l'aqueduc, qu'il longeait en le laissant du côté de la rade; il le recoupa à quelque distance près des restes d'une vieille tour à peine reconnaissable, et qui dut servir pour des signaux. Nous y étions à une demi-lieue environ de la ville."[41]

Bory de St. Vincent next observes that the valley of a small river, the Navarinitza, opens in front of him.[42] It is "... en ce point que la marine française avait établi son hôpital parallèlement à l'une des sinuosités du conduit d'eau et dans une excellent exposition." There follows a detailed description of the hospital itself, one that fits Baccuet's depiction of it precisely:

Ce bâtiment, construit en planches et dont la toiture était recouverte de cette grosse toile goudronnée dont on fait les prélats, présentait extérieurement à peu près la forme qu'on donne à l'arche de Noé dans les images où sont

65

---

38. Blouet 1831-1838, vol. 3, p. 47.

39. Mills at Yialova drew their power from the Yianouzaga River, Smyth's Kurbeh River.

40. Bory de St. Vincent 1836a, p. 135. This "hôpital militaire" is that built in the town of Navarino under Roux's supervision. On p. 133, Bory de St. Vincent describes it and the other buildings at the port: "... les magasins militaires, l'artillerie et l'hôpital, la douane grecque, avec un commissaire de police, occupaient le faubourg du port, où l'on débarque à l'aide d'une sorte d'estacade en madriers et en planches, qui se prolonge à quelques toises sur la mer."

41. The old signal tower, a "demi-lieue" (2 km) from the harbor, was at a place still called Vigla today.

42. Navarinitza was also called Pesili.

représentés les principaux traits de la Bible; au dedans on eût dit l'entrepont d'un vaisseau de ligne bien aéré et parfaitement tenu. Les maladies qu'on y envoyait se rétablissaient promptement, et du petit jardin qu'on avait planté en terrasse sur le devant, on apercevait vers le nord-ouest, dans l'étendue basse et marécageuse de la côte, les traces de ce camp de malheur, où quelques mois au paravant tant de soldats français étaient morts victimes du mauvais choix d'un emplacement, dont personne dès-lors ne voulait convenir avoir eu la funeste idée.[43]

Key to understanding the geography of these accounts is a map compiled by Captain W. H. Smyth for the British Admiralty in 1823; it is far more detailed than that published by the Expédition scientifique in its *Atlas* (Fig. 27).[44] Smyth's map shows the route of the road north from Navarino as well as the course of the aqueduct. Bory de St. Vincent mentions the map, and it is clear that he had it in hand as he was writing. The account of his journey corresponds to details on Smyth's map: for example, the road, as drawn, crosses the aqueduct once near the modern "Hotel Philip."

Bory de St. Vincent notes that the hospital was located "parallèlement à l'une des sinuosités du conduit d'eau" and that "L'embranchement de la route que nous laissâmes à l'est sur la droite, entre le mur de l'aqueduc et les parois de l'hôpital, conduisait à Koubeh ...". Blouet's account clarifies Bory de St. Vincent's text, since, in approaching the area from the north, he notes that "À gauche était établi l'hôpital militaire de l'armée française."

A third itinerary, "Route de Goubé a Navarin," corroborates information contained in the other two.[45] Blouet in this instance was traveling along the Kalamata road toward Navarino. He finds the French hospital ("... peu de temps après, nous voyons des hangars en planches qui servent d'hôpital aux malades de notre armée que les fièvres, fléau de ce climat, déciment...") at a distance of thirty two minutes from the port of Navarino, then notes that the road crosses the aqueduct seven minutes before reaching the port. He also records a fountain at the French hospital.[46]

In drawing no. 52 of the "hôpital de la marine," Baccuet has given us a view from the hospital towards Yialova that appears to have been intentionally designed to

---

43. Bory de St. Vincent 1836a, p. 136.

44. "Greece. The Bay of Navarino. The Antient Pylos. By Captn. W.H. Smyth, R.N. F.R.S." Dated 1823. Published 1830. National Maritime Museum, London, Image L4364. For Smyth's detailed necrology, see the "Report of the Council of the Forty-Sixth Annual Meeting of the Royal Astronomical Society." His Mediterranean surveys were conducted between 1814 and 1825 and, for Greece, they constitute an invaluable record of the coastal geography of Navarino at the end of the Ottoman period.

45. Blouet 1831–1838, vol. I, p. 7.

46. An unlabelled rectangular symbol on Smyth's map, shown in the bend of the aqueduct, immediately west of the fork where the roads to Gargaliani and Kalamata split, may represent the fountain. Today there is a fountain here, but it is dry and newer than the 19th century.

contrast the tranquility of the setting of the hospital with its polar opposite — the woes of the "camp de malheur" at Yialova below it in the marshy plain. This must be an imaginary camp, since the camp at Yialova would no longer have existed when the drawing was produced. Baccuet's rendering of it is formulaic, with tents arranged in regular rows. Neither Bory de St. Vincent nor Blouet mention any lingering French presence at Yialova.[47] Because of unhealthy conditions there, the French army had soon after Ibrahim's retreat in late fall of 1828 dispersed to Navarino, Methoni, and elsewhere, while many of the troops returned to France.

The view that Baccuet presents is broadly panoramic, encompassing far more than a single field of vision (Fig. 28). The contours of the various hills and ranges that form the background are wrong. Features of the landscape are exaggerated or misrepresented: for instance, the deep, v-shaped cleft inserted between the northern end of the island of Sphacteria and Paleokastro. The camp at Yialova is set too far east and seems to be pitched at the foot of the Aigaleon Range, whereas in reality several ridges intervene.

The manner in which Baccuet has chosen to frame the scene in the foreground may also be his own construct. The ridge of Ayios Vasilios, on which the hospital was built, consists of eroded marl; there are no prominent crags like that on which the church at the left rests. The present church of Ayios Vasilios is new. Is Baccuet depicting its predecessor, or is the representation entirely a picturesque invention, as are the travelers on the road beneath it?

Smyth's map and Blouet's description, taken together, do on the other hand help to locate the small building on the shore framed by French frigates in drawing no. 52. It is the "petit batiment en bois, destiné a la marine française, qui venait y faire de l'eau a l'epoque de notre voyage." The building must have been located at the mouth of the Pesili River, where Smyth marks a "watering place" and where there is a small headland. Here again Baccuet has simplified the landscape by eliminating an intermediate range of hills.

The "hôpital de la marine" is depicted in one other drawing — pl. ix of the *Atlas*, which was executed by Bory de St. Vincent himself (Fig. 30). Pl. ix, like Baccuet's no. 52, is highly interpretative. Bory de St. Vincent displaced the hospital from its true location to a point near the steep cliff on top of which the "Hotel Philip" now stands so as to allow it to be embraced within a single compositional frame, along with the fortress of Neokastro and the hill of Ayios Nikolaos behind it (Fig. 29). Pl. ix, like Baccuet's drawing no. 52, also encompasses a wide panoramic view that sweeps all the way to the southern entrance of the bay of Navarino.

The conceit of the drawing is that the artist was standing at the northern edge of the islet of "Kuloneski" (today, Helonaki or Helonisi) in the middle of the bay — an impossible position from which to achieve the perspective of the drawing. This de-

47. On the contrary, Bory de St. Vincent (1836, p. 136) speaks only of traces of the camp remaining.

vice, however, allowed him, as it did Baccuet, to contrast the violence of the recent past with the idyllic setting of the French hospital. The focal point of the composition is the French fleet, anchored above Kuloneski, on which bleaching human bones fascinate two French officers. These are not, however, those of victims of the Battle of Navarino. A more sinister message emerges from a dialectical reading of the visual representation alongside Bory de St. Vincent's text.

The call-out for pl. ix in the text falls at the end of a lengthy excursus on the cruelties and vicissitudes of war, including brutalities inflicted on Turks by Greeks.[48] Within this narrative the islet of "Kuloneski" represents one of the greatest acts of perfidy in the course of the entire Greek Revolution. Bory de St. Vincent describes how, after surrendering Navarino to Greek forces on the condition that the Turkish defenders would be delivered safely to Ottoman territory, the Orthodox bishop of Modon broke his word and left more than 400 prisoners to die on the islet. One of the French officers holds the skull of a child. The other figure represents Bory de St. Vincent himself, in a cameo role.

Elsewhere Bory de St. Vincent may have intended to pair art and text to illustrate the horrors that Greece had suffered in recent years. Drawing no. 19, although unpublished, recalls an incident experienced in their travels (Fig. 31):

> Des chèvres et des brebis, échappes aux derniers pillages de l'armée arabe, nourissaient de leur lait ces pauvres gens, parmi lesquels nous recontrâmes encore une femme sans langue avec une fille d'environ dix-sept ans, qui, ayant été esclave des Musulmans, parvint à s'échapper de leurs mains au moment où on l'embarquait pour l'Égypte. "Étant revenue au lieu de ma naissance," nous dit-elle, "je n'y trouvai plus que les ossemens de mes parens, disperses entre les murs écroulés de leur maison."[49]

ART AND SCIENCE IN THE SERVICE OF GREECE?

This brief contribution to *The New Griffon* has only scratched the surface of what might be possible through a complete analysis of the drawings of Navarino produced by the Expédition scientifique de Morée. Topographical studies in the field in preparation for this paper discovered previously undocumented remains of the Ottoman physical landscape, including sections of the aqueduct channel on the steep slopes west of the "Hotel Philip" (Fig. 32) and next to the modern highway between Vigla and Miden (Fig. 33). Its course corresponds to indications on Smyth's map.

No traces of the "hôpital de la marine" have yet been found and none may ever

---

48. Bory de St. Vincent 1836a, pp. 130-132.

49. Bory de St. Vincent 1836a, p. 159. In a romantic flourish, Baccuet set the vignette of mother and child against a fanciful background that recalls the warfare responsible for their miseries, including the fortress of Navarino and charging cavalry in a style that, as Ioli Vingopoulou has suggested to me, may invoke the spirit of Delacroix.

be. There has been extensive modification of the landscape in the area where it stood: long ago by the building of a center for wedding receptions at Miden, more recently by the re-routing of the highway to Gargaliani, as mentioned above. Its remains were, in any case, impermanent, as is clear from Bory de St. Vincent's description.

Perhaps of greater significance is the purpose for which Baccuet's art was prepared. Peltre must be partly correct in asserting that "les artistes envoyés par le gouvernement français ont voulu donner une image positive de la Grèce et oublier ce qui lui était étranger: c'est là peut-être le reflet de leurs propres choix, mais surtout des circonstances. La commission, avatar du 'philhellénisme' politique, devait avant tout montrer le génie d'un peuple, les ressources d'un pays qui pouvaient promettre à la France un avenir."[50] Bory de St. Vincent, in fact, writes in the preface to the first volume of the edition of his *Relation* published separately from the work of the Expédition scientifique de Morée that "il concevra combien on pourrait facilement régénérer un pays où languissent, toujours féconds et pourtant méconnus, tant d'éléments de prospérité."[51]

Yet an additional theme appears to emerge from an analysis of the both Baccuet's and Bory's drawings of the "hôpital de la marine": that both artist and author were concerned to express to a French public the effectiveness of the relief brought to Greece through the recent French military intervention. Bory de St. Vincent also wrote in his Preface that one of the objects of the Expédition scientifique de Morée was "de prouver que le généreux Gouvernement qui les [sc. Greece's present inhabitants] secourut ne prodigua point aveuglément la vie de ses soldats et les trésors de contribuables."[52] The drawings of the "hôpital de la marine" seem to show this best out of all those produced by the French artists who came to Greece in the service of science to produce an "iconographie officielle."

BIBLIOGRAPHY

Amaury-Duval, P. 1885. *Souvenirs (1829–1830)*, Paris.

Atlas = *Expédition scientifique de Morée: Section des sciences physiques* 5: *Atlas*, Paris 1831–1835.

Bennet, J., J. L. Davis, and D. Harlan. 2005. "The Fortress of Anavarin-i Cedid," in *A Historical and Economic Geography of Ottoman Greece: The Southwestern Morea in the 18th Century*, ed. F. Zarinebaf, J. Bennet and J. L. Davis, Princeton, pp. 241–281.

Bessan, J. F. 1833. *Souvenirs de l'expédition de Morée en 1828, suivis d'un Memoire historique sur Athènes, avec le plan de cette ville par J. F. Bessan*, Lalognes.

Blouet, A. 1831–1838. *Expédition scientifique de Morée: Architecture, sculptures, inscriptions, et vues du Péloponnèse, des Cyclades et de l'Attique*, 3 vols., Paris.

---

50. Peltre 1997, p. 104.
51. Bory de St. Vincent 1836b, p. xiii.
52. Bory de St. Vincent 1836b, p. xii.

Bory de Saint Vincent, M. 1836a. *Expédition scientifique de Morée: Section des sciences physiques* I: *Relation*, Paris.

Bory de Saint Vincent, M. 1836b. *Relation du voyage de la Commission scientifique de Morée dans le Péloponnèse, les Cyclades et l'Attique* I, Paris.

Duheaume, M. A. 1833. *Souvenirs de la Morée*, Paris.

Lacour, J.-L. 1834. *Excursions en Grèce pendant l'occupation de la Morée par l'armée française dans les années 1832 et 1833*, Paris.

Mangeart, J. 1830. *Souvenirs de la Morée, recueillis pendant le sejour des Français dans le Péloponnèse*, Paris.

Musset-Pathay, V.-D. 1829. *1828: Nouveaux memoires secrets, pour servir à l'histoire de notre temps*, Paris.

Pellion, J.-P. 1855. *La Grèce et les Capodistrias pendant l'occupation française de 1828 à 1834*, Paris.

Peltre, C. 1997. *Retour en Arcadie: Le Voyage des artistes français en Grèce au XIXe siècle*, Paris.

Roux, G. G. 1829. *Histoire médicale de l'armée française en Morée pendant la campagne de 1828*, Paris.

Schlumberger, G. 1910. *Mémoires du Commandant Persat 1806 à 1844.* Paris.

Saïtas, G., ed. Forthcoming. *Το έργο της Γαλλικής Επιστημονικής Αποστολής του Μοριά (1829–1832), I: Τμήμα Φυσικών Επιστημών*, Athens.

Vingopoulou, I. 1999. "Dessins originaux de Prosper Baccuet: Un Album à la Bibliothèque Gennadius," in *Enquêtes en Méditerranée: Les Expéditions françaises d'Egypte, de Morée et d'Algerie, Actes de Colloque, Athènes-Nauplie, 8–10 Juin 1995*, ed. M.-N. Bourquet, D. Nordman, V. Panayotopoulos, and M. Sinarellis, Athens 1999, pp. 333–349.

Vingopoulou, I. Forthcoming. "Ο χώρος στις εικόνες: τα χαρακτικά του Άτλαντα με τις απόψεις τοπίων και τα σχέδια του Prosper Baccuet στο Λεύκωμα της Γενναδείου Βιβλιοθήκης," in Saïtas, forthcoming.

Wolpert, A. D. 2005. "The Fortress of Anavarin-i Atik," in *A Historical and Economic Geography of Ottoman Greece: The Southwestern Morea in the 18th Century*, ed. F. Zarinebaf, J. Bennet, and J. L. Davis, Princeton, pp. 223–240.

EARLY NINETEENTH-CENTURY SMYRNA:
A HANDWRITTEN MAP WITH VIEWS OF THE CITY[1]

CRISTINA PALLINI

I. INTRODUCTION

"Smyrna hath so many advantages from its natural situation, that notwith-standing the great calamities which have befallen it by war, and most prodigious earthquakes, that no less than six times have overthrown, and almost utterly ruined it; yet it hath still been thought worth repairing, and restoring to all the beauty the art of its inhabitants could contrive to adorn with: notwithstanding also, that from some old tradition they expect the seventh, that shall be its utter ruin, never to be repaired."[2]

These words by the learned traveler Sir George Wheler well express the fate of Smyrna, rebuilt so many times (Fig. 34). In July 1688, some 13 years after Wheler's visit, a severe earthquake followed by fire destroyed the city; in July 1742, the city was further ravaged by a fire lasting five days; in July 1778, another disastrous earthquake was followed by fire. The full account of earthquakes, fires, plague epidemics, wars, and riots throughout the 18th century may make us wonder how many people could still have been living in Smyrna.[3] More recently, in September 1922, a fire destroyed its commercial center together with the Armenian, Greek, and European neighborhoods. Reconstruction along radically new lines and the compulsory process of ethnic relocation imposed by the Treaty of Lausanne were to erase any memory of the city known to Western travelers as "the little Paris of the Orient" and "infidel Smyrna" by virtue of its non-Muslim population.[4]

So many recurring calamities make us even more appreciative of every new visual source, in particular the two views and the fine hand-drawn map among the material held at the Gennadius Library. Together, they provide us with a "snapshot"

---

1. I began my studies on Smyrna in 2003 with a fellowship from the Aga Khan Program at MIT and continued in Athens, thanks to the Onassis Foundation; at that time, my focus was town planning and architecture before and after the fire of 1922. This contribution is a first attempt to understand what Smyrna was like before the urban transformations of the second half of the 19th century.

2. Wheler 1682, p. 240.

3. See Frangakis-Syrett 1992, pp. 43-74.

4. On the reconstruction of Smyrna after 1922 see A. F. 1927; Bilsel 1997; Yerolympou 1997; Georgelin 2005; Kolluoğlu 2002, 2007; Smyrnelis 2006.

of Smyrna before it was reshaped in the 19th century.[5] Intended as a guide to the missionary activity of the Reformed and the Capuchin Fathers, the map also owes its importance to its legend, which lists the most important public and religious buildings and associates specific neighborhoods with different ethno-religious groups.

2. THE TWO VIEWS

Both illustrations show the port area and are included in an "Album of 18 original drawings in sepia, of views in Phaleron, Sunium, Aegina, Chios, Smyrna, Pergamum" (ca. 32 x 19 cm).[6] Like many of the better-known views, the finest one shows Smyrna from the sea, bringing us closer to the waterfront (Fig. 35). Dominating the foreground is the old *bezesten*,[7] a multi-domed arcade with its long façade parallel to the shore. Close upon it, by the sea, stands the *han*[8] of the Cretans. Right behind the bezesten stands the fireproof Vizir han, described by Cazzaiti in the 18th century as "the largest in Smyrna, built of stone with a lead cladding, containing many rooms above for accommodating the merchants and spacious warehouses below for storing their goods. The building is a perfect square round a central courtyard surrounded by a long gallery with marble columns."[9] The whole complex bore witness to the large-scale building program implemented by local Ottoman authorities in the late 17th century (Fig. 36). [10] The view also shows two caïques, used for transporting people and goods from the ships in the bay to the wooden piers. They almost hide the old Crusader castle and the Hisar ("Castle") Mosque (late 16th century).[11] Mount Pagus appears in the background, crowned by a walled citadel. On its lower slopes are houses, minarets, and cypress trees, closely matching Théophile Gautier's vivid description: "What struck my eyes at that distance, was a great number of cypress trees, rising above the houses and blending their black cones with the white summits of the minarets; and a hill, still bathed in deep shadow, and surmounted by an

---

5. The map is dated 1822, but it may have been drawn on an earlier survey, or else modeled on a previous document. Remaking Smyrna in the 19th century included the implementation of railway and port works, new state-sponsored institutions, and new Western-oriented building types. See Batur 1993; Yerolympou 1997; Bilsel 2001; Zandi-Sayek 2001; Smyrna 2002; Hastaoglou-Martinidis 2003, 2010; Colonas 2005; Smyrnelis 2005, 2006; Pallini 2010a.

6. For a fine reconstruction of the port and market areas see Müller-Wiener 1980-1981, pp. 420-447.

7. The word *bezesten* indicated a special section in the heart of the bazaar where cloth was sold. Although the erection of bezestens can be traced back to the end of the 13th century, their diffusion for storing and marketing precious merchandise was characteristic of the Ottoman period. See Cezar 1983.

8. A *han* is large courtyard building serving as a warehouse for goods in transit, in many cases also functioning as a hostelry for the dealers. By keeping control of the entrance, communication between the street and the courtyard could be permitted or impeded.

9. See Cazzaiti 1972, pp. 61-62.

10. See Anderson 1989, p. 3.

11. Built by the Crusaders around 1260 to defend the entrance to the inner harbor, the castle was rebuilt by the Ottomans in 1472. The Hisar Mosque, still standing, occupies the site of the former (pre-13th century) Church of Jesus Christ, see Rougon 1892, p. 28.

old ruined fortress, the dismantled walls of which, standing out against the clear sky, formed an amphitheatre behind the houses of the town."[12]

The other view shows the inside of a han: around all sides of its elongated court-yard, wooden structures form a portico, with an arcade on the upper floor (Fig. 37). The arcaded access from the street is clearly visible. The ruined citadel appears much closer. All around the han are some fine tall buildings of the Turkish quarter.

3. THE MAP (FIG. 38)

The map (57 × 76 cm) is entitled "Pianta della Città di Smyrna per le due Parroc-chie Latine" (Map of the City of Smyrna for the two Latin Parishes), with all written information in Italian. In the oval cartouche in the upper left-hand corner, the title continues: "the territory belonging to the Parish of the Reformed Fathers is colored yellow and that of the Capuchin Fathers red, in accordance with the agreement reached in Constantinople on February 25, 1763."[13] The agreement concerned the new rules set by the Apostolic Vicar Franzosini, establishing the distinction between French Catholics, assigned to the Capuchin Parish of S. Polycarp, and non-French Catholics, assigned to the Parish of the Immaculate Conception run by the Reformed Fathers.[14] In the four almost illegible corners of the cartouche, the following can be deciphered: "by order of the Reverend Father Polycarp, Superior of the Capuchins / Smyrna, April 1822 / Bassi [?] of Piacenza, licensed engineer, made it."[15] On the right-hand part of the map is a legend in two sections: the upper part describes the "neighborhoods and various nations" living in the Parish of the French Capu-chin Fathers,[16] while the lower part gives similar information for the Parish of the Reformed Fathers.[17]

While listing the city's major thoroughfares and focal points of the port, the legend mentions some commercial structures in the bazaar, the locations of foreign consulates and religious legations, the main residential quarters and more recent neighborhoods, hospitals, and some areas devoted to specific products. The only reference to antiquity is the temple presumed to be of Asclepius. A series of notes

---

12. Gautier 1854, p. 56.

13. "Il terreno spettante alla Parrocchia dei P.P. Riformati è tinto di color giallo, e quello spettante alla Parrocchia dei P.P. Cappuccini tinto di color rosso. Secondo il regolamento fatto a Costantinopoli il 25 Feb. 1763."

14. See Hofmann 1935, pp. 454-455. The affiliation of Ottoman Catholics depended on the parish in which they lived, whereas Ottoman subjects possessing an agreement with the Ottoman Government according to which they could enjoy all the privileges of a given foreign nationality, were considered as Europeans and therefore were divided between French or non-French Catholics.

15. "Per Comm.ne del Rev.do P.re Polyc.po Sup.re dei Capp. / Smyrna l'aprile 1822 / Bassi [?] Piacentiae L'ingegnere Patentato Fecit."

16. "Discrizione delli Quartieri e delle varie Nazioni abbitanti sopra il territorio della Parrocchia dei P.P. Cappuccini Francesi."

17. "Delli Quartieri e delle varie Nazioni abbitanti sopra il Territtorio della Parrocchia dei P.P. Rif.ti."

comments on the different ethno-religious communities to be found in each part of the town. Observed from the sea (the north to the left of the document), the city is drawn in two dimensions with no distinction between built-up or green areas. The coastline is drawn with slight distortions, but the network of streams through the city from the River Meles and the location of each single well are clearly shown. The Caravan Bridge across the River Meles and the walled citadel on Mount Pagus (as well as the mouth of a tunnel at its base) are drawn in three dimensions. To understand the geography of the city with its narrow, winding streets, and the relative location of its buildings, the map and its legend must be coordinated .

4. WHAT THE MAP TELLS US: URBAN STRUCTURE AND QUARTERS (FIG. 39)

The Caravan Bridge across the River Meles was an obligatory point of entry into the city by land.[18] This single-arched masonry bridge — along with its picturesque surroundings — was extolled by every traveler who saw it. A cypress grove marked the site of a Turkish cemetery; here caravans began or ended their journeys: long strings of horses and camels came from Persia every year, smaller ones from all parts of Asia Minor in the fruit-season. Since the late 16th century, the commerce of the Aegean region had been focused upon Smyrna.[19]

Almost parallel to the stream of the River Meles, on approaching the city, the road crossed some "Turkish gardens rented by Greeks" and forked after entering the city gate, with one branch leading to the Frank Quarter, the other to the bazaar. This latter street— called the "Great Jirikilik/ Tirikilik[20] — separated the Jewish from the Turkish quarter and, after reaching the area of the "Bit Bazaar and other markets," continued on the lower slopes of Mount Pagus in the direction of Aydin. The roundish shape of the bazaar and its concentric streets are clearly shown in the map. The bazaar — where Greeks, Armenians, Jews, Turks, and English each had their different sections[21] — occupied most of the area of the former inner harbor, which had been filled in, perhaps partially with debris from the 1778 earthquake.[22]

---

18. In connection with the Caravan Bridge, the legend also mentions "the great road to Diana's Baths." This was one of the chief attractions northeast of Punta, consisting of numerous springs forming a large pool, also known as Halkapınar. The discovery of one complete statue and the head of another, thought to represent Artemis, led to the name "Diana's Baths."

19. See Goffman 1990; Hasluck 1918-1919.

20. The term "Jirikilik" may derive from the Turkish word "jirki" meaning "Kurd", whereas the term "Tirikilik" may come from the Turkish "Tilkilik," a name still indicating an east-west road to the feet of Mount Pagus close to the archaeological site of the Agora that today is called Anafartalar Caddesi. The toponym may be linked to the Tilkizade family, or according to Yasar Aksoy, writer and researcher from Smyrna, it may indicate the path followed by foxes (tilkiler) from Mount Pagus when they came to town in search for food. I wish to thank my friends Cenk Berkant and Melisa Urgandokur for sharing this information with me.

21. Frangakis-Syrett 1992, p. 34.

22. According to Müller-Wiener (1980-1981, pp. 429-431), around 1670-1680 this area was already much smaller than it used to be in antiquity and, by the beginning of the 19th century, the old port had disappeared,

This road led to Hisar Mosque and the new bezesten, built using marble purloined from the Roman theatre.[23] The old castle of Saint Peter also stood there, even though it no longer had strategic value. To the south of the bazaar, next to the Palace of the Pasha, stood the Turkish Customs for goods from Constantinople and the rest of the empire.

The road from the Caravan Bridge to Frank Street divided the two Catholic parishes. At the "Turkish Tannery," it entered the Armenian quarter, passing the Armenian church of St. Stefanos (1688) and reaching the Greek church of St. Fotini on Frank Street, one of the oldest churches in Smyrna, destroyed by the 1778 earthquake and rebuilt between 1785 and 1787. The map's legend locates all the foreign consulates — Dutch, Imperial, British, Prussian and French — on Frank Street, together with the Capuchin convent and church of St. Polycarp, the convent of the Reformed Fathers and their church of the Virgin, and the house of the Lazarists.

Visiting Smyrna in 1827–1828, Charles Colville Frankland, a commander in the British Royal Navy, described Frank Street as the most animated part of the city: "The modern city, as far as respects Frank Town, is comparatively well built and spacious; its houses are large and commodious and of stone. This part of it runs parallel to the sea, and has ready communication with a long quay, which of an evening becomes the promenade of the beau monde."[24]

At the southern end of Frank Street stood the old bezesten and the Frank Customs, established in 1675 for goods from Holland, France, England, and other non-Muslim countries. North of Gallasia (blue) Street, was Fassola Square, the commercial heart of Frank Street, where dyers and barrel makers were to be found, together with butchers and fishermen, as well as coffee houses.

The shore to the north of the bazaar — the "Marina line" — combined commercial and residential functions. Here western Europeans concentrated their consular representations, factories, and trading houses: their residences were equipped with stores and warehouses, linked to private wharves extending seaward. As the inner harbor had been filled up by the 19th century, the area between Frank Street and the Marina became a tightly built fabric of contiguous long houses that opened toward the shore through a series of closely spaced, narrow, and privately owned vaulted streets flanked by small shops, called verhanes.[25]

The legend also mentions the "Great Circle Street" (Via del Grande Giro) with its access from the Turkish Tannery. After crossing a stream, the road forked one branch led to the Lazaretto of St. Mark (a few hundred meters north of the Caravan Bridge) and continued towards Punta with its dry dock, while the other branch also

75

as shown in a map by Luigi Storari (1854-56). In addition Müller-Wiener observes that the largest hans forming the bazaar were all built or rebuilt after the disastrous earthquake of 1778.

23. See Wheler 1682, p. 242.
24. Frankland 1830, p. 267.
25. See Zandi-Sayek 2001, p. 50. For a map of the verhanes, see Goad 1905, reprinted in Atay 1998, p. 43.

led to Punta but by way of low-density quarters such as Tabahana, St. Anne, St. Catherine, St. Dimitris, and Keratochori.

A comparison between this map and that published by the British Admiralty 20 years later[26] shows that the stream flowing to Frank Street near the Prussian Consulate marked the boundary of the built-up area. The most recently developed urban areas included the quarters "of the Roses," "Manna Perivoli," and "dé Copries." At the heart of this area were the British, Dutch, Austrian, and Greek hospitals. The British Hospital was, according to the volunteer nurse Martha Nicol, "a large red building of three stories, describing a side and two half-sides of a square."[27] Like the Dutch Hospital, it accepted only its own nationals. The Austrian Hospital, also known as the Catholic Hospital of St. Antoine, had been founded by the Franciscans in 1710[28] and served patients regardless of nationality or religion. The Greek Hospital of St. Charalambos, the largest in the city, was founded between 1725 and 1747 and placed under British protection.[29]

5. CATHOLIC MISSIONS

The early spread and enduring presence of the Franciscans in the Levant as "Custodians of the Holy Land" may be traced back to St. Francis's visit to Egypt in 1219–1220 and his attempts at rapprochement with the Muslim world. In 1402, when the city was conquered by Tamerlane, Smyrna had five Catholic churches,[30] while at the beginning of the 17th century only two Franciscans were to be found in Smyrna.[31] Things changed soon thereafter, however, in line with the policy of the *Sacra Congregatio de Propaganda Fide*,[32] whose aim was to organize Catholic missions in the New World and centralize their activity in the old Orient as well.

A crucial step was the 1624 revival of the Smyrna episcopate, which had been established in 1344; a Dominican friar, bishop of Chios at the time, was to be appointed bishop of Smyrna.[33] The new wave of missions, also due to the Counter-Reformation, affirmed the growing international importance of the port. Following

76

---

26. "Map of Smyrna by Lieutenant Thomas Graves," 1836-1837, published in 1844, updated in July 1873 and October 1876.

27. See Nicol 1856, p. 32.

28. See Hofmann 1935, p. 463.

29. See Rougon 1892, pp. 58-63.

30. See Hofmann 1935, p. 438.

31. See Granella 2009.

32. The Sacred Congregation for the Propagation of the Faith was established in Rome in 1622 by Pope Gregory XV.

33. See Frazee 1983, pp. 127-128. The Dominicans had been present in Smyrna since the 14th century, as the port was on the route to Armenia, Persia, Turkmenistan, Russia, and China. At the beginning of the 18th century, when massive immigration of Armenian Catholics took place, the Dominican presence was strengthened. Around 1718 several Armenian Dominican friars founded a church and hospice to assist refugees in the hospital district.

the transfer of foreign consulates from Chios (the French in 1619, the British in 1621), the first two Jesuits arrived in Smyrna in 1623, representing the strongest expression of the Catholic revival.

The Reformed Fathers and the Capuchin Fathers, both offshoots of the Franciscans, were each in charge of a parish, the dividing line being the east-west road that entered the city from the Caravan Bridge and led to St. Fotini.[34] The Capuchins settled in Smyrna in 1628 with the help of the French consul Jean Dupuy. In 1629, they started building the church dedicated to St. Polycarp (still in existence), which the king of France had bought in 1637 and donated in perpetuity to the friars. Their convent was connected to the French consulate by a wooden gallery.[35]

The map makes no mention of the Jesuits who, in 1638–1640, erected their church at the north end of Frank Street. This may have been due to the fact that in 1782, ten years after the order had been suppressed, their missions and properties in the Levant were taken over by the Lazarists, who had built a church at Smyrna earlier, in 1698.[36] In 1782, the Lazarists opened a school, which burned down in 1797 and was re-established in 1802 as a secondary school for classical and commercial education.[37] Nearby was the convent of the Reformed Fathers[38] and the residence of the Archbishop[39] with the church of St. Mary, which was rebuilt in 1797 after the earthquake of 1778 and is still standing.[40]

While the Catholic population of Smyrna included Greek, Armenian, and Arab subjects of the Ottoman Empire as well as foreign colonies of French, Italians, Maltese, and Austro-Hungarians, the city also attracted many itinerant religious people on their way further east.[41] In 1833 the total number of Catholics in Smyrna amounted to 6354, including 1990 Ottoman subjects, 1042 Austrians, 440 subjects of the Kingdom of Sardinia, 1088 subjects of the King of Greece, 467 British, 653 French, 20

---

34. Almost the exact same boundary was adopted in 1877-1879 to separate the first and second municipal districts.

35. Notable for preaching and caring for the poor, the Capuchins had been founded in 1525 and from a very early date engaged in missions to Constantinople and the Venetian possessions in the Levant and along the Adriatic. Louis XIII of France and his prime minister Cardinal Richelieu strongly supported the Capuchins' missionary activity in the Ottoman Empire. In Smyrna, the Capuchins were responsible for the education of the *enfants de langue*, French boys aged nine or ten brought out to be trained at government expense; see Anderson 1989, p. 7; Cocchia 1867.

36. See Atay 1998, with Goad's map on p. 43.

37. See Zandi-Sayek 2001, p. 225. This complex is still in existence, though converted into a commercial high school (Ticaret Lisesi).

38. Aimed at reviving the simple way of life of St. Francis, the movement started in southern Italy and was also linked to the Counter-Reformation.

39. When, in the course of the 17th century, Bishop Subiano was transferred to Istanbul, Smyrna was downgraded to an apostolic vicariate: see Frazee 1983, p. 127. On March 18, 1818, Pope Pius VII re-established the Roman Catholic Archdiocese of Izmir. See Hofmann 1935, pp. 459-460.

40. A map and a description of the Franciscan Convent in 1710 can be found in Hofmann 1935, pp. 448-449.

41. See Anderson 1989, p. 7, and Zandi-Sayek 2001, pp. 214-215.

Prussians, 30 Spanish, 74 Russians, 148 Neapolitans, 16 Romans, 23 subjects of the Grand Duchy of Tuscany, 22 Dutch, 35 Swedish, 23 Danish, 23 Americans, plus 200 people whose nationality could not be ascertained.[42]

6. A PROTO-SOCIOLOGICAL SURVEY (FIG. 40)

While some historians have described Smyrna as "a mosaic city of various communities that existed in isolation from one another,"[43] others have noted that the different groups did not always consider themselves as members of mutually exclusive communities.[44]

The notes added to the map's legend may contribute to the clarification of the city's ethnic topography. In the parish of the French Capuchins (colored in red) only a few Catholics were to be found: this area covered the oldest part of the city, including "upper" and "lower" Smyrna, a division dating back to the Crusades, when the Turkish population was concentrated inside the citadel on Mount Pagus and the Latins were down in the harbor area.[45]

In the han of the Chiots (3) and the southern part of Frank Street (2), the notes tell us, were "many Greeks, many Lutherans and a few Catholics." At the Frank Customs (5) were "all Turks," but the nearby old bezesten (6) has "some Latins passing through." The seafront between the Frank and Turkish Customs and the market area behind it (7–15) were frequented by Turks, Greeks, "schismatic" Armenians,[46] and Jews. In the Arab mahalla[47] (21) there were also Jews, but the adjoining Turkish quarter (22) contained all Turks. On both sides of the road from the Caravan Bridge, the Armenian quarter extended across the two parishes (20 red and 23 yellow), containing both Latin (Uniate/Mekhitarist) and "schismatic" Armenians as well as Turks. Some notes refer to specific buildings: at the Dervişoğlu khan (23) "Greeks, Turks, and a few Jews;" at the Küçük Vezir khan (24) and neighboring area "Turks, Greeks, some Jews, some Lutherans, and a very few Catholics." At the "Pit called Yeraniou," next to the Church of St. Fotini are simply "Greeks." Only in the western stretch of the Kenurion (new) Mahalla was half the population supposedly Catholic, and at its eastern end (36 yellow) there were to be found mostly Catholics.

The parish of the Reformed Fathers (colored yellow) included the Frank Quarter and the non-Muslim districts that grew up during the 17th and 18th centuries, when the port of Smyrna became increasingly active due to trade between the Ottoman

78

---

42. Hofmann 1935, p. 459.
43. See Beyru 1993, p. 145.
44. See Zandi-Sayek 2001. Considering the Istanbul case-study, Gilardelli (2005) suggests a fresh approach to the spatial framework of inter-communal relationships.
45. Arıkan 1993. Around 1528-1529 a solid band of Muslim settlement extended from the citadel to the port, obliterating the ancient division between Crusaders and Turks, see Goffman 1993.
46. The largest group of Armenians had refused reunion with the Roman Catholic Church, recognizing as their head the patriarchs of Etschmiadzin (Caucasus), Aghtamar, and Jerusalem.
47. Arabic word (Turkish mahalle) for a quarter or district within a town or city.

Empire and major European countries.[48] Along Frank Street (2), from the convent of the Reformed Fathers (3) to the British Consulate (8) near Gallasia Street (4) almost all residents were Catholics. At Fassola Square (9–11), nearly all residents were Greeks. In the area of the Prussian (12) and French (13) consulates were Greeks and Catholics. Farther north, at Punta (15–16), there were a few Catholics and Greeks. Along the "Great Circle Street" (25), were Catholics and Greeks in equal parts; this street linked the more recent neighborhoods with large green areas such as the new quarter of St. Anne (17), which was inhabited by a few Catholics. In the St. Catherine quarter (18) were Catholics and Greeks in equal parts. Tabahana / "Ta da Bahana" (19: the name may come from the Turkish word *tabakhane*, meaning "tannery") was a Greek quarter. At St. Dimitris, around the church of the same name, there were mostly Greek-Catholics. In the quarters of "the Roses," "Manna Perivoli," and "dé Copries" mostly Catholics were to be found, as well as in the Hospitals District, the Kenurion Mahalla (36), Alongi Han, and Kioumour Han. At the Han Madame, in contrast, next to the Catholic church of St. Polycarp, were "a few Catholics, some Greeks and Lutherans, and a Turkish coffeehouse."

7. WHY STUDY EARLY 19TH-CENTURY SMYRNA?

Since the 1980s much has been written about urban development and architecture in connection with the "modernization" of the Levant's great ports of call (*les grandes échelles du Levant*), but much less is known about how these cities looked before their 19th-century remaking. Recent studies on Smyrna emphasize time and again the multicultural character of this city, defined as a "palimpsest of cultures" or as the "metropolis of the Asia Minor Greeks."[49] Smyrna might in fact be considered a "proto"-cosmopolitan city because its golden age belonged to the 17th century. So little has remained that reconstructing how Smyrna looked in the early 19th century requires us to correlate the visual and literary sources.

If we are to understand the complex settlement processes that shaped the city and its resulting anthropological makeup, a comparative approach may also help.[50] Perhaps we should start from Aleppo and Alexandria, both important international business centers before and after Smyrna. Moreover, the history of Smyrna helps us understand the refounding of Alexandria when, after Napoleon's Egyptian expedition, it was re-established within the orbit of the Western world. Indeed, in Smyrna and Alexandria we find similar settlement processes: a new quarter for consulates and European merchants linked to a pre-existing market area, the presence of religious "delegations" (legations, including the Franciscans and the Lazarists) hosting the first educational institutions, the creation of extraterritorial buildings for warehous-

48. For migratory movements following the rise of the port of Smyrna, see Goffman 1990.
49. See Batur 1993.
50. I first attempted a comparison between Alexandria and Thessaloniki in my Ph.D. dissertation (Pallini 2001) and later included my studies on Smyrna in Pallini 2010b.

ing and manufacturing, and, even more important, the "recurring problem" of city reconstruction. Following migratory movements from Europe and the rest of the Ottoman Empire, these settlement processes left their mark on the structure and architecture of the city.

The history of the growth of Smyrna and Alexandria brings to light examples of "space-based pluralism[51] providing the basic features to foster composite yet individuated cultural identities. City reconstruction here has had to face constant change more often than in most European cities. At the same time, it also gave Smyrna and Alexandria strong urban structures. It may be added that both cities were founded by Alexander the Great and his successors. When marching against the Persian Empire in 334 B.C., Alexander visited Mt. Pagus where, in a dream, the Nemeses told him to found a city for the Smyrneans.[52] Two years later, in 332 B.C., Alexander chose the location of Alexandria, having observed the potential advantages of a small port sheltered by an island, halfway along a narrow stretch of coastline between the Mediterranean and a huge coastal lake. Alexandria and Smyrna were isthmian ports located on routes connecting the Eastern Mediterranean with the Red Sea and the Persian Gulf, each situated in a natural corridor that extended far inland. Laid out in a grid pattern, both cities fully exploited the natural features of their sites, vital elements of their structure since the earliest days.[53] In considering these two ports —Alexandria with its famous Heptastadium,[54] later to become the site of the Turkish town, and the inner harbor of Smyrna, which also silted up and eventually accommodated the bazaar — it is clear how they provided each city with a basic framework within which settlements and their architecture could develop time and again. The heritage of such cities, we should remember, depends not merely on literary myths, nor even on the archaeological remains and the fine buildings that lined their dusty streets, but rather on their very urban structure, which has preserved the stamp of their foundation.

---

51. The presence of different groups found expression in the built environment: not only in the individual character of each ethno-religious quarter and in the architecture of churches, mosques and synagogues, but also in the monumentality of the main community buildings (schools, hospitals, and welfare structures). In the second half of the 19th century an architecture for a widest possible appreciation became a crucial issue: each group adopted certain exterior forms as a clear expression of its identity.

52. See Dumper and Stanley 2007, p. 189, and Cadoux 1938, pp. 94-97. After their city was destroyed by the Lydians in 589 B.C., the Smyrneans were scattered among the neighboring villages; Archaic Smyrna was eventually replaced by the new port city built by Antigonus I and Lysimachus on the opposite side of the gulf in the early Hellenistic period.

53. At Smyrna, the Golden Street encircled the northwest slopes of Mt. Pagus, avoiding the swampy plain for the greater safety of the routes from Ephesus and running from the Anatolian plateau towards the port. At Alexandria, the triumphal Canopic Street followed a depression in the strip of land between the sea and the lake, starting from the point where the Egyptian river system reached the seaport area.

54. A causeway seven stadia long (7 × 185 m = 1295 m) that connected the mainland with the island of Pharos.

BIBLIOGRAPHY

A. F. 1927. "Le plan d'aménagement de la ville de Smyrne," *L'Architecture*, 40.4, pp. 117–126.

Anderson, S. P. 1989. *An English Consul in Turkey: Paul Rycaut at Smyrna 1667–1678*, Oxford.

Arıkan, Z. 1993. "Izmir in the fifteenth and sixteenth centuries," in Batur 1993, pp. 59–70.

Atay, Ç. 1998. *Osmanlı'dan Cumhuriyet'e İzmir Planları* (*Plans of Izmir from Ottoman times to the Republic*), Ankara.

Batur, E., ed. 1993. *Three Ages of Izmir: Palimpsest of Cultures*, trans. V. T. Saçlıoğlu, Istanbul.

Beyru, R. 1993. "Social life in Izmir in the first half of the 19th century," in Batur 1993, pp. 145-216.

Bilsel, C. 1997. "Ideology and Urbanism During the Early Republican Period: Two Master Plans for Izmir and Scenarios of Modernization," *METU: Journal of the Faculty of Architecture*, 16.1–2, pp. 13–30.

Bilsel, C. 2001. "The Ottoman Port City of Izmir in the 19th Century: Cultures, Modes of Space Production and the Transformation of Urban Space," in *Seven Centuries of Ottoman Architecture, A 'Supra-National Heritage,'* ed. A. Batur, Istanbul, pp. 225–233.

Cadoux, C. J. 1938. *Ancient Smyrna: A History of the City from the Earliest Times to 324 A.D.*, Oxford.

Cazzaiti, M. A. 1972. *Geografia in dialogo con moltissime notizie istoriche cronologiche di Marco Antonio Cazzaiti, nobile di Corfu, Zante e Cefalonia, dedicata al Serenissimo Doge di Venezia, Alvise Pisani (Venice 1788)*, Athens. [= Μάρκου Αντωνίου Κατσαΐτη δύο ταξίδια στη Σμύρνη: 1740 και 1742, tr. and comm. P. K. Falpou, Athens 1972]

Cezar, M. 1983. *Typical Commercial Buildings of the Ottoman Classical Period and the Ottoman Construction System*, Istanbul.

Cocchia, R. 1867. *Storia delle Missioni dei Cappuccini*, Paris.

Colonas, V. 2005. *Greek Architects in the Ottoman Empire*, Athens.

Dumper, M., and B. E. Stanley, eds. 2007. *Cities of the Middle East and North Africa: a Historical Encyclopedia*, Santa Barbara, Calif.

Frangakis-Syrett, E. 1992. *The Commerce of Smyrna in the Eighteenth Century, 1700–1820*, Athens.

Frankland, C. C. 1830. *Travels to and from Constantinople in the years 1827 and 1828* I, London.

Frazee, C. A. 1983. *Catholics and Sultans: The Church and the Ottoman Empire 1453–1923*, Cambridge.

Gautier, T. 1854. *Constantinople of to-day*, trans. R. H. Gould, London.

Georgelin, H. 2005. *La fin de Smyrne: du cosmopolitisme aux nationalismes*, Paris.

Gilardelli, P. 2005. "Architecture, identity and liminality: on the use and meaning of Catholic spaces in late Ottoman Istanbul," *Muqarnas* 22, pp. 233–264.

Goad, C. E. 1905. "Plan d'assurance de Smyrne, Turquie," London [reprinted in Atay 1998, p. 43].

Goffman, D. 1990. *Izmir and the Levantine World, 1550–1650*, Seattle and London.

Goffman, D. 1993. "Izmir before the 17th century," in Batur 1993, pp. 70–83.

Granella, O. 2009. "I Cappuccini a Smirne (Izmir) e sulla costa egea," at http://www.eteria.it/missioni/251-I-i-cappuccini-a-smirne (last accessed April 23, 2011).

Hasluck, F. W. 1918–1919. "The Rise of Modern Smyrna," *The Annual of the British School at Athens* 23, pp. 139–147.

Hastaoglou-Martinidis, V. 2003. "The Advent of Transport and Aspects of Urban Modernisation in the Levant during the Nineteenth Century," in *The City and the Railway in Europe*, ed. R. Roth and M.-N. Polino, Aldershot, Hants, and Burlington, Vermont, pp. 61–78.

Hastaoglou-Martinidis, V. 2010. "The Cartography of Harbour Construction in Eastern Mediterranean Cities: Technical and Urban Modernization in the Late Nineteenth Century," in Toksöz and Kolluoğlu 2010, pp. 78–99.

Hofmann, G. 1935. "L'Arcivescovado di Smirne," *Orientalia Christiana Periodica* I, pp. 434-466.

Kolluoğlu, B. 2002. "The Play of Memory, Counter-Memory: Building Izmir on Smyrna's Ashes," *New Perspectives on Turkey* 26, pp. 1–28.

Kolluoğlu, B. 2007. "Cityscapes and Modernity: Smyrna Morphing into Izmir," in *Ways of Modernity in Greece and Turkey: Encounters with Europe, 1850–1950*, ed. A. Frangoudaki and C. Keyder, London and New York, pp. 217–235.

Müller-Wiener, W. 1980–1981. "Der Bazar von Izmir. Studien zur Geschichte und Gestalt des Wirtschaftszentrums einer ägäischen Handelsmetropole," *Mitteilungen der Fränkischen Geographischen Gesellschaft* 27–28, pp. 420–454.

Nicol, M. C. 1856. *Ismeer, or Smyrna and its British hospital in 1855*, London.

Pallini, C. 2001. "Architecture and City Reconstruction in Eastern Mediterranean Ports: Alexandria and Thessaloniki" (diss. IUAV, Venice)

Pallini, C. 2010a. "University and Trade Fair: Ideas and Projects for the Modernization of Izmir," in *Kuva-yı Milliye'nin 90 Yılında İzmir ve Batı Anadolu (Izmir and Western Anatolia in the 90th Years of the National Forces)* I, Izmir, pp. 107–114.

Pallini, C. 2010b. "Geographic Theatres, Port Landscapes and Architecture in the Eastern Mediterranean: Salonica, Alexandria, Izmir," in Toksöz and Kolluoğlu 2010, pp. 61–77.

Rougon, F. 1892. *Smyrne, situation commerciale et économique*, Paris and Nancy.

Smyrna 2002. *Smyrna: Metropolis of the Asia Minor Greeks*, Alimous.

Smyrnelis, M.-C. 2005. *Une société hors de soi. Identités et relations sociales à Smyrne aux XVIII et XIX siècles* (Collection Turcica 10), Paris.

Smyrnelis, M.-C., ed. 2006. *Smyrne, la ville oubliée? 1830–1930*, Paris.

Toksöz, M. and B. Kolluoğlu, eds. 2010. *Cities of the Mediterranean: From the Ottomans to the Present Day*, London.

Wheler, G. 1682. *A Journey into Greece in Six Books* 3, London.

Yerolympou, A. 1997. *Μεταξύ Ανατολής και Δύσης: Βορειοελλαδικές πόλεις στην περίοδο των οθωμανικών μεταρρυθμίσεων*, Athens.

Zandi-Sayek, S. 2001. "Public Space and Urban Citizens: Ottoman Izmir in the Remaking, 1840–1890" (diss. Univ. of California, Berkeley).

82

MAP LEGEND

Description of the neighborhoods and the various nationalities living in the Parish of the French Capuchin Fathers

1. Church and Convent of the Capuchin Fathers
2. Frank Street
3. Han of the Chiots (2–3: some Greeks, many Lutherans, few Catholics)
4. The so-called "Marina" line
5. Frank Customs (all Turks)
6. Old Bezesten (some transient Latins)
7. Castle with Marabout (7 – 14: Turks, Greeks, schismatic Armenians and Jews)
8. Great Mosque
9. New Bezesten
10. Turkish Customs
11. Pasha's Palace

12. Temple of Asclepius
13. Jewish Quarter
14. Great Jirikilik / Tirikilik [*Tilkilik*]
15. Bit Bazaar and other markets (cf. 7 to 14)
16. St. Stefanos Armenian Church (16–20: Turks and schismatic Armenians)
17. Ho Min. Agà [?]
18. City Gate
19. Caravan Bridge and Great Street to the Baths of Diana
20. Armenian Quarter
21. Arab Mahalla (Turks and Jews)
22. Turk Mahalla (all Turks)
23. Dervis Oglou Han (Greeks, Turks, and a few Jews)
24. Kouciouk Visir Han (24–27: Turks, Greeks, some Jews, some Lutherans, and a very few Catholics)
25. Sta Galÿadica [?]
26. St. Fotinì Greek Church
27. The Three Streets
28. To the Pit called Yeraniou (Greeks)
29. Kenitrou [?] Mahalla (from the left side of n. 29 to n. 32 is the Parish of the Capuchin Fathers, almost half of its population was Catholic)
30. House of the Dominican Fathers
31. The last house of the Bakciati [?] Quarter facing the entrance to the Greek Hospital
32. Entrance to the Cassan Chio [?] Han, today called Stravohano Han
33. French Hospital
34. French Cemetery
N.B.: Numbers 1, 33, and 34 are in the Parish of the Reformed Fathers.

Neighborhoods and various nationalities living in the Parish of the Reformed Fathers
1. So-called Street of the Marina
2. Frank Street
3. Archbishop's Residence, Church and Convent of the Reformed Fathers
4. Gallasia Street
5. House of the Lazarists
6. Dutch Consulate
7. Imperial Consulate
8. British Consulate
9. Fassola
10. Dyers
11. Barrel makers
12. Prussian Consulate
13. French Consulate
14. Tirato Cori, Village [Kerato Chori?]
15. Punta
16. Dry-dock
17. St. Anna Quarter

18. St. Catherina Quarter

19. la da Bahana (Tabahane) Quarter

20. St. Marco Lazaretto for Catholics affected by plague

21. Turkish Gardens rented to Greeks

22. Ta da Bahana [*Tabakhane*] Turkish Tannery

23. Armenian Quarter

24. St. Dimitris Quarter

25. Great Circle Street

26. Quarter of the Roses

27. Quarter of St. Mana Perivoglia [Manna Perivoli]

28. Quarter dé Copries

29. So-called Street of Impurity

30. Hospital Quarter

31. British Hospital

32. Dutch Hospital

33. Austrian Hospital

34. Hospice and Garden of the Reformed Fathers

35. Greek Hospital

36. Kenurion [new] Mahala

37. Alongi Han

38. Kioumour Han

39. Han Madame

N.B.: Nos. 1 – 8, nearly all Catholics; Nos. 9–11, nearly all Greeks; Nos. 12–13, Greeks and Catholics; Nos. 15–16, a few Catholics and Greeks; No. 17, a few Catholics; No. 18, Catholics and Greeks in equal numbers; No. 19, Greeks; No. 23, Latins and schismatic Armenians; No. 24, Greeks, mostly Catholic; No. 25, Catholics and Greeks in equal numbers; Nos. 26–38, mainly Catholics; No. 39, Han Madame, a few Catholics, some Greeks and Lutherans, a Turkish coffee shop.

CONSTANTINOS SIMONIDIS IN THE GENNADIUS LIBRARY

PASQUALE MASSIMO PINTO

Constantinos Simonidis (1820?–1890?) is well known as the skilful 19th-century forger of several Greek manuscripts on papyrus and parchment. He has recently become a topic of debate, since his ingenious hand has been seen as the most plausible candidate for the forging of the so-called "Artemidorus Papyrus."[1] But Simonidis was also the author of a certain number of publications. He wrote in different languages and published in different countries, or at least circulated, a variety of pamphlets and booklets on several subjects. He also provided a list of his own writings which is richer than the extant publications.[2] These "books" — we will use this term for the sake of convenience — claim to contain original or/and reliable material, but in fact they adroitly mix fact and imagination, genuine ancient texts and fabrications, research by others, and pure fiction (though some were credited with containing authentic scholarship and reviewed as such in journals and newspapers). They are also disconcerting on account of the game of identities that the author plays. Because of their technical features and contents, they are puzzling from a bibliographic point of view, too. Readers can get a sense of all this by scrolling down the list below. Nevertheless, Simonidis' books were sufficiently weird and scarce to appeal to a book collector like Joannes Gennadius (1844–1932).

The collection of books by Simonidis that is in the Gennadius Library today was first brought to the attention of the scholarly world in 1993 by a French classicist, the distinguished epigraphist Olivier Masson (1922–1997), who had come upon Simonidis accidentally while he was studying forged Greek inscriptions. The article that Masson wrote for *The Griffon* on that occasion was entitled, significantly, "Constantin

* This paper is the revised version of a presentation made at the Gennadius Library on October 23, 2010, as a Cotsen Traveling Fellow. I would like to thank the ASCSA and its Director, Prof. Jack Davis, for granting me the opportunity to spend research time in the Gennadius Library. I am also very grateful to the Gennadius Library's Acting Director, Dr. Irini Solomonidi, and to all the staff for their kind help and support, as well as to the Director, Dr. Maria Georgopoulou, for inviting me to contribute a paper to this issue of *The New Griffon*.

1. See most recently Canfora 2008 and 2010, where a rich bibliography relevant to Simonidis can be found. Greek sources connected with Symi, Simonidis' birthplace, and with the Greek community of Alexandria in Egypt, where Simonidis is supposed to have spent the very last part of his life, offer much useful information, e. g., Chaviaras 1889; Firippidis 1931; Chatzifotis 1964 (one of the many contributions of this scholar to the biography of Simonidis).

2. Simonidis 1864, on the verso of the "Contents" page (leaf A). Cf. Stewart 1859, 24–25; Chaviaras 1889, 582–583; Elliott 1982, 170–172.

Simonidis et Jean Gennadius: Le Faussaire et le Bibliophile."[3] As we shall see, the interest of the "bibliophile" in the books and pamphlets of the "forger" was indeed a strong and a lifelong one. And this is the main reason why the Gennadius Library houses to date the largest collection of "Simonideia" in the world, as far as is known.[4]

It may therefore be worth trying to describe this collection and to outline its history, making clear that much information has been obtained from the typewritten Catalogues which Joannes Gennadius himself made of his own library, which have proved to be a valuable source of documentation.[5]

The Gennadius Library preserves today 29 items corresponding to 19 titles, including several duplicates.[6] I will list them by title (omitting the mottos on the title-page), in ascending current call number order, together with brief notes. Some of the items from Gennadius' personal library are accompanied by the shelf-mark (GC) that Gennadius assigned to them in Vol. 3 Part 2 of his Catalogue (pp. 65–71: "J.– Appendix. The publications of Constantine Simonides the Notorious forger of ancient Greek MSS."). The same call number for different items means that they were bound in the same volume or purchased by Gennadius already bound together.

A LIST OF SIMONIDIS' WORKS IN THE GENNADIUS LIBRARY
I) BB 1226.1

> Ἡ πρὸς τοὺς ἐξ Ἑβραίων πιστοὺς Ἐπιστολὴ τοῦ Ἀποστολικοῦ πατρὸς Βαρνάβα ἥ περ ἀνακαλυφθεῖσα ἐν Ἄθωνι τῷ ͵αωλζ ὁλόκληρος ὑπὸ Κ. Σιμωνίδου διδάκτορος τῆς φιλοσοφίας. Ἐκδίδεται τανῦν ἐπὶ τῇ βάσει ἑπτὰ ἀρχαίων χειρογράφων δαπάνη καὶ ἐπιμελείᾳ Γ. Δ. Ῥοδοκανάκη. Ἐν Σμύρνῃ ͵αωμγ´ [1843].

In Greek. This document is a couple of newspaper pages from the appendix of a journal published in Smyrna, the Ἀστὴρ τῆς Ἀνατολῆς (*Star of the East*), no. 26, August 1, 1843 (pp. 425–426). The article actually contains the first part of Simonidis' rare work bearing this title, which the Gennadius Library does not hold.[7] It concerns one

---

3. Masson 1993a. During the same years, Masson found himself dealing with Simonidis in an entire series of papers: Masson 1993b, 1994; Masson and Fournet 1992.

4. Other collections of considerable extent are in the British Library (London), the Bodleian Library (Oxford), and the libraries of Harvard University (Cambridge, Mass.). In Greece, books by Simonidis are kept in the University Library of Crete (4 items), the University Library of Thessaloniki (5 items), the Korais Library of Chios (1 item), the Korgialenios Library of Cephalonia (1 item), and the Municipal Center for Historical Research and Documentation of Volos (1 item). In Athens, a few copies of Simonidis' works can also be found in the National Library, the University Library, the Library of Parliament, the Library of the Academy of Athens, the Library of the Benaki Museum, and the Library of the German Archaeological Institute. A census of the extant copies all over the world is currently being carried out.

5. These catalogues are in the Gennadius Library as well (call no. BB 768).

6. The Library also holds a series of items concerning Simonidis which likewise come from Gennadius' private collection: Lykurgos 1856a, 1856b; Stewart 1859; *Report* 1859.

7. A copy of this pamphlet, which formerly belonged to Nikolaos Politis, survives in the Central Library of the Aristotle University of Thessaloniki (call no. BS2900.B2G8 1843).

of the apocryphal texts of the New Testament, the so-called *Letter of Barnabas*, of which Simonidis pretended that he had found a more correct text.

2) BB 1226.2

Συμαῖς ἢ Ἱστορία τῆς ἐν Σύμη Ἀπολλωνιάδος Σχολῆς ἰδίως δὲ τῆς ἁγιογραφικῆς καθέδρας καὶ πρόδρομος τῶν ἀνεκδότων Ἑλληνικῶν χειρογράφων. Ἄρχεται δὲ ἡ Ἱστορία αὕτη τῷ τριακοστῷ ἑβδομηκοστῷ ἑβδόμῳ ἔτει μ. Χ. ἀφ᾽ ἧς ἐποχῆς ἵδρυται ἡ Σχολὴ καὶ λήγει τῷ χιλιοοστῷ ἑκατοστῷ τεσσαρακοστῷ ὀγδόῳ μ. Χ. ὅτε καὶ κατεστράφη ὑπὸ τῶν Σταυροφόρων. Συγγραφεῖσα μὲν ὑπὸ Μελετίου ἱερομονάχου τοῦ ἐκ Χίου, τῷ ͵ασλς᾽ μ. Χ. Ἐκδοθεῖσα δὲ τὸ πρῶτον ὑπὸ Κωνσταντίνου Σιμωνίδου ἀπαραλλάκτως μετὰ σημειώσεων καὶ προλεγομένων. Δαπάνη τῶν καθότι τυπογράφων. Ἀθήνησι, τύποις Καραμπίνη καὶ Βάφα. (Παρὰ τῷ ὁδῷ Ἀδριανοῦ) 1849.

In Greek. This copy is a gift of Damianos Kyriazis (the date of accession is recorded on the first page: "June 1953 Kyriazis 10217"). The *Συμαῖς* (*Symais*) is a history of the great men of Simonidis' native island, Symi. The history, which looks as if it were written by a monk of Chios in the 13th century, while Simonidis features only as editor, was exposed as a forgery by Alexander Rangavis in *Pandora* 2 (1851), pp. 595–601.

3) BB 1226.3 [GC 5371]

Ὀρθοδόξων Ἑλλήνων θεολογικαὶ γραφαὶ τέσσαρες. Α΄. Νικολάου ἐπισκόπου Μεθώνης λόγος πρὸς τοὺς Λατίνους περὶ τοῦ ἁγίου Πνεύματος ὅτι ἐκ τοῦ Πατρὸς οὐ μὴν καὶ ἐκ τοῦ Υἱοῦ ἐκπορεύεται. Β΄. Γενναδίου τοῦ Σχολαρίου ἀρχιεπισκόπου Κωνσταντινουπόλεως καὶ οἰκουμενικοῦ Πατριάρχου τὸ περὶ ἐκπορεύσεως τοῦ Παναγίου Πνεύματος ἐπιστολιμαῖον πρῶτον βιβλίον. Γ΄. Τοῦ ἐν ἁγίοις πατρὸς ἡμῶν Γρηγορίου ἀρχιεπισκόπου Θεσσαλονίκης τοῦ Παλαμᾶ ὁμιλία περὶ πίστεως ἐν ᾗ καὶ τῆς κατ᾽ εὐσέβειαν ὁμολογίας ἔκθεσις. Δ΄. Τοῦ ἐν θεολόγοις καὶ ἰατροῖς κλεινοτάτου Γεωργίου Κορεσσίου τοῦ ἐκ Χίου Συντομία τῶν Ἰταλικῶν ἁμαρτημάτων τοῦ ἀριθμοῦ. [...] Πρῶτον ἤδη τὰ πάντα ἐν Λονδίνῳ ὑπὸ Σιμωνίδου, διδάκτορος τῆς φιλοσοφίας, ἐκδιδόμενα ἅμα τῇ τοῦ Νικολάου Μεθώνης εἰκόνι καὶ ἐξ πίναξιν ἐπιγραφῶν ἀρχαίων καὶ σημειώσεσιν ἱστορικαῖς. London. Published by David Nutt. 270. Strand. 1859.

In Greek. This copy bears the *ex libris* of Joannes Gennadius and a handwritten dedication by Simonidis on the title page: Βασιλειάδῃ πρεσβυτέρῳ Κ. Σιμωνίδης φιλίας καὶ ἀγάπης μνείας ἕνεκα. τῇ 8/20 Ἰουνίου 1862. Here again, Simonidis features only as editor. The book brings together four theological treatises by Nicholas of Methone (12th century), Georgios Gennadios Scholarios (15th century), Gregory Palamas (14th century), and Georgios Coressios (17th century, reader of Greek at the University of Pisa and opponent of Galileo Galilei). Nicholas of Methone's *On the Holy Spirit* also circulated separately (London 1858, see Gennadius' note below). In addition,

Simonidis published letters by scholars and other texts concerning the *Shepherd of Hermas*, another of his favorite New Testament apocrypha.

4) BB 1226.4 [GC 5376]

Archaeologische Abhandlungen. I. *Ueber die Echtheit des Uranius*, Von Constantinos Simonides. München, 1856. Druck von Carl Robert Schurich.

In German. This copy is bound in a volume containing seven items by and concerning Simonidis that bears the bookplate of Gennadius. The front endpaper of this pamphlet has a handwritten note by Gennadius: "Extremely rare." It is the first issue in a series of which no further numbers were published. The treatise concerns the palimpsest manuscript of an unknown ancient historian named Uranius that Simonidis had forged and succeeded in selling to the King of Prussia in 1855 after deceiving some of the best German philologists of the time. A sample edition was even published by the Clarendon Press of Oxford, but the copies were called in as soon as the fraud was exposed. Several copies slipped through the net, however, though Gennadius never got his hands on any of them; the Library today has no copy of the work. Simonidis persisted in defending the authenticity of his fabrication.

5) BB 1226.4 [GC 5372]

Ἐγκώμιον Κωνσταντίνου Ἀκροπολίτου καὶ Μεγάλου Λογοθέτου εἰς τὸν ἅγιον καὶ θεόστεπτον βασιλέα Κωνσταντῖνον τὸν Μέγαν καὶ ἰσαπόστολον. Ἐκδοθὲν πρῶτον ἤδη ὡς ἔχει ἐν χειρογράφοις ὑπὸ Κωνσταντίνου Σιμωνίδου ὁ καὶ τοῖς ἐθελοκακοῦσι τῷ ἐκδότῃ ὁ αὐτὸς ἀνατίθησιν. Εὑρίσκεται ἐν Λονδίνῳ ἐν τοῖς βιβλιοπωλείοις τῶν Κ. Κ. Λογγμάνου, Βράουνος, Γρῆν καὶ Λογγμάνου, ΑΩΝΓ΄. The Panegyric of that Holy, Apostolic, and Heaven-crowned King, Constantine The Great, composed by his Head Logothetes Constantine Acropoliti, faithfully copied from the MSS., and now for the first time published, by Constantine Simonides, who dedicates the work to those who bear the editor no good will. London: Longman, Brown, Green, and Longmans. 1853

In Greek. This copy is bound together in the same volume as the previous item. It contains the edition of a work of the 13th–14th-century hagiographer Constantinos Akropolitis; cf. D. M. Nicol, *Dumbarton Oaks Papers* 19 (1965), pp. 249–256. Simonidis claimed to have published a more reliable text.

6) BB 1226.4 [GC 5373]

Ἐπιστολιμαία περὶ ἱερογλυφικῶν γραμμάτων διατριβὴ παρὰ Κ. Σιμωνίδου διδάκτορος τῆς φιλοσοφίας κ.τ.λ. κ.τ.λ. κ.τ.λ. ὃς καὶ τῷ κυρίῳ Κωι. Ἰωσήππῳ Μαϋέρῳ ἀνδρὶ παιδείᾳ κεκοσμημένῳ παντοίᾳ καὶ μέλει διαφόρων ἐταιριῶν κ.τ.λ. κ.τ.λ. κ.τ.λ. εἰς φιλίας ἀϊδίου τεκμήριον ἀνατίθησιν. Εὑρίσκεται ἐν μὲν τῷ Λονδίνῳ παρὰ τῷ κυρίῳ Δαυῒδ Νουττίῳ, 270, Στράνδ, ἐν δὲ τῇ Λιβερπούλῃ παρὰ τῷ κυρίῳ Α. Χολδενίῳ. ΑΩΞ. *A Brief dissertation on hieroglyphic letters by Constantine Simonides, Ph. D. etc. etc. etc.* London: David Nutt, 270, Strand. Liverpool: A. Holden. 1860.

In Greek and English. It is bound in the same volume as the previous item. The text is a bilingual treatise with continuous pagination. This copy bears a handwritten dedication by Simonidis: "To the Editor of the Times with the Author's Compliments." The editor of the *Times* around 1860 was John Thaddeus Delane (1817–1879), whose library was sold at London in February 1899. This item, like the two following nos., concerns another of Simonidis' major interests, Egypt and its hieroglyphs.

7) BB 1226.5 [GC 5379]

Memnon. Archäeologische Monatsschrift, redigirt von Const. Simonides aus Stagira, Dr. philos. etc. etc. Erster Jahrgang. I. Band. I. und 2. Heft für Januar und Februar. München 1857. Commission-Debit von Lampart & Comp. in Augsburg. Μέμνων. *Σύγγραμμα ἀρχαιολογικὸν κατὰ μῆνα ἐκδιδόμενον ὑπὸ τοῦ συγγράφοντος αὐτὸ Κ. Σιμωνίδου τοῦ Σταγειρίτου διδάκτορος τῆς φιλοσοφίας κ.τ.λ. κ.τ.λ. κ.τ.λ. Ἔτος Α'. Τόμος πρῶτος φυλλάδια δύο κατὰ μῆνα Ἰαννουάριον καὶ Φεβρουάριον. Πρῶτον καὶ δεύτερον. Ἐν Μονάχῳ. ‚ΑΩΝΖ'.*

In Greek and German. This copy bears the *ex libris* of Joannes and Anthi Gennadius. It consists of the first three issues of a bilingual monthly journal written entirely by Simonidis, of which nothing further was published.

8) BB 1226.6 [GC 5382]

Concerning Horus of Nilopolis, the hierogrammatist of his native place, son of Ammouthis and Thessais. With notices of his works. By Constantine Simonides, Ph. D. etc. etc. etc. London: Trübner & Co., No. 60 Paternoster Row. 1863.

In English. This same volume, which bears the bookplate of Joannes Gennadius, also contains the next item (no. 9.) The book is entirely based on documents and details invented by Simonidis, starting with the author's very name, Horus, which according to Simonidis was the real name of Horapollo, the Greek writer who studied hieroglyphic writing in antiquity.

9) BB 1226.6 [GC 5383]

The Periplus of Hannon, King of the Karchedonians, concerning the Lybian parts of the Earth beyond the Pillars of Herakles, which he dedicated to Kronos, the greatest God, and to all the Gods dwelling with him. London: Trübner & Co., No. 60, Paternoster Row. 1864.

In English. This work is bound in the same volume as the previous item. It contains the edited text and commentary along with the lithographed facsimile of a papyrus that Simonidis forged using Hanno's *Periplus*, a work actually handed down to us through the medieval manuscript tradition, as his basis.

10) BB 1226.68 and BB 1226.68 copy 2

> *Αὐτόγραφα τοῦ διδάκτορος καὶ ἱππότου Κωνσταντίνου Λ. Φ. Σιμωνίδου ἐξαχθέντα ἐξ ἐπιστολῶν καὶ ἑτέρων αὐτοῦ ἐγγράφων, καὶ περιέχοντα ποικίλην ἀρχαιολογικὴν ὕλην λίαν σπουδαίαν, ἅπερ καὶ ἐκδίδονται αὐτογραφίᾳ ὑπὸ Καλλινίκου Ἱερομονάχου τοῦ Θεσσαλονικέως τῇ ἀδείᾳ τοῦ συγγραφέως καὶ Κωνσταντίῳ τῷ Α' πρῴην Κωνσταντινουπόλεως πατριάρχῃ ἀνδρὶ σοφῷ λίαν καὶ παντοίᾳ ἀρετῇ κεκοσμημένῳ εἰς εὐγνωμοσύνης ἀϊδίου τεκμήριον πανευλαβῶς καθιεροῦνται ὑπὸ τοῦ ἐκδότου καὶ ταπεινοῦ αὐτοῦ θεράποντος. Ἔκδοσις πρώτη. Ἐν Μόσχᾳ. Ἔτει σωτηρίῳ ,αωνγ'. Μηνὸς Αὐγούστου η'.* [1853]

In Greek. Nos. 10–16 contain the weirdest of Simonidis' products. Consisting of lithographed handwritten leaves in Greek, all assigned to the pen of one of Simonidis' aliases, the monk Kallinikos of Thessaloniki, they contain several texts that we also find in his printed pamphlets, plus other short writings and letters on his favorite subjects: Egypt and hieroglyphs, the *Shepherd of Hermas*, ancient Greek inscriptions, papyri, theological and historical texts, and so on. All are dated Moscow 1853 or, in the second edition, Odessa 1854, but the actual place of "publication" is disputable.

The call numbers BB 1226.68 and BB1226.68 copy 2 were assigned to two volumes containing the same four lithographed pamphlets (see also nos. 11–13) and bearing the following title engraved on the spine: Κ. ΣΙΜΩΝΙΔΟΥ / ΑΡΧΑΙΟΛΟΓΙΚΑΙ / ΕΠΙΣΤΟΛΑΙ / Α'. Β'. Γ'. Δ'. / ΕΚΔΟΣΙΣ / ΜΟΣΧΑΣ / Α'. / ,ΑΩΝΓ'. Some of the pages of the Αὐτόγραφα in the copy BB 1226.68 are out of order: 1–2, 3–4, 9–10, 11–12, 7–8, 5–6, 13–14, 15–16.

11) BB 1226.68, BB 1226.68 copy 2, and BB 1226.69

> *Ἤθη καὶ ἔθιμα τῶν ἀρχαίων Αἰγυπτίων ἐξαχθέντα μὲν ἐξ ἱερογλυφικῶν μνημείων καὶ κυρίως ἐκ τοῦ ἀγάλματος τοῦ Ἀρχιερέως τῶν Διοσπολιτῶν Ψαμμεχούθωνος ὑπὸ τοῦ διδάκτορος τῆς φιλοσοφίας καὶ ἱππότου Κωνσταντίνου Σιμωνίδου, καὶ πρὸς τὸν αὐτοῦ προστάτην Ἀλέξανδρον Σκαρλάτου Στούρτζαν, τὸν μυστικὸν σύμβολον τοῦ τε ἀοιδίμου αὐτοκράτορος πασῶν τῶν Ῥωσσιῶν Ἀλεξάνδρου τοῦ πρώτου, καὶ Νικολάου τοῦ πρώτου γραφέντα καὶ σταλέντα, ἐκδοθέντα δὲ πανομοιοτύπως ταῦτά τε καὶ ἄλλα σὺν τούτοις τοῦ αὐτοῦ ἀνδρὸς φιλολογικὰ ἔργα λίαν σπουδαῖα ὑπὸ Καλλινίκου Ἱερομονάχου τοῦ Θεσσαλονικέως, καὶ ἀνατεθέντα τῷ αὐτῷ τοῦ συγγραφέως προστάτῃ Ἀλεξάνδρῳ Στούρτζᾳ τῷ κλεινοτάτῳ καὶ πάσης Ἑλλάδος εὐεργέτῃ καὶ μουσῶν μουσηγέτῃ εὐγνωμοσύνης ἕνεκα. Ἐν Μόσχᾳ. Ἔτει σωτηρίῳ ,αωνγ'. Μηνὸς Αὐγούστου ΙΑ.* [1853]

In Greek. 16 leaves. Title page + subsequent pages numbered from α΄ to ι΄, followed by five unnumbered pages containing text.

Call no. BB 1226.69 was assigned to a collection of five lithographed pamphlets bound together; see also nos. 12–15 (cf.n. 26 below).

12) BB 1226.68, BB 1226.68 copy 2, and BB 1226.69

> Σπουδαῖον ὑπόμνημα περί τε τῶν ἑξ καὶ ὀγδοήκοντα ἀπογράφων τῶν Ποιμενικῶν γραφῶν τοῦ ἀποστολικοῦ Πατρὸς Ἑρμᾶ, υἱοῦ Ἀσυγκρίτου τοῦ Λαοδικέως, καὶ περὶ τῶν μονῶν ἐν αἷς ὑπῆρχον ἀποτεθησαυρισμένα. Συντεθὲν παρὰ Κωνσταντίνου Σιμωνίδου τοῦ διδάκτορος καὶ ἱππότου, καὶ ἀποσταλὲν τῷ Παναγιωτάτῳ καὶ Σοφωτάτῳ Πατριάρχῃ Κωνσταντίῳ τῷ Πρώτῳ, ᾧ καὶ καθιεροῦται ὑπὸ τοῦ πρώτου αὐτοῦ ἐκδότου Καλλινίκου Ἱερομονάχου τοῦ Θεσσαλονικέως, ἅμα δ᾽ αὐτῷ καὶ πάντα τὰ λοιπὰ, τὰ συνεχόμενα σεβασμοῦ ἕνεκα. Ἐν Μόσχᾳ τῇ κ͞ τοῦ μηνὸς Αὐγούστου τοῦ ἔτους ΑΩΝΓ΄. [1853]

In Greek. Title page + 22 numbered pages.
BB 1226.68 copy 2: this copy is incomplete, as pp. 20–21 are missing.

13) BB 1226.68, BB 1226.68 copy 2, and BB 1226.69

> Κωνστίνου (sic) Σιμωνίδου διδάκτορος καὶ ἱππότου Μεταγραφαὶ αὐτόγραφοι, ἐκδοθεῖσαι ἐν Μόσχᾳ λιθογραφίᾳ τῷ ‚αωνγ΄ ἔτει ὑπὸ Καλλινίκου Ἱερομονάχου τοῦ Θεσσαλονικέως καὶ καθιερωθεῖσαι τῇ ἱερᾷ σκιᾷ τοῦ ἀοιδίμου Βενεδίκτου τοῦ Συναίου τοῦ παιδείᾳ καὶ ἀρετῇ κεκοσμημένου παντοίᾳ [1853]

In Greek. Title page + pages numbered from α΄ to ιβ΄.
BB 1226.68: this copy is incomplete, as pp. ιγ΄–ιε΄ are missing.

14) BB 1226.69

> Κ. Σιμωνίδου τοῦ διδάκτορος καὶ ἱππότου Σύμμιγα (sic). Ἐκδοθέντα ὑπὸ Καλλινίκου Ἱερομονάχου τοῦ Θεσσαλονικέως, καὶ ἀνατεθέντα τῷ φιλτάτῳ αὐτοῦ Σίμωνι, τῷ τοῦ συγγραφέως φιλοστόργῳ πατρὶ, ἀνδρὶ καλῷ κἀγαθῷ καὶ τῆς πατρίδος κοινῷ εὐεργέτῃ. Ἐν Μόσχᾳ. Μηνὶ Σεπτεμβρίῳ, ἐν ἔτει ΑΩΝΓ΄. [1853]

In Greek. At the end this copy includes three unnumbered pages which can also be found in Ἤθη καὶ ἔθιμα κτλ.

15) BB 1226.69

> Αὐτόγραφα τοῦ διδάκτορος καὶ ἱππότου Κ. Λ. Φ. Σιμωνίδου ἐξαχθέντα ἐξ ἐπιστολῶν καὶ ἑτέρων αὐτοῦ ἐγγράφων, καὶ περιέχοντα ποικίλην ἀρχαιολογικὴν καὶ ἱστορικὴν ὕλην λίαν σπουδαίαν, ἅπερ καὶ ἐκδίδονται αὐτογραφίᾳ ὑπὸ Καλλινίκου Ἱερομονάχου τοῦ Θεσσαλονικέως τῇ ἀδείᾳ τοῦ συγγραφέως καὶ Κωνσταντίῳ τῷ Α΄. πρώην Κων-

σταντινουπόλεως πατριάρχῃ, ἀνδρὶ σοφῷ λίαν καὶ παντοίᾳ ἀρετῇ κεκοσμημένῳ, εἰς εὐγνωμοσύνης ἀϊδίου τεκμήριον πανευλαβῶς καθιεροῦται ὑπὸ τοῦ ἐκδότου καὶ ταπεινοῦ αὐτοῦ θεράποντος. Ἔκδοσις δευτέρα. Ἐν Ὀδησσῷ. Τῷ ΑΩΝΔ'. Ἰαννουαρίου α'. [1854]

In Greek. A pretend second edition of the work listed at no. 10; it differs from the first edition only in regard to the title page.

16) BB 1226.7, BB 1226.7 copy 2 [GC 5384], BB 1226.7 copy 3, and BB 1226.7 copy 4

K. Σιμωνίδου τοῦ διδάκτορος καὶ ἱππότου Σύμμιγα (sic). Ἐκδοθέντα ὑπὸ Καλ-λινίκου Ἱερομονάχου τοῦ Θεσσαλονικέως, καὶ ἀνατεθέντα τῷ φιλτάτῳ αὐτοῦ Σίμω-νι, τῷ τοῦ συγγραφέως φιλοστόργῳ πατρὶ, ἀνδρὶ καλῷ κἀγαθῷ καὶ τῆς πατρίδος κοινῷ εὐεργέτῃ. Ἔκδοσις δευτέρα ἐπηυξημένη. Ἐν Ὀδησσῷ. Ἐκ τῆς λιθογραφίας Βράουονος. Ἐν ἔτει ΑΩΝΔ'. Μηνὸς Ἰαννουαρίου εἰκοστῇ πρώτῃ. [1854]

In Greek. A pretend second edition of what is listed at no. 14. It differs from the first edition by the addition of five pages at the beginning (numbered from α' to ε') and four pages at the end (κε'–κη'). The three unnumbered pages which can be found at the end of the first edition are missing in all these copies.

BB 1226.7: this copy bears a handwritten dedication by Simonidis to the National Library of Greece (τῇ τῶν Ἑλλήνων Ἐθνικῇ Βιβλιοθήκῃ. Σιμωνίδης).

17) BB 1226.8q [GC 5380]

Fac-similes of certain portions of the Gospel of St. Matthew, and of the Epistles of Ss. James & Jude, written on papyrus in the first century, and preserved in the Egyptian Museum of Joseph Mayer, Esq. Liverpool. With a portrait of St. Mat-thew, from a fresco painting at Mount Athos. Edited and illustrated with notes and historical and literary prolegomena, containing confirmatory fac-similes of the same portions of Holy Scripture from papyri and parchment MSS. in the monas-teries of Mount Athos, of St. Catherine on Mount Sinai, of St. Sabba in Palestine, and other sources. By Constantine Simonides, Ph. D. Hon. Member of the Historic Society of Lancashire and Cheshire, &c. &c. &c. London: Trübner & Co., No. 60 Paternoster Row. ͵ΑΩΞΑ' = 1861 = MDCCCXLI.

In English. It bears the ex libris of Gennadius. A clipping from a sale catalogue is pasted on the second endpaper. A leaf containing what looks like experiments with a pigment is pasted on the fourth endpaper. Handwritten dedication on the title page: Τῷ καθηγητῇ Γούνσωνι Κ. Σιμωνίδης φιλίας ἕνεκα τῇ κβ/δ ὀκτ. ͵αωξβ' [September 22/ October 4, 1862]. The dedicatee might be William Mandell Gunson (1822–1881), Fel-low of Christ's College, Cambridge. The book deals with New Testament papyri from the collection of Joseph Mayer. The pretend originals are reproduced in lithographs.

18) BB 1226.9q [GC 5381]

Λείψανα ἱστορικά. Α΄. Ὁ Θηβαικὸς κώδηξ διαλαμβάνων περὶ τῶν τῆς Λυβικῆς Καρχηδόνος εἴκοσι καὶ δύο πρώτων δυναστῶν. Ἔστι δὲ γεγραμμένος ἐφ᾽ ἑνὸς τεμαχίου αἰγυπτιακοῦ παπύρου Ασαχαμ (εὐφύλλου τουτέστι) καλουμένου αἰγυπτιστί. Β΄. Ἀνδροσθένους Διοδώρου τοῦ Θασίου μικρὸν λείψανον ἐκ τῆς τρίτης βίβλου τῶν Οἰκιστικῶν γεγραμμένον ἐπὶ παπύρου αἰγυπτιακοῦ Μαραβα καλουμένου τουτέστιν σκληροῦ ἐν ᾧ καὶ μικρὸν χωρίον ἐκ τῶν παντοδαπῶν ἀναγνωσμάτων Διοτίμου μεταγενοῦς τοῦ Ἀδραμυττηνοῦ. Γ΄. Ἱστορικὰ τεμάχια ἀνεπίγραφα γεγραμμένα καὶ ταῦτα ἐπὶ παπύρου Γουμα Εγχουιρα καλουμένου αἰγυπτιστί τὰ πρωτότυπα δὲ τούτων σώζονται πάντα ἐν τῷ τῆς Λιβερπούλης αἰγυπτιακῷ Μουσίῳ. Ἐν αὐτῷ γὰρ καὶ ἀνεκαλύφθησαν ὑπὸ Κωνσταντίνου Σιμωνίδου διδάκτορος τῆς φιλοσοφίας κ.τ.λ. κ.τ.λ. κ.τ.λ. ὑφ᾽ οὗ καὶ πρῶτον ἤδη ἐκδίδονται καὶ ἀνατίθενται τῷ ἱππότῃ καὶ προξένῳ τοῦ βασιλείου τῶν Ἑλλήνων κυρίῳ κυρίῳ Σταματίῳ Ν. Φραγκοπούλῳ ἀνδρὶ καλῷ καὶ ἀγαθῷ καὶ λίαν ἀγαθοέργῳ εὐγνωμοσύνης ἕνεκα. ΑΩΞΔ΄. [Liverpool 1864]

In Greek. It bears the *ex libris* of Gennadius. It deals with papyri of ancient Greek historians from the collection of Joseph Mayer. The pretend originals are reproduced in lithographs.

19) T 2253

"Τὰ ὄργια."

In Greek. A newspaper article written by Simonidis for the *Aἰών* (*The Age*), 16/28 July, 1847, while he was in Athens. It is connected with the smear campaign against the American evangelical missionary Jonas King, in which Simonidis played an active role.

All the items in the preceding list come from Gennadius' personal library, except nos. 1 (BB 1226.1), 2 (BB 1226.2), and 19 (T 2253). Nos. 1 and 19 were placed in the Gennadius Library afterwards, whereas no. 2 comes from the donation of Damianos Kyriazis (d. 1948). As we understand from the note in Gennadius' typewritten Catalogue reproduced below, this item in fact replaced another copy of the *Symais* that did come from Gennadius' personal collection. The latter was recorded as missing from the Gennadius Library in the inventory of 1973, together with two other items with which it was bound,[8] a small seven-page booklet containing an announcement for the publication of a hagiographic manuscript (something that so far I have not come across in any other library[9]), and a copy of the so-called *Kefalleniakà*, a fake

8. According to the former shelf-marks attributed by Gennadius, they were GC 5368–5370. I owe this information to the kindness of Gabriella Vasdeki, the Library's Secretary.
9. Actually, another copy was in the possession of Spyridion Lampros (it bore a dedication by Simonidis to Lampros' father), cf. «Νέος Ἑλληνομνήμων» 17 (1923) 40.

history of Kefalonia ascribed to the ancient historian Eulyros, who remains only a name, as no work of his actually survives.[10] The loss of the *Kefalleniakà* is particularly regrettable, since we also understand from Gennadius' note that the book bore Simonidis' handwritten dedication to Gennadius' father, Georgios (1786–1854).[11] This suggests that Simonidis' name was probably familiar to Gennadius from the time he was still living at his family's home.

The remaining items are the result of the joining of two different sets of books. The first set includes books by Simonidis that Gennadius had put together before 1923, which is the date when the latter's typewritten Catalogue of Greek Classics was completed. The books in this group were purchased at different sales of private libraries or from booksellers' catalogues and have been in the Gennadius Library since its opening in 1926. They are the items to which the call numbers BB 1226.3, 1226.4, 1226.5, 1226.6, 1226.7 copy 2, 1226.8q, and 1226.9q were assigned.

The second set, on the other hand, comes from a very late purchase by Gennadius. In April 1931, one year before his death, he bought one lot of Simonidis items at a sale of books. As he recorded in his Catalogue (see below), he purchased them without even inspecting the lot.[12] Their provenance is significant. The lot came from the last sale (April 1931) of the library of John Eliot Hodgkin (1829–1912), an engineer and collector who had been one of the English friends of Simonidis, or rather one of his supporters and patrons.[13] The new acquisitions arrived in August 1931 with the very last shipment of books to the Gennadius Library. They now have the call numbers BB 1226.68, BB 1226.68 copy 2, 1226.69, 1226.7 copy 3, 1226.7 copy 4. It should be noted that in this case as well, two items recorded in the 1931 catalogue are missing; they probably never reached the Library (see n. 25 below). This set includes some very rare publications by Simonidis, which it seems are found exclusively, or almost exclusively, in the Gennadius Library: Ἤθη καὶ ἔθιμα τῶν ἀρχαίων Αἰγυπτίων κτλ. (3 copies: BB 1226.68, BB 1226.68 copy 2, and BB 1226.69), Μεταγραφαὶ αὐτόγραφοι κτλ. (3 copies: BB 1226.68, BB 1226.68 copy 2, and BB 1226.69), and the 1854 Odessa editions of the Αὐτόγραφα (1 copy: BB 1226.69)[14] and the Σύμμιγα (3 copies: BB 1226.7 copy 2, BB 1226.7 copy 3, and BB 1226.7 copy 4).

We must leave BB 1226.7, which contains a further copy of the "Odessa edition" of the Σύμμιγα, aside because it is difficult to say where it actually comes from. This

---

10. An edition of Simonidis' *Kefalleniakà* will be published shortly by M. R. Acquafredda (Bari, Edizioni di Pagina).

11. The book is not recorded in the manuscript catalogues of Georgios Gennadius' personal library, which are likewise preserved in the Gennadius Library (F 146–149).

12. This was also emphasized by Masson (1993a, pp. 9–10).

13. Most of Simonidis' extant papers come from the bequest of Hodgkin's papers to the British Museum and are now in the British Library. I will try to explore the connections between Simonidis and Hodgkin in another paper.

14. Another copy of the "second edition" of the Αὐτόγραφα is in fact held by the Bibliothèque Nationale, Paris (J 6227).

item is not recorded in the Catalogues of Gennadius and moreover bears a puzzling handwritten dedication by Simonidis to the National Library of Athens.[15]

To sum up, a schematic overview of the "Simonideia" which incontestably come from Gennadius' private collection follows:

First Group (acquired before 1923):
BB 1226.3
BB 1226.4
BB 1226.5
BB 1226.6
BB 1226.7 copy 2
BB 1226.8q
BB 1226.9q

Second Group (purchased 1931):
BB 1226.68
BB 1226.68 copy 2
BB 1226.69
BB 1226.7 copy 3
BB 1226.7 copy 4

As already mentioned, the very last installment of books sent by Gennadius to Athens was accompanied by a supplement to his typewritten Catalogue which also included a comprehensive note about Simonidis and his career. This is not the rule in Gennadius' Catalogues; on the contrary, Simonidis is one of the very few authors to which Gennadius devoted a note. It therefore offers something of a clue to the special interest that Gennadius had in Simonidis. The first record of this interest is in the preface that Gennadius wrote in 1915 for Dowling and Fletcher's *Hellenism in England*. In it Gennadius discussed the connections between Simonidis and the sham Prince Demetrios Rhodocanakis. According to Gennadius, Simonidis had a relevant part in the forging of the documents with which Rhodocanakis supported his claims.[16]

Gennadius had in fact already appended a brief note on Simonidis to the end of his list of "Simonideia" in Vol. 3 Part 2 of his *Catalogue of Greek Classics* (p. 71),

---

15. I can only conjecture that, if it came from a Gennadius, it had been sent to Gennadius' father, as he was one of the founders of the National Library of Athens. We should note that this title is not included in the few Simonidis items kept in the National Library at Athens.

16. Dowling and Fletcher 1915, pp. 41–42, 48. Gennadius is the only source connecting Simonidis to Rhodocanakis' impostures. He repeated the assertion in 1923, in the note reproduced below, and also collected a considerable number of documents (books, pamphlets, catalogues, etc., which are now in the Library) concerning Rhodocanakis, including the extraordinary dossier put together by Legrand (1895) to expose the deceptions of the false prince.

completed in 1923. This note provides an early indication of his intention to build up a complete collection, or at least the fullest possible collection, of "Simonideia," though some titles would continue to evade his grasp:

"The above 16 items are all very rare and constitute an almost complete set of the Author's publications. He himself gives (on the vo. of the 2nd. l. of No. 5383) a list of 42 works of his.[17] But it is suspected that some are imaginary publications intended to support the claims made in his forgeries. I have ascertained, for instance, that No. 7, "Ἡ πρὸς τοὺς ἐξ Ἑβραίων πιστοὺς Ἐπιστολὴ τοῦ Ἀποστολικοῦ πατρὸς ἡμῶν Βαρνάβα", which purported to have been issued in Smyrna in 1843, was (as the copy I saw betrayed), printed in England at about 1860[18] in order to support certain claims of Prince Rhodocanakis (see Biographies Catalogue No. 43–57) who was an intimate friend of his, and whom he has schooled in the art of inventing, in like manner, non extant publications. The only other work of Simonides of which I saw a copy in the library of the late Sir James Donaldson, Principal of St. Andrews University, was this: -

Διοκλέους Δαμόρου τοῦ Καρυστίου ἡ περὶ ὑγιεινῶν ἐπιστολὴ καὶ Τρυφίλου Πρα- ξιάδου Διδ. τῆς φιλος. καὶ καθιεροῦται τῷ Κυρίῳ Ἰωάννῃ Λύδδῃ, ἀνδρὶ φιλτάτῳ λίαν καὶ εἰς τὰ μάλιστα φιλομούσῳ. Ἐν Λονδίνῳ 1865. -16ο., 8+15 p. No printer's name but evidently from Clayton's press, whose types I could well recognise."[19]

Finally, the document most relevant to Gennadius' interest in Simonidis is repro- duced here. It is the extensive note from the Catalogue of 1931,[20] which is a brief but precious assessment of the life and career of Simonidis that shows how intriguing Gennadius found him. We have already referred to this note above, as it contains a detailed description of the books that Gennadius had just purchased.

C. THE SIMONIDES FORGERIES

1640. The appendix to the third section of my Catalogue of Greek classic literature gives a list of the publications of Constantine Simonides, the notorious forger of Greek MSS. (Nos. 5368–5384). That collection of seventeen items is, as far as I know, the completest extant. And it may be appropriate and convenient to add here a brief account of the man and his exploits. Simonides, in his adventurous ca-

17. See n. 2 above.

18. As a former librarian noted in the margin of this page, Gennadius' statement is complicated by the fact that part of the pamphlet had already been published at Smyrna in the Ἀστὴρ τῆς Ἀνατολῆς, August 1, 1843 (no. 1 in the List above).

19. Donaldson's library was bequeathed to the University of St. Andrews, but I have not so far been able to obtain any information from the Library there. Gennadius omitted some words of the title after Πραξιάδου: Ὑλλαριμέος λείψανα. Ἐκδίδονται δὲ ὑπὸ Κ. Σιμωνίδου. Other copies of this pamphlet survive in the Bodleian Library, Oxford (I Delta 598, with the handwritten dedication by Simonidis to William Bollaert), and the University Library at Strasbourg (C.121.362).

20 Sixth Instalment of Accessions to The Gennadius Library provisionally catalogued according to subjects. No. 1615–2161, and Index of Names. Whitegates, August 1931, 8–18 (no. 1640).

reer, visited many lands, and his various publications (always issued in few copies) marked his roaming footsteps from Athens and Constantinople, to Mount Sinai, and to the monasteries of Athos; also to Moscow and | Odessa, and thence to Vienna, Leipzig, Paris and London, with visits to Oxford and to Manchester. [From his dated letters he seems to have been in the island of Lemnos on July 1839. He must have studied in Athens, and have begun publishing there from 1847 to 1850. In Mount Athos he arrived in October 1851, in Alexandria in January 1852, and in Sinai in April of the same year, returning to Alexandria and Cairo in May and August 1852. We next hear of him in Moscow in September 1853, and in Odessa in January 1854; and again in Moscow in August 1857. In London he was in 1853, in Leipzig in 1856, and in England (London, Liverpool and Manchester, the centers of Greek Communities) at times from 1858 to 1864].[21] There is some record of him in the *Encyclopaedia Britannica*. In the article on Henry Bradshaw it is stated that Bradshaw "had a share in exposing the frauds of C. Simonides who had asserted that the Codex Sinaiticus, brought by Tischendorf from the Greek monastery of Mount Sinai, was a modern forgery of which he was himself the author. Bradshaw exposed the absurdity of these claims in a letter to the *Guardian* (January 26, 1863)."[22] Much to the same effect is recorded under O. H. Coxe the English Librarian, who published a | *Report on the Greek Manuscripts yet remaining in the Libraries of the Levant*, London 1858. The late Sir Frederick Madden, Keeper of the *MSS.* in the British Museum, had much to do with the exposure of Simonides, as related by J. A. Farrer in *Literary Forgeries*, 1907. But the personality and appearance of Simonides is best described by the Comte de Marcellus, in *Épisodes littéraires en Orient*, Paris, 1851. He describes him as taciturn, gloomy and suspicious, dressed always in black. He testifies to the sedentary and industrious life led by him, and also to his indifference to gain, and expresses his belief that during the whole time he was in France he made no attempt to sell any of his *MSS*.[23] But when he went to Germany and settled at Leipzig, his mind, or his habits, underwent a change. He was not only himself suspicious, but the cause of that suspicion was aroused in other men. "He forged a palimpsest – not an easy thing to do – which is preserved in the Imperial Library at Vienna."[24] Of his friend and disciple Rodocanachis (of Manchester), for whom he invented a whole princely genealogy, mention is made in the appendix referred to above.

Such, in brief, was this extraordinary man, of whom it may be said that he practiced his marvellous dexterity as a calligraphist, not so much for gain, as for the |

---

21. This addition was inserted by Gennadius at the bottom of p. 9 of his Catalogue.

22. The affair was recalled by Prothero (1888, pp. 92–99), one of Bradshaw's biographers.

23. I was not able to find any reference to Simonidis in *Épisodes littéraires en Orient*, but the description quoted by Gennadius matches the one given by Marcellus in a letter to *L'Athenaeum Français* (February 23, 1856, 156–157) reproduced by Masson (1994, p. 377).

24. The reference is to the palimpsest of the *Shepherd of Hermas* now in the National Library of Vienna (Suppl. Gr. 119), cf. Gastgeber 2001, esp. pp. 105–106.

satisfaction he felt in being able to hoodwink scholars much more learned than himself. For he was not a profound scholar, and while his palaeographic calligraphy was admirable, the texts he invented and then clothed with his penmanship, left him open to exposure by both Greek and foreign critics. Moreover he laboured under the presumption of most adventurers in underestimating the chances of detection, or of the probabilities of the actual facts cropping up. I heard the story of his discomfiture at Oxford, when one of the older Dons, when examining the *MSS.* offered by Simonides, first took up one of them, the most inviting, and carefully smelling it, layed it aside at one end of the table saying deliberately: "Fifteenth century." He then took up another, and submitting it to the same scrutiny, deposited it at the other end of the table declaring with a smile: "Nineteenth century", and so on through the whole lot of the goods offered, to the undoing of Simonides who, when exhibiting his wares, mixed his own fabrications with genuine *MSS.* which he had collected — by what means we can well imagine — during his visits to Greek monasteries. But he had overlooked the fact that his productions still exhaled the odour of the chemicals he employed in giving his parchments the appearance of age. The same thing happened at the British Museum, when, on his first visit, he offered documents all | of which Sir Frederick Madden rejected as spurious; but on the day following he submitted another lot the whole of which was acquired for the nation as genuine.

Many such incidents, and indeed the whole guilt and immorality of Simonides's traffic in literary products, the proprietorship of which could not be established as avowable and honest, were passed in significant silence, and were not even for a moment considered by the public officials, who were primarily concerned with what genuine Greek *MSS.* they could choose out of offers made possible only by purloinment and deliberate fraud. These public Museums are now the custodians and expositors of the fruits of his dishonesty and theft. But the Gennadeion Library can avow openly how it came by the collection of its Simonidea, – both those already catalogued, and the important accessions just acquired. Of these I will now give some account.

On the two last days of the month of April just lapsed Messrs Hodgson, of 115 Chancery Lane, disposed by public sale of the Library of John Hodgkin of Three Mile Cross, Reading. Lot 478 of the sale Catalogue read as follows:

" Simonides Opuscula. Facsimile of a purported Original Greek MS. with A. L. s. from J. A. Farrer, author of *Literary Forgeries*. Morocco, t. e. g. n. d. &c. 6 small | folio vols. With a Dissertation on Hieroglyphic Letters, 1860".

This rather muddled description sufficed to convince me of the importance of the lot offered, and without inspecting it, I had the lot purchased for me. It now forms a material addition to the collection already in the Library. Let me go minutely through the items referred to in the Lot.

1640. A. – The "Dissertation" is a duplicate of No. 5373 of our Catalogue of Greek Classics. Another item contained in the Lot but not mentioned therein is a duplicate of No. 5371, identical in pagination and other respects, but with what appears to be an earlier title page, as follows:

B. – Νικολάου τοῦ ἁγιωτάτου Ἐπισκόπου Μεθώνης λόγος πρὸς τοὺς Λατίνους περὶ τοῦ Ἁγίου Πνεύματος, ὅτι ἐκ τοῦ Πατρὸς, οὐ μὴν καὶ ἐκ τοῦ Υἱοῦ ἐκπορεύεται. Πρῶτον ἤδη ἐκδιδόμενος ὑπὸ Κωνσταντίνου Σιμωνίδου διδάκτορος τῆς Φιλοσοφίας. Ἐν Λονδίνῳ τύποις Γιλβέρτου καὶ Ῥιβινγτῶνος, ‚αωνη‛ (1858).[25]

It is the copy presented to John Hodgkin and bears this inscription: "Τῷ Κυρίῳ Κυρίῳ Ἰωάννη Ε. Χοδγκινίῳ Σιμωνίδης φιλίας εἰλικρινοῦς μικρὸν δῶρον, τῇ 2 Δεκεμ. 1860".

C. – To Hodgkin is also addressed a short undated Autograph Letter from Farrer returning to him some of Simonides' *MSS* and tracings, which Farrer apparently utilised in | his work on *Literary Forgeries*.[26]

These two facts point to friendly and close relations between Simonides and Hodgkin, who was an eminent Lawyer, a Quaker in persuasion, and whose library shows a love and tendency to what is strange and uncommon. He had evidently befriended Simonides and purchased more than one copy of his productions. Most of these, I have met with here for the first time. They are all lithographed from Simonides' beautiful handwriting on the one side only of very thick paper of brownish or blueish tint.

D. – A small Fo. volume bound in brown morocco gilt and lettered "Simonidis Opuscula".[27] This vol. contains the following dissertations:

α΄. Σπουδαῖον ὑπόμνημα περὶ τοῦ τῶν ἐξ καὶ ὀγδοήκοντα ἀπογράφων τῶν ποιμενικῶν γραφῶν τοῦ ἀποστολικοῦ Πατρὸς Ἑρμοῦ, υἱοῦ Ἀσυγκρίτου τοῦ Λαοδικέως, καὶ περὶ τῶν μονῶν ἐν αἷς ὑπῆρχον ἀποτεθησαυρισμένα, συντεθὲν παρὰ Κωνσταντίνου Σιμωνίδου τοῦ διδάκτορος καὶ ἱππότου, καὶ ἀποσταλὲν

---

25. The first two items in this description are not in the Gennadius Library and their accession is not recorded anywhere.

26. The letter is pasted onto the front endpaper of the volume bearing the call number BB 1226.69 and containing the works described just below under D. Here is the text of the letter from Farrer to Hodgkin: "50, Ennismore Gardens, Prince's Gate. / Dear Mr. Hodgkin, I am leaving all the papers I took away the other day, except the curious uncial tracing, which seems to be from the Shepherd of Hermas. This I am anxious to compare at the Brit. Museum / with Tischendorf's Facsimile of the same at the end of his Codex. I expect your volume of Lithograph letters contains a treatise by Simonides on Αγιογραφια, on the Church Art of Mt. Athos. A letter I found / from Alexander Sturzas (at least I think he is meant by A. S. S.) is dated from Odessa, April 14, 1852, and acknowledges the receipt of it. If so, the presumption is that the other letters were really also lithographed about that time. My arrangement of the papers is quite [*a word was probably left out*], but will, I hope, / facilitate reference for future use, should such ever be required. Yours very truly J. A. Farrer».

27. BB 1226.69 (containing nos. 11–15 of the List).

τῷ Παναγιωτάτῳ καὶ Σοφωτάτῳ Πατριάρχῃ Κωνσταντίῳ τῷ Πρώτῳ, ᾧ καὶ καθιεροῦται ὑπὸ τοῦ πρώτου αὐτοῦ ἐκδότου Καλλινίκου Ἱερομονάχου τοῦ Θεσσαλονικέως, ἅμα δ᾽ αὐτῷ καὶ πάντα τὰ λοιπὰ τὰ συνεχόμενα σεβασμοῦ ἕνεκα. "Μὴ τὰ ἀρέσκοντα, ἀλλὰ τὰ ὠφελοῦντα λέγε".

Ἐν Μόσχᾳ τῇ κ´ τοῦ μηνὸς Αὐγούστου, ἔτους ΑΩΝΓ´. (1853) (22 leaves).|

β´. Κωνστίνου (sic) Σιμωνίδου διδάκτορος καὶ ἱππότου Μεταγραφαὶ αὐτόγραφοι ἐκδοθεῖσαι ἐν Μόσχᾳ λιθογραφίᾳ, τῷ ‚αωνγ´ ἔτει, ὑπὸ Καλλινίκου Ἱερομονάχου τοῦ Θεσσαλονικέως, καὶ καθιερωθεῖσαι τῇ ἱερᾷ σκιᾷ τοῦ ἀοιδίμου Βενεδίκτου τοῦ Σιναίου, τοῦ παιδείᾳ καὶ ἀρετῇ κεκοσμημένου παντοίᾳ. (t. p. and 5 l.)

γ´. Κ. Σιμωνίδου τοῦ διδάκτορος καὶ ἱππότου Σύμμιγα, ἐκδοθέντα ὑπὸ Καλλινίκου Ἱερομονάχου τοῦ Θεσσαλονικέως καὶ ἀνατεθέντα τῷ φιλτάτῳ αὐτοῦ Σίμωνι, τῷ τοῦ συγγραφέως φιλοστόργῳ πατρὶ, ἀνδρὶ καλῷ κἀγαθῷ καὶ τῆς πατρίδος κοινῷ εὐεργέτῃ.
Ἄριστος ἡδονῇ ὁ τῶν σπουδαίων ἔρως. Τροφὴ γὰρ ἀθάνατος ἡ τούτων μελέτη.
Ἐν Μόσχᾳ. Μηνὶ Σεπτεμβρίου ἐν ἔτει αωνγ´ (t. p. and 27 l.)

δ´. Αὐτόγραφα τοῦ διδάκτορος καὶ ἱππότου Κ. Λ. Σιμωνίδου ἐξαχθέντα ἐξ ἐπιστολῶν καὶ ἑτέρων αὐτοῦ ἐγγράφων, καὶ περιέχοντα ποικίλην ἀρχαιολογικὴν καὶ ἱστορικὴν ὕλην λίαν σπουδαίαν, ἅπερ καὶ ἐκδίδονται αὐτογραφίᾳ ὑπὸ Καλλινίκου Ἱερομονάχου τοῦ Θεσσαλονικέως τῇ ἀδείᾳ τοῦ συγγραφέως, καὶ Κωνσταντίνῳ τῷ Α´ πρώην Κωνσταντινουπόλεως πατριάρχῃ, ἀνδρὶ σοφῷ λίαν καὶ παντοίᾳ ἀρετῇ κεκοσμημένῳ | εἰς εὐγνωμοσύνης ἀϊδίου τεκμήριον πανευλαβῶς καθιεροῦται ὑπὸ τοῦ ἐκδότου καὶ ταπεινοῦ αὐτοῦ θεράποντος.
Ἔκδοσις δευτέρα. Ἡσίοδος ἐν Ἔργοις καὶ Ἡμέραις, 291
Ἐν Ὀδησσῷ τῷ ‚αωνδ´ Ἰανουαρίου α´ (t. p. and 15 l.)

ε´. Ἤθη καὶ Ἔθιμα τῶν ἀρχαίων Αἰγυπτίων ἐξαχθέντα ἐξ ἱερογλυφικῶν μνημείων καὶ κυρίως ἐκ τοῦ ἀγάλματος τοῦ Ἀρχιερέως τῶν Διοσπολιτῶν ψωμμαχούθωρος, ὑπὸ τοῦ διδάκτορος τῆς φιλοσοφίας καὶ ἱππότου Κωνσταντίνου Σιμωνίδου, καὶ πρὸς τὸν αὐτοῦ προστάτην Ἀλέξανδρον Σκαρλάτον Στούρτζαν, τὸν μυστικὸν Σύμβολον τοῦ ἀοιδίμου αὐτοκράτορος παντῶν (sic) τῶν Ῥωσσιῶν Ἀλεξάνδρου τοῦ πρώτου, καὶ Νικολάου τοῦ πρώτου, γραφέντα καὶ σταλέντα, ἐκδοθέντα δὲ πανομοιοτύπως ταῦτά τε καὶ ἄλλα σὺν τούτοις τοῦ αὐτοῦ ἀνδρὸς φιλολογικὰ ἔργα λίαν σπουδαῖα ὑπὸ Καλλινίκου Ἱερομονάχου τοῦ Θεσσαλονικέως καὶ ἀνατεθέντα τῷ αὐτῷ τοῦ Συγγραφέως προστάτῃ Ἀλεξάνδρῳ Στούρτζᾳ τῷ κλεινοτάτῳ καὶ πάσης Ἑλλάδος εὐεργέτῃ καὶ μουσῶν μουσηγέτῃ, εὐγνωμοσύνης ἕνεκα.
"Εὐτυχεῖς οἱ ὑπὲρ τῆς ἀνθρωπότητος ἐργαζόμενοι"
Ἐν Μόσχᾳ, ἔτει Σωτηρίῳ ‚αωνγ´ (1853) μηνὸς Αὐγούστου 11 / (t. p. and 8 l.)

E and E[bis]. – Two small Fo. vols. bound alike in brown calf, and containing a copy each of the Dissertations δ', ε', α', and β' of the preceding volume,[28] with this difference, that the δ' Dissertation is here said to be first issued in Moscow in 1853, instead of the second, issued in Odessa in 1854. The quotation also is from the Iliad, N 729–733, instead of Hesiod. There is also some difference in the ornamental handwriting of the title page; but the text of the subsequent 15 leaves is identical.

F and F[bis]. – Two small Fo. vols. bound alike in half calf, and containing each a copy of the Dissertations γ' of the "Opuscula" volume,[29] but with some difference in the text, the title being marked: "Ἔκδοσις δευτέρα ἐπηυξημένη", issued, not at Μόσχᾳ, but ἐν Ὀδησσῷ, ἐκ τῆς Λιθογραφίας Βράουνος ἐν ἔτει ‚αω54 (sic) μηνὸς Ἰανουαρίου εἰκοστῇ πρώτῃ. (t.p. and 31 l.).

(No. 5384 of our Catalogue of Classics seems to be another copy of this).[30]

At l. 14 of this vol. is the text of a poem entitled Ὁ παράξενος Κακοήθης, of which the 100 lines all end in – αζει:

Ὅ, τι πέρνει νὰ χαράζῃ
Ἀρχινῆ νὰ ἀλαλάζῃ |
Καὶ τὸν κόσμον νὰ τρομάζῃ
Πλὴν κὶ ὁ ἴδιος ταράζει
Καὶ τὰ ροῦχα του τινάζει, &c.

and Simonides adds that the Author of these humorous lines was: I. Ρ. Νερουλλος· "σατηρίζει δὲ διὰ τούτου Ὑπουργόν τινα τῆς ἐποχῆς του εἰσέτι ἐν τῇ ζωῇ ὄντα. Πιστεύω δὲ ὅτι τὸ παρ' ἐμοὶ σωζόμενον χειρόγραφον ἐστὶ τὸ τοῦ ποιητοῦ αὐτόγραφον". Many more remarks of equal interest might be added to each of the items here described. But it is time to return to the main purpose of this list.

It can be said, in conclusion, that the connections between the forger and the bibliophile have turned out to be much closer than expected. Exactly why Gennadius decided to include a collection of the rare publications of a notorious counterfeiter and swindler within the "grand design" of his great Greek library remains unclear. In fact, Simonidis' name had probably been familiar to Gennadius since the time when he was still living with his family: we have seen that his father possessed at least one book by Simonidis. Gennadius' interest was probably rekindled in the years of his youth, when he first arrived in London at the beginning of the 1860s and began to work in a Greek import-export firm. That was a time when Simonidis was popular, and certainly well known in the Greek communities of England.

---

28. BB 1226.68 and BB 1226.68 copy 2 (each containing nos. 10–13 of the List).

29. BB 1226.7 copy 3 and BB 1226.7 copy 4 (each containing no. 16 of the List).

30. The reference is to BB 1226.7 copy 2.

Gennadius' search for Simonidis' books went on until the very last years of his activity as a book-collector. In the meantime, Gennadius had also tried to get his hands on the books that made up Simonidis' personal library, the tools with which he worked. He in fact managed to obtain one of them and today it is the only book from Simonidis' library in the Gennadius Library: a copy of the *Hieroglyphs of Horapollo Nilous* by Alexander Turner Cory, published in London in 1840. It bears a few autograph notes of the owner and a beautifully handwritten *ex libris*: Καὶ τόδε Κ. Σιμωνίδου | ἐν Λονδίνῳ 1854 Απριλ. 6/18.[31]

BIBLIOGRAPHY

Canfora, L. 2008. *Il papiro di Artemidoro*, Rome and Bari.

Canfora, L. 2010. *Il viaggio di Artemidoro. Vita e avventure di un grande esploratore dell'antichità*, Milan.

Chatzifotis, I. M. 1964. "Νεο-Σιμωνίδεια," Ἀνάλεκτα (of the Patriarchal Library of Alexandria) 13, pp. 115–128.

Chaviaras, D. 1889. "Σιμωνίδης (Κωνσταντίνος)," in Λεξικὸν ἱστορίας καὶ γεωγραφίας 7, ed. S. I. Voutiras, Constantinople, pp. 580–583.

Dowling, T. E., and E. W. Fletcher. 1915. *Hellenism in England: A Short History of the Greek People in this Country from the Earliest Times to the Present Day*, London.

Elliott, J. K. 1982. *Codex Sinaiticus and the Simonides Affair*, Thessaloniki.

Firippidis, N. S. 1931. "Σιμωνίδεια," Ἐκκλησιαστικὸς Φάρος 30, pp. 567–582.

Gastgeber, C. 2001. "Der Falscher Konstantinos Simonides (1820–1867)," in *Kopie und Fälschung*, ed. C. Gastgeber, Graz, pp. 93–108.

Legrand, É. 1895. *Dossier Rhodocanakis. Étude critique de bibliographie et d'histoire littéraire*, Paris.

Lykurgos, A. 1856a. *Enthüllungen über den Simonides-Dindorf'schen Uranios*, Leipzig.

Lykurgos, A. 1856b. *Enthüllungen über den Simonides-Dindorfschen Uranios*, 2nd ed., Leipzig.

Masson, O. 1993a. "Constantin Simonidis et Jean Gennadius: Le Faussaire et le Bibliophile," *The Griffon* 3.1, pp. 7–15.

Masson, O. 1993b. "François Lenormant (1837–1883), un érudit déconcertant," *Museum Helveticum* 50, pp. 44–60.

Masson, O. 1994. "Le faussaire grec C. Simonides à Paris en 1854, avec deux lettres inconnues de Sainte-Beuve et un récit du Comte de Marcellus," *Journal des savants* 1994, pp. 367–379.

Masson, O., and J. L. Fournet. 1992. "À propos d'Horapollon, l'auteur des *Hieroglyphica*," *Revue des études grecques* 105, pp. 231–236.

Prothero, G. W. 1888. *A Memoir of Henry Bradshaw*, London.

Report 1859. *Report of the Council of the Royal Society of Literature on some of the Mayer papyri and the palimpsest MS. of Uranius belonging to M. Simonides*, London.

Simonidis, K. 1864. *The Periplus of Hannon*, London.

Stewart, C. 1859. *A Biographical Memoir of Constantine Simonides*, London.

---

31. The book was used by Simonidis for his own work *Concerning Horus of Nilopolis* (no. 8 in the List above).

EDWARD LEAR'S CRETAN DRAWINGS

STEPHEN DUCKWORTH

The Gennadius Library holds an exceptional collection of Edward Lear's drawings of Greece, including those of Crete. This article focuses on Crete and Lear's journey to Crete in 1864, the only visit he paid to the island, then in Turkish hands. His journal survives and forms an essential accompaniment to the drawings he made. It was first published in 1984, together with illustrations in color of several of the drawings held not only by the Gennadius Library but by other institutions and individuals [1]. The Gennadeion holds 90 of these drawings, but at least as many have been dispersed since the late 1920s.

The research on which much of this article is based has sought to identify the locations which Lear sketched in some 185 consecutively numbered drawings of Crete. By finding the provenance and other details of many of these drawings after Lear's estate was dispersed, the Cretan locations have been identified and are listed with a map showing Lear's route (Fig. 41). A current record has been built up of the nature of the dispersal, including the exhibition history of particular drawings, and details of the drawings and watercolors which can be accessed at public institutions. [2]

The Cretan journey was Lear's last significant visit to what is now Greece. Later on, he stopped briefly at Corfu in 1866 and 1877 en route to other destinations or to visit his old valet and his family. So, the Cretan drawings represent the culmination of his recording of Greek topography. Dr. Fani-Maria Tsigakou commented, "I believe that the largest and more serious pictorial contribution to our knowledge of nineteenth century Greece was made by Lear." [3]

EDWARD LEAR IN CRETE

Lear traveled to Crete from Athens, arriving in Hania towards the west end of the island on April 11, 1864. He had first considered visiting Crete only in February of that year, but had planned the journey by mid-March and read Robert Pashley's *Travels in Crete* (1837), which he carried with him to Crete. [4] Throughout his seven weeks in Crete, Lear kept a detailed journal, described thus by Rowena Fowler:

---

1. By Rowena Fowler; a revised second edition appeared the next year (Fowler 1985).
2. Earlier research on all Lear's Greek and Cretan drawings was carried out by Dr. Fani-Maria Tsigakou for her unpublished thesis: see Tsigakou 1977.
3. Tsigakou 1997, p. 68.
4. Fowler 1985, p. 12.

"He offers us, first, a detailed and sometimes minute-by-minute commentary on the landscape of Crete and, second, an impression of the ups and downs, physical and mental, of an artist travelling on foot over difficult country. He is good on people, food, birds and flowers, disappointing on language, literature and local culture; he notes a few dialect words but, although he knew Fauriel's *Chants populaires de la Grèce moderne* (1824–5) he makes no mention of any folk music or poetry. The weather was generally foul, and in the evening the rigours of Cretan hospitality matched the physical strain of the day's travelling."[5]

Lear based himself in Hania, which is spelled at least five different ways on his drawings, from "Canea" to "Khania." He stayed just outside the town in Halepa, in a room owned by the Dutch Consul, and then with the British consul Hay and his family, also in Halepa. No less than 25 nights were spent in the Hania area, but in day or overnight journeys from there, and in two much more significant expeditions, he covered much of the west and center of the island. One of the latter was to the west, as far as Kissamos, and the other was a large clockwise circuit of Mount Ida via Rethymnon and Herakleion. Until the end of the first week of May he was plagued by bad weather. "And what consolation is it to hear that such late rains were never known before as are in Crete this year? — much as we English tell foreigners that east winds and bitter cold in June, long dreary rains through July and August, and fogs in September are 'quite extraordinary and never occurred before the present year'." (journal, April 21).[6]

Lear initially had qualms about his visit to Crete and retained an ambivalent attitude throughout his stay, though his mood improved once the weather was better. "I much doubt Crete being a *picturesque* country in any way, or that it will repay much trouble in seeing it. Its antiquities etc. *so* old as to be all but invisible; its buildings, monasteries, etc. nil; its Turkish towns fourth-rate. Rats O! and gnats" (April 15). But a few days later he wrote (in Greek in his journal) "since it's necessary to 'do' Crete, let's do it well" (April 22).

His description of Turkish towns as fourth-rate is borne out by his detailed descriptions of Hania, Rethymnon, and Herakleion. He saw some antiquities, in particular at Aptera, south of Suda Bay, and at Polyrrhinia, south of Kastelli Kissamos at the west end of the island. He relied on Pashley for information on these places but called the latter Palaiokastro, the local name. Lear also traveled near the site of Knossos, then of course still unrevealed , and Gortyn in the Messara plain in south-central Crete, where the Roman remains were very visible. But at none of these does he show great interest in the history or nature of the visible remains.

Of the monasteries and their monks, he is less scathing than he had been when

---

5. Fowler 1985, pp. 12-13.
6. The journal extracts given here and later are taken from Fowler 1985, pp. 36, 89, 90, 99, and 103.

he visited Mount Athos in 1856. At that time, he wrote to Chichester Fortescue about Athos, that it was "so gloomy – so shockingly unnatural – so lonely – so lying – so unatonably odious seems to me all the atmosphere of such monkery."[7] Lear approached the monasteries he visited in Crete with some suspicion, but then responded in terms of his own perception of each *hegoumenos* (abbot). On the Akrotiri peninsula near Hania, he visited Aghia Triada and Aghios Ioannis (Gouverneto), and the ruined monastery at Katholiko (Fig. 42). Then came Gonia monastery on the Rodopos peninsula east of Kastelli Kissamos, and later in his travels Asomatos and Arkhadi monasteries in central Crete west of Mount Ida.

He had intended to stay at Asomatos monastery in the Amari valley on May 19. But he was not impressed by the abbot's welcome and went on to the monastery of Arkhadi despite the long walk that he had already taken that day and some disagreement from his companions. He was well received at Arkhadi. He liked the abbot, Hegoumenos Gabriel, who was "a man of the world, ...very jolly and pleasant."

As his travels progressed, particularly after he left Rethymnon for Herakleion by ship for his longest expedition through central Crete (from the 9th to the 20th of May), Mount Ida, the highest mountain in Crete, became something of an obsession. Lear was always anxious to find good views of it to sketch, but was constantly disappointed by the existence of clouds or by bad vantage points: "Ida always covered, the truth being that she is unwilling to have comparisons made by a distinguished landscape-painter" (May 19), and at Arkhadi "Ida *would* be lovely, and the whole scene delightful, but clouds stopped all" (May 20).

Thankfully for his artistic ambitions for the visit to Crete, on an overnight visit to Phre south of Hania in his last week Lear at last achieved excellent views of Ida both in the evening and early morning. "The view of Ida is by far the best I have yet seen, and truly fine. Never till now have I had much respect for Ida. A dream-like vast pile of pale pink and lilac, with endless gradations and widths of distance, and the long curve of sand from Rethymnon hills to Armyró" (May 24).

Lear had hoped to get to Sphakia in the south and also perhaps to Selino in the far southwest, but after the good Ida views he abandoned the idea, thinking the Sphakian mountains would be an anticlimax. It is somewhat odd that despite the time he spent in the west in Hania, he pays little attention to the White Mountains above Sphakia and looming to the south of him. Only on May 29, two days before his departure, does he acknowledge that "the Sphakian mountains, though now almost snowless, are very grand."

There is an intimate link between Lear's journal and the large number of drawings he produced while in Crete. Of the drawings on which details have been found (described in the next section), his journal records when he made the drawing in some 90 of the cases. Unless long distances had to be covered, he often stopped

---

7. Quoted in Noakes 2004, p. 123

to draw three or four times each day, and sometimes more. While the longer-term prospects of making an income from worked-up watercolors or from a book based on these travels must have had some influence, the urge to draw was an essential part of his motivation and perseverance, as witness the Ida obsession referred to earlier.

Franklin Lushington, Lear's friend and literary executor, wrote,

"Lear never set out on a journey to any of the new lands he visited throughout his life, without previously exhausting and digesting all the literature on the subject that he could collect; and in the journey itself he was a model traveller. He knew perfectly what he wanted to do and was not to be put off from doing it. He was impervious to discomfort and fatigue, and almost to illness that might have quelled the stoutest energy. He gained an eye for at once seeing the distinctive local character of all varieties of scenery, and a hand for reproducing it on paper or canvas, sometimes with laborious fullness and finish, sometimes with a few swift incisive strokes and broad simplicity of effect, always with a thorough truth of representation, and the highest appreciation of whatever poetical beauty the scene he was drawing contained."[8]

Lear carried his methodical approach into the annotation of his drawings. He numbered these consecutively for each particular journey, also noting the date, almost always including the time of day and the location, on each drawing. This has made the location attributions resulting from this research all the more certain.

Lear's more specific drawing technique was also well described by a contemporary, Hubert Congreve, who knew Lear in the last 20 years of his life: "When we came to a good subject, Lear would sit down, and taking his block from George, would lift his spectacles and gaze for several minutes at the scene through a monocular glass he always carried; then, laying down the glass, and adjusting his spectacles, he would put on paper the view before us, mountain range, villages and foreground, with a rapidity and accuracy that inspired me with awestruck admiration... They were always done in pencil on the ground, and then inked in sepia and brush washed in colour in the winter evenings."[9]

Placing Lear's work in a wider artistic context are Robert Wark's comments in the introduction to an exhibition catalogue of Lear's drawings in 1962:

"It is clear at a glance that his basic style and approach remain constant; he works essentially with line supplemented with washes of tone or color. But as he matures, the line becomes freer and more calligraphic; the objects represented (whether hills, trees or buildings) become more simplified and stylized;

8. Franklin Lushington, "Introduction," to Tennyson 1889, written a year after Lear's death. Lear had intended one scene of Crete to appear in such a volume, but the number of illustrations was severely restricted in the published edition.

9. Congreve, preface to Strachey 1911.

the washes of color become more arbitrary. These tendencies give mature Lear water colors a rather two-dimensional but lively and decorative quality that brings to mind certain twentieth-century drawings. Lear is by no means unique in developing this type of stylized linear draftsmanship. Earlier men like Francis Towne and John White Abbott had similar interests. All of these men looked at landscape with an eye for pattern and shape; they attained a degree of monumentality and grandeur through simplification and stylization; the primary tool of each was line."[10]

While Lear's particular use of line makes his drawings instantly recognizable as attributable to him, he was also interested in color and made copious notes on the drawings themselves of the color wash he would intend for later application, or for use in a developed watercolor. As Dr. Fani-Maria Tsigakou noted specifically about some of his Cretan drawings,

"In 'Mount Psiloritis from Fre' (Fig. 43), vigorously brushed purple and brown watercolour fills the outline of the mountain and by contrasting the dark mass with a lemon sky Lear conveys the effect of early morning '4.30 A.M. before sunrise'.[11] In the view of Lake Kourna (Fig. 44) he suggests with grey-green and blue washes the warm haze that hangs over the lake on a hot summer morning.[12] 'Rethymnon' (Fig. 45) is economically washed in green, yellow and ochre; while the view is drawn in outline, the colours lend unity to the middle ground details and at the same time produce a warm light; the bright red spots on the men's waistcoats and belts break the monotony and give depth to the composition."[13]

Finally, Lear seemed to enjoy his drawing, not least as a relief from the rigors of walking long distances and the uncertainty of comfort at the end of the day. Often drawings are annotated with idiosyncratic notes to himself : "froggs," "many night-ingales and asses that is to say donkeys" (Greek script with a mixture of English and Greek words), "there are beeeaters who eat the bees," and so forth.

During his time at Halepa with Mr. and Mrs. Hay, he made alphabet and numeral drawings for Madeleine, their young daughter. He was fond of her, and she of him. On May 26, near the end of his stay, she had been funny at the family lunch. Lear went out in the afternoon with George and sketched the Arab encampment just outside the walls of Hania.[14] In the foreground are two odd little figures which look as though they could have come from a nonsense rhyme, and below them Lear has written:

---

10. Wark, introduction to *Drawings* 1962.

11. Lear 167, Gennadius Library Collection. This paragraph is taken from Tsigakou 1977, p. 83.

12. Lear 77, Gennadius Library Collection.

13. Lear 90, Gennadius Library Collection.

14. Lear 174, Gennadius Library Collection. Cf. Fowler 1985, p. 102.

"There was a young person of Crete
Whose toilet was far from complete."[15]

He could have continued:

"She dressed in a sack, spickle-speckled with black,
That ombliferous person of Crete."[16]

But instead he went into Hania and bought some toys for Madeleine.

THE CRETAN DRAWINGS TODAY

Lear referred to "196 drawings — & a vast number of small bits" when penning out and coloring his Cretan sketches back in England in the summer of 1864.[17] As already mentioned, his working practice was to number his drawings consecutively, as well as to date them and (usually) give the time of day. In fact, his last drawing as he left the island by ship from Hania on May 31, 1864, was numbered 179. At least three of the numbers have A and B supplements on separate drawings, making 185 in all.

Then there was the vast number of "small bits." In the course of this research 53 drawings of Crete without a number, or without a recorded number, have been found. Some of these probably fall into the numbered category but at least 31 of the 53, judging partly by size and content, would have been Lear's "small bits." Most of the subjects are small, colorful male and female figures in Cretan dress, mules, and small landscape sketches (Fig. 46). There may well have been many more "small bits," since destroyed or dispersed.

I have prepared a complete listing of both these categories of drawings showing, in addition to Lear's number if applicable, the Cretan location illustrated, date, time and size of drawing where known, as well as the provenance, present owner, exhibition history, and other notes of relevance.[18] The map in Figure 1 and the accompanying Table show how the numbered drawings correspond to Lear's drawings over the seven weeks of his stay in Crete.

The Gennadius Library acquired 90 of these drawings in 1929, the year in which most of Lear's works were put on the market. When Lear died in 1888, the unpublished original journal of his Cretan visit, together with at least a part of a later version that had been somewhat edited and intended eventually for publication, was left with other journals, letters, and papers for his friend and literary executor, Franklin Lushington.[19]

15. 'The late Vivien Noakes confirmed to the author (pers. comm.) that to her knowledge this is the only Lear drawing inscribed with the lines of a limerick.

16. Lear 1861, unpaginated.

17. Fowler 1985, p. 15.

18. Duckworth 2011.

19. Fowler 1985, p. 17

Edward Lear's Travels and Drawings in Crete

Date	Places drawn	Drawing numbers
April 12–20	Hania and immediate surroundings, including Suda Bay and Mournies	1–19
April 21–22	Akrotiri peninsula and monasteries	25–31
April 23–25	Hania and Mournies	32–36
April 26-27	Platania, Ghonia, and Cape Spadha	39–51
April 28–30	Topolia, Polyrinia (Palaiokastro)	57–59
May 3–4	Aptera	67–73
May 5	Exopoli, Lake Kourna and Episcopi	74–79
May 6–9	Rethymnon and Perivolia	81–100
May 9–10	By sea to Herakleion, Mount Ida	105–110
May 10–12	Knossos, Mount Juktas, Herakleion	111–120
May 13–14	Mount Juktas, Kani Kastelli, Dhaphnes	122–131
May 15–16	Venerato, Aghios Thomas, Plain of Messara	132–142
May 16–18	Aghii Deka, Gortyn, Pobia	143–152
May 18–20	Petrokephali, Aghios Ioannis, Paximadhi islands, Apodhoulou, Arkadi monastery, Perivolia	153–158
May 22–25	Machairi, Apokorona, Aptera, Suda Bay, Phre, and Mount Ida	159–172
May 26-31	Hania	173-179

Note: Gaps in the sequence of numbered drawings indicate that no drawings with these numbers have yet been identified.

The history of the Gennadius acquisition is well known, but Haris Kalligas' preface to the exhibition catalogue for "Edward Lear's Greece," shown in Thessaloniki in 1997, is worth repeating:[20],

"The celebrations for the opening of the Gennadius Library took place in Athens on April 23 1926, after which John and Florence Gennadios returned home, in Surrey. The collections were already in the Library and his financial resources very limited. His mania for collecting had not, however, left him. On 23 February 1929 he received a letter from the house of Craddock & Barnard, in which they announced they had 'recently purchased the entire collection of drawings by Edward Lear, left by him to his great friend Sir Franklin Lushington', about 140 of which were views of Greece. They offered the lot at a price of £25. He hastened to reply, asking to see a small selection, as was suggested. Three days later, on 26 February, in the letter accompanying the selection they mention: 'We think, when you examine these, you will agree that the price of £25 for the whole lot is quite reasonable'. Immediately after examining the drawings and returning them the next day 27 February, he wrote to Edward Capps, President of the Managing Committee of the American School, in Princeton urging him to purchase them for the Gennadius. 'The collection is simply magnificent' and the price is 'absurdly low', he remarked and awaited his answer by cable before March 10."

After delays due to Capps' absence and an extension of the time limit, Gennadius received the cable "Accept. Pardon delay. Capps." As a result 188 drawings, far more than originally quoted, were shipped to the Gennadius Library. Ninety of these are from the Cretan visit of 1864. Fourteen additional Lear drawings of Greece were acquired in 1940 from Craddock & Barnard at a low price by Gennadius Library Director Shirley H. Weber. One further drawing was given to the Library in 1972 by Philip Hofer, the American collector and author. These additional items were drawn in 1849, and hence are not of Crete.

After the successful purchase, Gennadius invoiced the Library for his shipping costs: special box made by bookbinder £5.7.6, and cartage, freight, and insurance £4.6.4. He wrote again to Dr. Capps on May 30, 1929: "That wonderful Lear collection has been preserved in a strong and most suitable box and this in a deal box has just been despatched to Athens, where I am sure you will enjoy examining it. It is a precious and rare collection acquired at a ridiculously low price."[21]

Lear was in Crete from April 11 to May 31, 1864. Interestingly, the earliest numbered drawing in the Gennadius collection was made on April 27 and all the rest are from

20. Tsigakou 1997, p. 5.
21. Gennadius Library, American School of Classical Studies, Joannes Gennadius Archive, Series VI, Box 14, Folder 14.2.

May 3 onwards. Only 29 of the 117 numbered drawings sketched from that date until the end of his stay are not in the Gennadius Library.

It is not certain how Craddock & Barnard, who were print dealers based in Tunbridge Wells, Kent, at the time, acquired "the entire collection of drawings by Edward Lear." Philip Hofer refers to the sales which took place by the order of Sir Franklin Lushington's "daughters" in February and March of 1929.[22] One of these, a Sotheby's "Valuable Printed Books" and other related items sale, took place between March 25 and 28; it comprised seven lots of Lear items, including one containing 30 volumes of his private diary from 1858 to 1887 that are now in the Houghton Library of Harvard University. The volumes included the 1864 Cretan journal. This sale therefore happened after the Craddock & Barnard acquisition.

An auction by Hodgson and Co. of London took place earlier, on February 21, two days before Joannes Gennadius received the letter from Craddock & Barnard. The Hodgson sale had 16 Lear lots, but included 150 drawings at most, and mentioned locations only in Italy, Malta, Egypt, and England. It seems almost certain, therefore, that Craddock & Barnard acquired their substantial holding of Lear drawings by direct purchase from Sir Franklin's daughter Mildred (as no other daughter seems to have been alive by then) before the public sales. Mildred's father was born in Kent. It is thought that she was living near Tunbridge Wells and so may have had some previous contact with Craddock & Barnard. Sadly, she died on April 1, 1929, aged 63, just after the sales had taken place.

111

A direct purchase seems to be confirmed by an entry in the Craddock & Barnard exhibition catalogue of 1937 referred to below, which states: "The collection of drawings from which those included in the catalogue have been selected was bequeathed by Lear to Sir Franklin Lushington, from whose daughter we purchased the entire collection." Craddock & Barnard were chiefly dealers in Old Master prints as well as more contemporary etchings, lithographs, and other forms of prints. They later moved to London and eventually closed in 1986. A search of what is believed to be their last remaining archive, in the University College London Special Collections, showed only purchase and sale records for prints, and went back only to 1939.

Craddock & Barnard continued to sell Lear drawings actively in the 1930s, however. In October and November 1929, the Howard Gallery in London held an exhibition in which 57 drawings owned by the firm were offered at prices from three to ten guineas, many times the sale price quoted to Joannes Gennadius; demand was poor.[23] A further Craddock & Barnard exhibition of 97 Lear "watercolour landscapes" took place in November 1931 at the Alpine Club Gallery, London, which included just one of Crete. The same firm held an exhibition in Tunbridge Wells of "One Hundred Landscape Drawings (in pen and water-colours) by Edward Lear,"

22. Hofer 1967, p. 60.
23. Hofer 1967, p. 60.

probably in 1937. [24] Lots 58 to 63 were drawings from Crete, priced between two and fifteen guineas. So, in this period and subsequently, Lears of Crete began to reach individual collectors.

Auction records from the 1930s to the mid-1950s show virtually no evidence of additional sales of any Lear drawings. There had been one major sale, by Sotheby's, of the Earl of Northbrook's Lear collection later in 1929 which further flooded the market. [25]

However, some individual collectors were beginning to create large collections, in particular William B. Osgood Field and Philip Hofer, both from the U.S. Philip Hofer's book describes the subsequent development of collecting, commencing with Angus Davidson's biography of Lear in 1938, and an exhibition at The Fine Arts Society in London in the same year which achieved about 80 sales at under £10 average price, including one of Crete.

During this period, Professor R. M. Dawkins, Bywater and Sotheby Professor of Byzantine and Modern Greek Language and Literature at Oxford University, must have been building up a fine collection of Cretan drawings. He had been Director of the British School of Archaeology in Athens from 1906 to 1914, excavated at Sparta, Melos, and Sikinos, served as an interpreter around the coasts of Crete in the First World War, and was an expert on dialect folk tales in Asia Minor. He published *The Cypriot Chronicle of Makhairas* in 1932, and *The Monks of Athos* four years later. [26]

After Dawkins' death in 1955, his collection was sold by Sotheby's on November 30, 1955, under the title "a collection of Mediterranean views by Edward Lear." Dawkins had acquired what must have been the largest group of Cretan drawings after that of the Gennadius Library. Forty-two drawings or sheets of drawings were sold in 24 lots; Lear's identifying numbers were not given in the sales catalogue, and many of the drawings were clearly his "small bits." Twelve of these drawings, however, are certainly specific drawings numbered by Lear: details of location, date, and time of drawing as well as measurements make the attribution possible. A further 10 probably fill in gaps in the list of identified drawings because of the dates and locations given.

No less than 12 of the lots were purchased by the dealer Agnew's. Other dealers who made purchases at the Sotheby's sale were The Fine Arts Society (3), Colnaghi (2), Spink (1), and Finch (1). Sales to individuals were to "Hon. S. Runciman" (2), "Heathcoat-Amory" (2) and "W. C. Wilder" (1). Lots at the sale comprising only a single drawing sold for between £30 and £80 each, a substantial increase on 1930s prices. Information kindly provided by Agnew's indicates that 33 drawings from their 12 lots were sold to 21 individuals by early 1957. Sales were assisted by publication

---

24. The catalogue is undated but the National Art Library at the Victoria and Albert Museum acquired their copy in 1937.
25. Hofer 1967, p. 60.
26. These details are from his obituary in the *The Oxford Magazine* 73 (1955), No. 23 (June 1955).

of the firm's 83rd exhibition catalogue in 1956, which included several of the Cretan drawings.

No other substantial sale of Cretan drawings has come to the London auction market since, but from the 1960s onwards there has been a steady supply of Lear drawings generally, and a trickle of auction sales of Cretan ones. Only 21 of the latter have been traced. From prices that are known (usually but not consistently including buyer's premium), the average price in the 1990s was £3,600, and in the past decade £5,800. The highest known price at auction, however, was £14,000 in the 1980s!

My research has also confirmed the existence of at least nine worked-up water-colors of Cretan scenes produced by Lear, probably based on drawings from his journey. These watercolors would have been for particular clients, and four were purchased by Rev. Henry Fanshawe Tozer, who travelled in Crete; he later left them to the Ashmolean Museum in Oxford. No oil paintings or engravings of Crete by Lear are known.

Of the 185 numbered drawings, 124 have been definitively identified by location and with some provenance. Of these, 100 are in public institutions, while the remaining 24 are known or presumed to be held by individuals or dealers. Of the remaining 61, probable provenance has been established for 13, for the most part through the Dawkins sale in 1955, but no trace has been found of the remaining 48.[27] It is possible to indicate the likely locations of the latter ones with the help both of Lear's diary and of the dating of the drawings whose provenance is known. Several may have been destroyed; the rest do not appear to have come to the auction market since the 1930s. Several dealers have been helpful in providing access to stock books, but no further numbered drawings were identified through this source.

The institutions holding Cretan Lears are as follows (all from the numbered series except where stated):

- Gennadius Library, Athens, Greece (89 numbered drawings, 1 unnumbered)
- Museum of Art, Rhode Island School of Design, U.S.A. (5 drawings)
- Ashmolean Museum, Oxford, U.K. (4 watercolors, 1 drawing)
- National Galleries of Scotland, Edinburgh, U.K. (1 watercolor, 1 drawing)
- British Museum, London, U.K. (1 drawing)
- Houghton Library, Harvard University, U.S.A. (1 drawing)
- Toledo Museum of Art, Ohio, U.S.A. (1 drawing)
- National Art Gallery, Wellington, New Zealand (1 drawing)

Finally, my research has established the exhibition history of the numbered drawings. There has only been one Lear exhibition confined to drawings of Crete. It was mounted in Athens in 1966 by the Academy of Fine Arts and the Gennadius Library

---

27. The drawings with no recorded numbers may include some of these, but the information recorded is insufficient to establish a possibility.

to commemorate the great Cretan uprising of 1866–1869. Sixty-two drawings were shown, probably all from the Gennadius Library collection.

Two major exhibitions based on Lear's Greek drawings in the Gennadius collection have subsequently been organized:

- "Edward Lear in Greece," which travelled to eight American institutions in 1971–1972 under the auspices of the International Exhibitions Foundation. Its catalogue contained 25 Cretan drawings.
- "Edward Lear's Greece from the Gennadeion Collections," held at the Cultural Center of the National Bank of Greece in Thessaloniki from June 12 to July 12, 1997, as part of the festivities for the Cultural Capital of Europe. The exhibition was curated by Fani-Maria Tsigakou, who also wrote the exhibition catalogue, containing 17 Cretan drawings.

A range of other exhibitions has also taken place since the 1950s in which Edward Lear's drawings of Crete have appeared, usually with other work by the artist from his wider travels. Prominent among them was the Royal Academy of London exhibition on Lear in 1985 which included one drawing from Crete, along with some delightful "nonsense" sketches of moufflons chasing the artist around the mountains of Crete.[28] Two such exhibitions were at the Fine Arts Society in London, which has mounted at least five other exhibitions of Lear's works, with or without other artists, between 1938 and 2004. Other exhibitions were organized in London, Edinburgh, Oxford, and at four venues in the United States.

As the bicentenary of Edward Lear's birth in 1812 approaches, perhaps there may be more. I would be grateful for information to add to the record when further sales of Lear's Cretan works occur.[29]

BIBLIOGRAPHY

Drawings 1962. *Drawings by Edward Lear: An Exhibition at the Henry E. Huntington Library and Art Gallery, November through December, 1962,* San Marino, Calif.

Duckworth, S. 2011. "Edward Lear's Drawings of Crete – 11 April to 31 May 1864" (unpublished paper, 2011).

Fowler, R., ed. 1985. *Edward Lear: The Cretan Journal,* 2nd ed., Athens and Dedham.

Hofer, P. 1967. *Edward Lear as a Landscape Draughtsman,* Cambridge, Mass.

Lear, E. 1861. *A Book of Nonsense,* 3rd enlarged ed., London.

---

28. The catalogue notes (Noakes, Maas, and Runciman 1985, p. 182), "The moufflon is in fact the wild goat of Corsica and Sardinia; that of Crete is called the agrimi, and is now only found in the region of the Samarian Gorge. These drawings (Cat.92b) were made after Lear's return from Crete when he was staying with the Prescotts in Roehampton."
29. I can be reached by e-mail at stephenduckworth@btinternet.com

Noakes, V. 2004. *Edward Lear: The Life of a Wanderer*, 4th ed., Stroud.

Noakes, V., J. Maas, and S. Runciman, eds. 1985. *Edward Lear 1812–1888. Catalogue of a 1985 Exhibition at the Royal Academy of Arts*, London.

Strachey, C., ed. 1911. *Later Letters of Edward Lear to Chichester Fortescue, Lady Waldegrave and others*, London.

Tennyson, A. 1889. *Poems of Alfred, Lord Tennyson. Illustrated by Edward Lear*, London and New York.

Tsigakou, F.-M. 1977. "Edward Lear in Greece" (Diss. University College London).

Tsigakou, F.-M. 1997. *Edward Lear's Greece from the Gennadeion Collections*, Thessaloniki.

ION DRAGOUMIS - EXILED TO CORSICA:
A VISIT TO THE GREEK COLONY OF CARGÈSE IN MAY 1918

ELEFTHERIA DALEZIOU

"I do not know why I am in Corsica. It is a thing I never fancied: to be an exile and to live in Corsica."[1] (Fig. 47)

With these words, Ion Dragoumis introduced his diary entries recorded in a notebook in which he practiced his English while in exile in Corsica from May 1917 to June 1919. The notebook is part of his personal papers at the Gennadius Library Archives of the American School of Classical Studies at Athens, a repository of outstanding collections that are in many ways unique. The papers of the diplomat, thinker, and politician Ion Dragoumis reached the Archives along with the papers of his father Stephanos, his brother Philippos, and other members of the family in 1960, when Philippos S. Dragoumis entrusted the papers of one of the most important and well-known political families of Greece to the Gennadius Library. The papers of his brother, Ion Dragoumis, were to remain closed to the public, according to the deed of gift, until the year 2000.

Ion Dragoumis's visit to the village of Cargèse during his exile in Corsica, the place to which 800 Greeks from the Mani region emigrated in the 17th century, is the focal point of this article. Using this as a point of reference, we have the chance to follow Ion's negotiations with the Corsican authorities to grant him permission to leave Ajaccio, the capital of the island, and visit Cargèse. The description of the visit, as Dragoumis himself records it in English in his notebook and through his letters to members of his family, is also vividly recorded in a series of photos and postcards of the village found among his papers and in the pages of his Greek diaries. The visit to Cargèse is a captivating episode during his time on the island of Corsica.

The paper includes extracts of his notebook in English along with excerpts from his correspondence with members of his family.[2] Personal correspondence and diaries are a wonderful source of historical information, providing us with details, which are direct, intimate, and revealing both of the person and of his times. Both capture the moment and the personality of the writer and are an important tool in the hands of historians seeking to interpret a particular period in a person's life.

---

1. Gennadius Library, American School of Classical Studies, Αρχείο Ίωνος Δραγούμη, Ενότητα VI, Φάκελος 44, Υποφάκελος 8, Τετράδιο "English," entry dated March 29/April 11, 1918.
2. All transcriptions and translations are by the author. Ion Dragoumis and his mother Eliza corresponded in French, while his correspondence with the rest of the members of his family is in Greek, French, and English.

Ion Dragoumis, son of the politician Stephanos Dragoumis, was a career diplomat. Early in his career he served in the Greek diplomatic missions in Western and Eastern Macedonia, East Roumelia, and Thrace. He was also a member of the Greek diplomatic corps in St. Petersburg, Alexandria, Rome, Berlin, and London.[3]

With the outbreak of the Great War in 1914, Greece had declared its neutrality. Greek Prime Minister Eleftherios Venizelos's pro-Entente stance was challenged in the political arena. Many Greek politicians had expressed their disagreements either with his belief that Greece's vital interests could be secured only in association with Great Britain or with his decision to offer Greek help to the Entente Powers, thereby violating his country's neutrality.[4] Members of high-profile families in the Greek political arena such as Rallis, Mavromichalis, Theotokis, and Dragoumis had expressed their objections and denounced Venizelos's tactics. The rift between Venizelos and his political enemies deepened.

Ion Dragoumis resigned his diplomatic post and was elected as a member of the Greek Parliament in the general elections of 1915. At the elections Venizelos emerged victorious once again, redoubling his efforts to bring the country into the war on the side of the Entente, but they were in vain. Venizelos handed his government's resignation to the King on October 4, 1915; the next day, Entente troops landed at Salonica, responding to an earlier invitation from Venizelos. In May 1916, Bulgarian troops crossed into the Struma region and occupied Fort Rupel. There were protests on the Greek side, but the government, with Skouloudis as Prime Minister, declared that it was beyond the country's means to defend the fort.[5] Both the Allied and the Central Powers had now entered and occupied Greek territories. In June 1916, General Sarrail, the French commander of the Allied forces stationed in Salonica, declared a state of siege in Macedonia and troops soon landed at Piraeus.

Ion Dragoumis had expressed his criticisms vehemently through the pages of *Politiki Epitheorisi*, the journal he was co-editing with Athanasios Nikolaidis.[6] He considered this foreign intervention in the internal affairs of Greece outrageous. Greece became divided into two radically opposed political camps. With Allied support, Venizelos forced King Constantine to abdicate, and Greece entered the fight on the side of the Allies in July 1917. Ion Dragoumis was sent into exile along with other prominent members of the Athenian political scene.

Ion Dragoumis arrived in Corsica in June 1917 together with his fellow exiles,

---

3. Biographies of Ion Dragoumis in Greek: Paraschos 1936 and Delta 2008. See also http://www.ascsa.edu. gr/index.php/archives/ion-dragoumis-biographical-note.

4. In March 1915 Venizelos had offered to provide Greek military assistance to the Dardanelles campaign to the Allied Powers but King Constantine had not consented.

5. The Archives of the Gennadius Library also hold the papers of Stephanos Skouloudis (1838–1928): http://www.ascsa.edu.gr/index.php/archives/stephanos-skouloudis-finding-aid/. For the period of his premiership, see in particular Αρχείο Στέφανου Σκουλούδη, Ενότητα II, Φάκελοι 13–20.

6. For the journal *Politiki Epitheorisi*, see Αρχείο Ίωνος Δραγούμη, Ενότητα IV, Φάκελος 25.

among them Dimitrios Gounaris, Victor Dousmanis, the Metaxa family, the Merkouri family, and the Pesmazoglou family, he lived at the Hôtel Continental at Ajaccio.[7] (Fig. 48) Ion commented about his exile and political conditions in Greece in those turbulent years:

> When the present war is over and the minds of men are appeased and calm again, the impartial historian will furnish the impartial reader with a rather gloomy page of Greek history; he will give a faithful picture of the wrongs inflicted on a small but brave nation by the governments of strong powers.
>
> The fate of Greece will be seen in its real light, not differing very much from the fate of Belgium during this war. Nevertheless two main differences may be noted between these two lands; first, that Greece did not think it proper to oppose the invaders arms in hand; and second, that Belgium did not count among her countrymen a politician so reckless and so unconscientious as Mr Venizelos.
>
> In this last respect we cannot blame foreigners, as we must throw the fault on some of Greece's own children.[8]

The works and days of Ion Dragoumis on the island of Corsica are documented by four different sources: his Greek diary entries, the notebook in English, a group of photos in a small photo album labeled "Corsica," and finally by an abundance of personal correspondence, incoming as well as outgoing, deposited along with the rest of his papers in the Gennadius Library Archives.[9] His diaries, which cover his time both in Corsica and on the island of Skopelos, have been published.[10] Extracts from Dragoumis's English notebook and a few of the letters exchanged with his family, as well as a small selection of photos, are presented here for the first time. The family correspondence includes numerous letters and postcards to and from Ion and his family, his parents Stephanos and Eliza Dragoumis, his sisters Natalia,

119

7. Dimitrios Gounaris (1866–1922) was a Greek politician and political opponent of Venizelos. Exiled to Corsica in 1917, he returned to Greece in 1920, becoming prime minister in April 1921. After the Asia Minor disaster in November 1922, he was held responsible for the catastrophe, found guilty of treason in the so-called "Trial of the Six" and executed. Victor Dousmanis (1861–1949) was a Greek military officer, a royalist and Chief of the General Staff.

8. Gennadius Library, American School of Classical Studies, Αρχείο Ίωνος Δραγούμη, Ενότητα VI, Φάκελος 44, Υποφάκελος 8, Τετράδιο "English."

9. The catalogue of the collection can be accessed online: http://www.ascsa.edu.gr/index.php/archives/ion-dragoumis-finding-aid. A selection of photos from the rich Dragoumis family archive along with items from the personal and professional correspondence of Ion Dragoumis have been digitized and are now online on the School's digital collections webpage: http://www.ascsa.net/research?q=collection%3ADragoumis;v=list.

10. Dragoumis 1987. The diaries included in this edition are found in Αρχείο Ίωνος Δραγούμη, Ενότητα II, Φάκελος 2, Υποφάκελος 5, Τετράδιο "Αιάκιο 1918–1919," Υποφάκελος 6, Τετράδιο "1919," and Υποφάκελος 7, Τετράδιο "1920."

Chariclea, Effi, Zoi, Alexandra, and Marika, and his brothers Philippos, Alexandros, and Nikos, as well as his aunt Marika N. Dragoumi, his father's sister, and his grandmother Eufrosyni.[11]

Ion was in constant touch with his family during his exile. At times, difficulties in communication were reported by parties at both ends. In addition to the distance and the ongoing war, French censorship also played a major role

April 5/18 1918

I received some letters and some post cards from Athens. My mother is very uneasy about everything that happens in Greece; it is why she encourages me, telling me to face the state of the affairs calmly. I don't see why I should not. She tells me that both my brothers have been exiled to Crete, and my nephew also.[12] The elder of my brothers was secretary at the Ministry of Foreign Affairs and had been sent out of office just as Mr Venizelos had come in office last summer; now his presence in Athens is probably considered as dangerous to the interests of Mr V and his folk (people). My younger brother, a young man of 27, and already a major of artillery, who distinguished himself as lieutenant during our war against the Bulgarians in 1913, as my nephew did also, my sister's son, lieutenant of artillery, are also considered as dangerous in Athens. Two of my friends have been sent with them to Crete for the same reason; and numerous other persons shared their lot. In one of my mother's letters the number of these persons is mentioned, but the always intelligent censorship has erased it all together. The phrase (sentence) of the letter, relative to these events was this (like this): 'Your two brothers, with their...... companions have just left for Crete and shall (sic) be distributed in the three towns of the island.' From this last member of phrase (part of the phrase), one may easily understand that they are numerous, so much the more so that the letter adds that they have been embarked on two ships. And this forwarding is not the sole one. Numerous others have been done before. The Greeks exiled or expelled or driven out of their homes and actually in prison or dispersed all over the world by the English and French governments and their ally Mr Venizelos, may fairly be estimated as amounting to the number of 20.000 souls. And considering that most of them are more or less prominent members of the greek society, one may repeat with the great Roman historian Tacitus 'Solitudinum facient, pacem appelant' (sic) (They are making solitude and they call it peace). Who was the king or general who after having wildly subdued a Polish insurrection in

120

11. Family correspondence, both incoming and outgoing: Αρχείο Ίωνος Δραγούμη, Ενότητα Ι.Β., Αλληλογραφία Οικογενειακή Εισερχόμενη και Εξερχόμενη. It must be noted that thanks to Philippos S. Dragoumis, who collected Ion's letters to most members of his family, the Gennadius Library Archives hold both the incoming and the outgoing family correspondence of Ion Dragoumis.

12. Ion refers here to his brothers Philippos and Alexandros Dragoumis and his nephew Mikis Melas, the son of his sister Natalia and Pavlos Melas.

Warsaw shedding much blood announced his fear to the world by the words: 'L'ordre regue á Varsovie!' The case of Greece at present is much like that of Poland in the past; and besides those who have been exiled, there are others who have been killed or shot or ….., for having resisted the foreign intrusion in internal affairs, and remaining faithful to their King.[13]

THE VISIT OF ION DRAGOUMIS TO CARGÈSE IN MAY 1918

In May 1918, Dragoumis had already been on the island of Corsica for almost a year. The detainees resided in a hotel, received proper meals, and were allowed to take walks in the surrounding area of the city of Ajaccio. Since the first months of his arrival in Corsica, he had expressed his desire to visit the village of Cargèse on the west coast of the island. A Greek colony had been established in Corsica in the area of Paomia in 1676 by 800 Greeks from Oitylon in the Mani; in 1774 they moved, settling in Cargèse on the island's west coast.[14]

Ion wrote to his sister Alexandra during the first two months of his arrival on the island

> * Ο Νίκος, θυμάσαι, είχε έλθει εδώ κάποτε προ πολλών χρόνων. Το έχει φαίνεται η μοίρα μας να ερχόμαστε εδώ, τα αγόρια. Φτάνει να μην εξακολουθήσει η μοίρα μου να μοιάζει με του Νίκου. Και αυτό μπορεί να γίνει, αλλά δε το πιστεύω. Είναι και ένα χωριό ελληνικό, Καρυές, που θέλω να πάω αν μ' αφήσουν.[15]

In general, no permission was required for the exiles to wander around the town and the surrounding area. Every now and then, however, restrictions were imposed and they were confined to the gardens surrounding their hotel.[16]

In his notebook entry dated May 11, 1918, Dragoumis described in great detail

---

13. Αρχείο Ίωνος Δραγούμη, Ενότητα VI, Φάκελος 44, Υποφάκελος 8, Τετράδιο "English." Dragoumis nods; the quotation from Tacitus (Agricola 30) should read solitudinem faciunt, pacem appellant.

14. For a short history of the Greek colony of Cargèse, see Nicholas 2005 and Michalopoulos 1998.

15. Translation: "Nikos, you remember, had visited the island sometime many years ago. It seems that it is our destiny to come here, I mean us the boys. Hopefully my fate will not continue to resemble Nikos'. Although this is possible, I do not believe it. There is a Greek village, Cargèse, which I really want to visit if they let me." Nikos Dragoumis (1874–1933) was Ion's eldest brother. Αρχείο Ίωνος Δραγούμη, Ενότητα Ι.Β Αλληλογραφία Οικογενειακή Εξερχόμενη, Φάκελος 5, Υποφάκελος Αλεξάνδρα Ξύδη-Κριεζή, Ίων προς Αλεξάνδρα, 3 Ιουλίου 1917.

16. Ion wrote to his sister Alexandra on March 27/April 9, 1918: "Είμαι καλά, χωρίς πολλή διάθεση αυτό τον καιρό. Μας είχαν περιορίσει στον περίβολο του ξενοδοχείου για καμμιά δεκαριά μέρες, μα τώρα μας άφησαν να περιφερόμαστε κ(αι) παίρνω τα βουνά κ(αι) τα δάση κ(αι) τα περιγιάλια. [I am fine now, not in a very good mood, however. We had been confined to the grounds of the hotel for some ten days, but now we are left free to wander again, so I take to the mountains, the woods, and the seashore.]" Αρχείο Ίωνος Δραγούμη, Ενότητα Ι. Β Αλληλογραφία Οικογενειακή Εξερχόμενη, Φάκελος 5, Υποφάκελος Αλεξάνδρα Ξύδη-Κριεζή, Ίων προς Αλεξάνδρα, 27 Μαρτίου/9 Απριλίου 1918.

how he managed to obtain permission to make the trip to Cargèse. He understood that he was not a "free man," but was determined to get the permission. The life of a detainee could not have been an easy one for a person like Ion Dragoumis. In Corsica, he had the opportunity to do more things for himself, like reading and practicing his English, learning Russian, or even entertaining himself by playing tennis, walking, or hiking. He was freed from his political or other obligations but unable to communicate his thoughts and ideas to his fellow Greeks. He may have perceived the whole idea of getting the permission from the Corsican authorities as a small personal victory, worthy enough to be recorded in his notebook and described to his family:

Ajaccio, May 11/24 1918

How I negotiated with M. le Prefet an excursion to Cargèse.

At four I went and called on the Prefect. I sent in my card; the usher came back in a few minutes saying that 'M. le Prefet est accompagné' that is: he is busy with somebody. So I sat on a bench in the hall; the bench was padded with a sort of green velvet stuff that had become yellowish from use and age. Various persons were passing every now and then; there was the telegraph boy bringing telegrams and giving them to the usher; a very short soldier with twisted moustaches opened a door and came to say something to a man standing at the end of the hall; from another door stepped in one elderly woman in a black shawl accompanied by a young girl in a hat, probably her daughter; they didn't know where to go and asked me where Mr. Santini was... I neither knew where he was nor who he was; so I told them to put that question to the man who was walking up and down and who was the usher. It seems that they found their way to M. Santini, for I lost them from sight. Then entered an elderly man, rather tall; his face was like a saint's image in a greek church; he wore a beard, his eyes and cheeks were ascetic and hollow, his whole appearance would have been that of hermit if he wore not a jacket and had not a stout belly, contrasting very curiously with the traits of his face. He must have been a distinguished land-owner. His whole appearance seemed to me very sad. After him came in a short gentleman of a certain age whose clothes were rather shabby. What was he? Who knows? Then I heard the faulted voice of an old woman; it was that of the only florist of Ajaccio; she looked very ill and discussed something with a certain amount of excitement with an employé of the prefecture in eye-glasses and a small hand. This one looked very important and talked as though he were going to solve the most serious affairs of the state. Another old woman in a black shawl came in afterwards, accompanied by her daughter in a black hat; who was rather pretty. They shook hands with one of the clerks who had a fair thick moustache and then sat next to me on the green or yellow velvet bench. They waited for the secretary general who, according to an inscription hanging on the wall, ought to be there at four because he gave audiences from four to five, but who had not come that afternoon; a thing that seemed to impress disagreeably the young and pretty girl, who looked very impatient. I suppose she was conscious of her charms and thought that nothing could resist them; she evidently believed that nothing provoking or vexatious could ever happen to her; it is why she insisted upon seeing the secretary general although he was not there.

A high official of the prefecture then passed in front of me holding, in an important way, heaps of papers. He passed twice and looked at me disdainfully. He probably recognized in me an assassin.

When I saw the usher seating himself on his chair before his table and beginning to read aloud to himself the morning paper 'Jeune Corse' I became rather impatient, but refrained from saying anything after a moment's thought. I was on the point of forgetting that I was not a free man. There I tried to take delight in the idea that I was actually having the experience of the feelings of a prisoner, and that gave me some joy and humour.

But as the prefect was making me wait too long, I rose and went to the usher and asked him if M. le Prefet would receive me. 'I don't insist upon seeing him just now I said, but if he has not the leisure to receive me I would rather ask him to fix an hour when I could meet him.' The usher left the paper and went into the Prefect's room. In a few minutes I was ushered in.

M. le Prefet was exceedingly amiable. I reminded him that he once had the kindness to allow me to visit Cargèse but that he had afterwards sent to me Mr. Rénaud to ask me to postpone my excursion until the days became longer, M. Rénaud had even mentioned the month of May as being the proper time for visiting that Greek colony. It is why I came now to ask M. le Prefet for the permission to undertake that trip. I added that I was very much interested in ethnological studies. The Prefet having asked me with whom I intended to go to Cargèse and by what means of locomotion, I suggested a carriage, as I could not hope to be allowed to use a motor car since I knew that M. le Prefet himself did not use his own car. He was quite pleased with this remark and justified himself by saying that a prefet was meant to give always the good example; he began then relating various cases when he hired a carriage for his wife so that she should not be seen using the motor car of the prefecture. I ventured to state that few officials were so highly conscious of their duties, and I expressed my sorrow for the news I had read in the newspapers according to which he would soon leave off. He explained to me at length his family interests and how he had himself asked to be transferred to the continent. His father in law was ill, his wife was in a constant state of anxiety, his eldest boy ought to finish his university studies; his younger child did not learn well in the schools here; and after all the new position he would have was more lucrative thought not so much in view as the situation of a Prefect. He talked to me about his career, how young he had entered the public service, how young he had become a sous-prefect and how young he had been promoted to a prefet.

I don't know how we came to talk about political affairs at any rate he began and I told him that most of the bad things they say in France against us are mere legends, and that it was a pity that some of the French representatives in Greece had made grave mistakes etc.

Laughing amiably he changed the subject of conversation by telling me that he would give me next day a safe-conduct if I would be so good as to call on him at five. I thanked him, adding that I hoped this time Mr Rénaud would have no objection to put forward. He smiled, and I continued: 'Because you know a police official has always a narrow way of considering things; his duties require him to be so.' M. le Prefet with a knowing smile insisted upon assuring me, first that <u>he</u> is the master and not Mr Rénaud and then that the mind of a prefet is not comparable with that of a commissaire de police, and he told me again to come next day for the permission.

We shook hands very cordially, he accompanied me to the door, I bowed and he bowed; and now the only thing that remains to be seen is, if I'll receive today the 'laissez passer' he promised to give me, and if tomorrow morning I will be rolling in a carriage in the direction of Cargèse.[17]

Dragoumis was joined by Dimitrios Gounaris as well as George and Eirini Pesmazoglou.[18] The group embarked on their two-day excursion on May 15/28, 1918. Cargèse stands in the middle of the island and the road was covered using two one-horse carriages, according to the memoirs of George Pesmazoglou.[19] They stayed overnight at the Hotel Cyrnos in the village and the next day they started exploring the area with the help of the Greek teacher Pierro Stefanopoli. Both Dragoumis and Pesmazoglou underlined the particular *maniatiki* pronunciation of the teacher in their accounts. Few, however, were the inhabitants who spoke perfect Greek (Fig. 49).

Dragoumis describes the excursion quite vividly in letters to his family and in the pages of his Greek diary, as well as in his English notebook:

Ajaccio May 17/30 1918
The prefect gave me the permission to go to Cargèse. But as he is a man

17. Αρχείο Ίωνος Δραγούμη, Ενότητα VI, Φάκελος 44, Υποφάκελος 8, Τετράδιο 'English.'
18. George Pesmazoglou (1890–1984), a young politician at the time, member of the Parliament. He was followed in exile by his family.
19. Pesmazoglou 1979, p. 82.

who cannot give something for nothing, he ordered out the same day two of the Greek exiles to leave Ajaccio and to be transferred to Corte, by way of punishment.

I have no intention to describe Cargèse, as I am not in a descriptive mood, but I may give you some dry information in a few sentences; more geographical than anything else. Cargèse, village or borough of 1050 or 1100 inhabitants, once Greek and now more or less mixed up, is situated on the southern side of a promontory (I love the situation). Somebody told me there that 350 men and women remain Greek, the rest of the inhabitants being Latins. That only means that there is a difference of religion between them; but it may be also that the 350 are of a purer Greek blood (Fig. 50).

The women are prettier than at Ajaccio; I saw two or three beauties. Many of the women and the men are Greek types. Two or three families speak Greek at home and their children are the only ones that talk our language. Besides there are also some old men and women who speak Greek. They have the pronounciation (*sic*) and accent of their original country in Greece (of Magna) and instead of some words we use now, they use others, more antiquated. Both their pronounciation (*sic*) and these words give to their talk a certain charm. The teacher is an old man with a beautiful beard; we found him in the school as he was shutting the shutters, the lesson being ended and the few children, who learn or do not learn Greek at school, having gone off. He told us: 'This is the French school, but I give Greek lessons twice a week to the boys and twice to the girls; I have about twenty pupils, the other children having no desire to learn Greek; which is not a compulsory lesson; on Mondays and Fridays I teach the boys, on Tuesdays and Saturdays the girls; on Wednesdays I have a rest; and on Thursdays I give no lesson, that day being a holiday. The Greek lesson is part of a program after all the others, from four to half past five, so that the children when they come to me are tired. My name is Peter Ragatsaki Stephanopoli. I have three sons and I lost one at the war. I don't know if he is alive or dead. For more than three years I have received no news from him. A hundred young men of this village have gone to the war and sixty of them are lost. (the percentage is enormous 60/100). I am very glad to meet you; may I show you the village? ; He knew my brother, who had gone to Cargèse some years ago and he was very moved when he heard that I was his brother. And we went about with him; he showed us everything, the narrow streets, some old houses, the two churches, the school, the post-office etc. On the eastern hill is a tower built by the inhabitants, so as to dominate the sea and look after the dangers of the pirates incursions, said Mr Peter Ragatsaki Stephanopoli. The tower built on the eastern hill is Genoese. I mounted on this hill next morning and saw the mountains, steep and strange of Paomia on the one side, and the capes, promontories, mountains and gulfs of Sagona and Prata on the other; a beautiful view. On several hills you see the usual Genoese towers rising above the sea and overlooking the plains. Early in the morning on Sunday I went to the spring out of the village, the spring with the best water. I met there Mrs Pesmazoglou talking with an old man. Later on we went to the Greek church, dedicated to Saint Spyridon. The innkeeper's daughter, a rather intelligent though very nervous girl, finds that two churches are too many for a village like Cargèse; she meant, I suppose, that two religions were too many; anybody seems to be of her mind and I am sure that in fifty years the Greek church will have become Latin. Poor people they are too tired to remain Greeks any longer. Already many Greeks become Latin when they are cross with the priest. Even one of the priests, having quarreled with the other one, went to Ajaccio and asked the bishop to allow him to change. The bishop was too glad to reinforce Latinism.

The Greek priest's name is Papa-Kaissaris Kottis, a very smart and good looking man of fifty, the richest proprietor of the village, and who seems to be much more given to the care of his material interests than to divine pre-occupations. He is not married as all Greek priests are, 'because,' as he said, 'people here are not used to see married priests and it would impress them disagreeably if I married; since 80 years, the Greek priests here don't marry.' After church we took his photograph at the church door and then we went about with him for half an hour. I walked to buy post-cards and he showed me the way to a shop opposite the post-office, where I chose some cards with views of Cargèse on them. Two young persons were the sellers; the priest called a third one, a young girl of a lovely Greek type and very much like him, so much so that we immediately fancied that it must be his natural daughter, since he was not married. Her name was Rose (Fig. 51).

I don't see why it would impress badly the inhabitants of Cargèse if the priest married, since it does not impress them that he has a beard and is not clean-shaven like the catholic priests. He has also short hair and not like the Greek priests and wears a catholic hat when he is in the street, although during the service he wears the regular Greek hat, with the black veil hanging behind. The service is read in Greek according to all the usages. The hymns are also sung in Greek; the melodies are a bad mixture of Latin and Greek tunes; but you feel still the reminiscence of their genuine Greek origin. Three images hanging on the walls of the Gothic church that seems as a Greek church, are real ancient icons coming from Greece, as also the 'epitaphios', dating, as the priest told us, from the 12th century.

We saw a shoe-maker working on a low little table in the street and talked with him in our language. Another old man, sitting beside him, spoke also Greek. We took their photograph. Next day the shoe-maker was in church and after the service he stayed with us a little; he seemed to have great pleasure in the company of his fellow countrymen and to feel a sort of nostalgia for his ancestral country. He looked at us in a strange loving way (Fig. 52).

The priest, when he heard who we were, tapped on Mr Gounaris' arm saying sympathetically: 'Never mind, you shall soon be back in Greece; all these things will be over.' And another man, when he heard that we were exiles said: 'It is just like us. They have done the same things to us' (alluding probably to their exile from Paomia and the troubles they once had with the Corsicans).

The innkeeper's daughters talked to us in French about many interesting things and principally on topics relating to the small Greek colony and the life of its inhabitants. For the lack of sufficient workmen, many of the properties are not cultivated but transformed into pasture lands. Vineyards produce good crops and the wine is not bad. The Cargèsians have boats—and you see them on the shore of the small creek on the southern part of the promontory—they fish lobsters and sell them to Ajaccio, whence they are expected to Marseilles and to Nice. Women don't trouble to work; they are ladies and wear hats and elegant dresses of townswomen— we saw them all in church on Sunday—they stay at home usually making embroideries and the young girls wait for the rich man who will ask their hand. "They all want to catch some millionaire!" as the eldest daughter of the innkeeper phrased it. "And if anything is heard about them before they marry, and they afterwards don't happen to marry the man with whom they flirted, then they are lost; they can't possibly marry and they remain old maids for life." I was extremely sorry for them as I fancied them living cloistered up and retired in that small country with nothing else to do but gossip and make embroideries.

The moon was beautiful on Saturday night and many young girls, women and children and a few men took their walk on the road leading to Sagone. They did not go very far. Some young soldiers on leave and (……..) were singing Corsican songs. The silhouettes of the trees on the road were black and the sea shore behind them. The horses were illuminated by the rays of the moon, a perfect chiar-oscuro![20]

It must have been a moving experience for all of them. Pesmazoglou wrote in his memoirs, "We set off the evening of the next day and arrived at Ajaccio late at night under the moonlight and full of excitement."[21]

Ion Dragoumis wrote to his sister Alexandra about the trip:

---

20. Αρχείο Ίωνος Δραγούμη, Ενότητα VI, Φάκελος 44, Υποφάκελος 8, Τετράδιο "English."
21. Pesmazoglou 1979, p. 83.

Πήγα στην ελληνική αποικία, στις Καρυές. Ο δάσκαλος εκεί, ονομάζεται Πέτρος Ραγατσάκης Στεφανόπολις, εγνώρισε τον Νίκο που είχε μείνει εκεί μια εβδομάδα (τη Μεγάλη Εβδομάδα) κ(αι) όταν του είπα το όνομά μου κ(αι) ότι ήμουν ο αδελφός του Νίκου καταχάρηκε, μου έσφιξε με συγκίνηση το χέρι κ είπε: 'Τι καλός που ήταν! Μας έστειλε όταν επήγε στην Ελλάδα διάφορα βιβλία για το σχολείο.' Οι γέροι μόνο μιλούν ελληνικά κ(αι) οι γριές. Είναι όμως και δυο τρείς οικογένειες που μιλούν ακόμη στο σπίτι τα ελληνικά. Μιλούν ελληνικά μανιάτικα, με προφορά κ(αι) λέξεις από τη Μάνη. Πήγα κ(αι) στην εκκλησία την Κυριακή κ(αι) άκουσα τη λειτουργία ελληνικά, ύστερα από ένα χρόνο που δεν την είχα ακούσει. Ο παπα-Καίσαρης Κώτης είναι καλοντυμένος κ(αι) καθαρός παπάς, με γένια περιποιημένα κ(αι) καλοκομένα (σχεδόν σαν του κ. Αλέκου Σκουζέ) κ(αι) φορεί στο δρόμο καπελάκι φλάρου, εις την εκκλησία βάζει το καλημαύχι του με ένα βέλο που κρέμεται πίσω. Η εκκλησία έχει τρείς παλιές εικόνες παρμένες στα 1676 από τη Μάνη όταν ήλθαν οι άποικοι στην Κορσική, κ(αι) έναν επιτάφιο του 12ου αιώνος καθώς μου είπε ο παπα-Καίσαρης. Και είναι ο παπα-Καίσαρης ο πλουσιώτερος άνθρωπος του χωριού, φροντίζει περισσότερο τα συμφέροντά του παρά την εκκλησία, αν κ(αι) δε μπορώ να πώς πώς η εκκλησία δεν είναι καλά περιποιημένη. Μόνο που είναι γοτθικού ρυθμού. Αυτά για τις Καρυές. Είναι κ(αι) άλλα πολλά να σου πω π.χ. η τοποθεσία του χωριού είναι θαυμάσια — μα τελειώνει το χαρτί κ(αι) εχτύπησε η καμπάνα για το φαγί, κ(αι) πρέπει να φάγει ο άνθρωπος για να ζήσει, αν κ(αι) δεν πεινώ σήμερα.........[22]

Dragoumis cannot escape physically from his exile but he does struggle to keep his spirits up:

22. Αρχείο Ίωνος Δραγούμη, Ενότητα Ι.Β Αλληλογραφία Οικογενειακή Εξερχόμενη, Φάκελος 5, Υποφάκελος Αλεξάνδρα Ξύδη-Κριεζή, Ίων προς Αλεξάνδρα, 21 Μαΐου 1918. Translation: "I visited the Greek colony of Cargèse. The teacher there is a man called Petros Ragatsakis Stefanopolis — he met Nikos who had stayed here for a week (Holy Week). When I told him my name and that I was Nikos's brother, he shook my hand with emotion and said: "What a nice man he was! He sent us many books for the school when he went back to Greece." Only the old men speak Greek, and the old women. There are, however, two or three families who still speak Greek at home. They speak Maniote Greek, with the pronunciation and words of Mani. I went to the church as well on Sunday and listened to the liturgy in Greek, after a year since I last did it. The priest, Father Kaisaris Kottis, is a very well-dressed man and clean, with a well groomed beard (similar to Mr. Alekos Skouzes'), and he wears a hat in the street; when he is in church he wears his kalimaukion with a veil hanging behind. The church has three old icons brought from Mani in 1676 when they arrived to Corsica, and a 12th-century epitaphion, as Father Kaisaris told me. The priest is the richest man in the village; he takes better care of his own affairs than of the church's, although I have to admit that the church is very well looked after, only its style is Gothic. That is all for Cargèse. There are many more things I might tell you, e.g. the location of the village is marvelous— but I will soon run out of paper and the bell for dinner is ringing. Man must eat to live, even if I do not feel hungry today..."

Διαβάζω πάντα, κάνω ρούσικα μαθήματα, παίζω τένις σπάνια, παίζω σπα-
νιότερα βιολί, γράφω λίγο όταν έχω όρεξη, απαντώ στα γράμματα που μου
γράφουν, κάθομαι, συλλογίζομαι, ονειρεύομαι, κοιμούμαι, τρώγω κ(αι) ξυπνώ
κ(αι) πάλι τα ίδια κ(αι) τα ίδια, κ(αι) περπατώ (λιγότερο όμως παρά το χειμώ-
να κ(αι) την άνοιξη). Πήγα στην ελληνική αποικία στις Καρυές, κ(αι) ίσως την
ερχόμενη εβδομάδα κάμω κ(αι) μιάν άλλη εκδρομή σε κανένα 'αξιοθέατο'
μέρος. Αλλ' όλα αυτά δεν αντικαθιστούν την ελευθερία....[23]

The papers of Ion Dragoumis at the Gennadius Library of the American School of
Classical Studies at Athens constitute a vast and vivid source of information for the
man himself, revealing both his multidimensional personality and his times, a turbulent
yet fascinating period of modern Greek history that lies open to researchers. The
episode of his visit to Cargèse during his 1917–1919 exile in Corsica is merely one
snapshot of his life and activities as recorded in his archive.

Ion Dragoumis returned to Athens in November 1919, having spent six more
months in exile on the island of Skopelos after he left Ajaccio. Greece was now on
the side of the victors and pursuing her interests in the peace negotiations in Paris.
While in exile, Dragoumis had written and submitted two memoranda to the Peace
Conference, on Greece's position and territorial desiderata after the end of the
war.[24] Back in Athens, he again embarked on his political career and his writing. But
these did not last long. On July 30, 1920, an attempt was made to assassinate Greek
Prime Minister Eleftherios Venizelos at the Gare de Lyon in Paris. The incident was
made known in Athens the next day. Dragoumis was stopped and arrested by the
police on his way back to Athens from Kifissia on July 31, 1920; while he was being
transferred to the police station, he was shot dead.[25] Ion Dragoumis finally found the
freedom he had so long desired, but the thread of his life was cut short, a casualty
of the turbulent passions that still tormented Greek political life.

23. Αρχείο Ίωνος Δραγούμη, Ενότητα Ι.Β Αλληλογραφία Οικογενειακή Εξερχόμενη, Φάκελος 5, Υποφάκελος Αλεξάνδρα Ξύδη-Κριεζή, Ίων προς Αλεξάνδρα, 2/15 Ιουνίου 1918. In translation: "I read always, I
am taking Russian lessons, I play tennis rarely, and I play the violin even more rarely, I write a bit when I
am in the right mood, I answer the letters people send me, I sit, I think, I dream, I sleep, I eat and I wake
up, and I do the same things over and over again, and I walk (less than the winter and the springtime). I
visited the Greek colony of Cargèse and maybe next week I will make another excursion to a place 'worth
seeing.' But all these things do not substitute for freedom..."
24. Material on Ion Dragoumis's two memoranda submitted to the Paris Peace Conference can be found
in Αρχείο Ίωνος Δραγούμη, Ενότητα V, Φάκελοι 33–36.
25. For material related to the assassination of Ion Dragoumis and the ensuing murder trial, see Αρχείο
Ίωνος Δραγούμη, Ενότητα VIII, Φάκελοι 50–59.

BIBLIOGRAPHY

Delta, P. 2008, Ίων Δραγούμης, ed. A. Zannas, Athens.

Dragoumis, I. 1987. Φύλλα Ημερολογίου Στ' (1918–1920), ed. Th. Sotiropoulos, Athens.

Michalopoulos, D. 1998. "Οι Έλληνες του Καργκέζε," Το Βήμα, 15 February 1998 [= http://www.mani.org.gr/apodimoi/kargarthro/kargkeze_arthro.htm.]

Nicholas, N. 2005. "A History of the Greek Colony of Corsica," Journal of the Hellenic Diaspora 16, pp. 33–78.

Paraschos, K. 1936. Ίων Δραγούμης, Athens.

Pesmazoglou, G. I. 1979. Το Χρονικόν της Ζωής μου (1889–1979), Athens.

ALIKI ASVESTA studied History at the University of Paris I and did graduate work in Greek historiography at the University of Paris IV, the École des hautes études en sciences sociales, and the Ionian University of Corfu. She has long been involved in the creation of an electronic index of the Gennadius Library's collection of rare books by 16th–19th century travelers within the Gennadius Travelers' project, which combines geographical itineraries with themes such as the natural environment, human settlement, pre-industrial techniques, and political institutions as contained in the accounts of travelers. Her research and publications address various aspects of travel literature and history.

MARIA CHRISTINA CHATZIIOANNOU studied History at the University of Athens (Ph.D.) and at the Scuola di Perfezionamento di Storia Medievale e Moderna, Università di Sapienza, Rome. A researcher at the National Hellenic Research Foundation (EIE) in Athens since 1981, she currently serves as Research Director and Coordinator of the Social and Economic History section of the Institute for Neohellenic Research (17th–20th centuries) there. In addition to teaching undergraduates and graduates at the Universities of Crete and Athens, she has written and/or edited ten books and numerous articles on topics in modern social and economic history. She is currently engaged in a comparative study of merchants and business enterprises in the Mediterranean (18th–20th centuries), and of Greek business and other financial and social networks in Britain.

131

ELEFTHERIA DALEZIOU is a historian and trained archivist with a B.A. in History, an M.Phil., and a Ph.D. in Modern History from the University of Glasgow. She also earned an M.Litt. in Archives and Records Management from the University of Dundee. She is currently employed as a Reference Archivist at the Gennadius Library Archives of the American School of Classical Studies at Athens.

JACK L. DAVIS is currently the Director of the American of Classical Studies at Athens and holds the Carl W. Blegen chair in Greek archaeology at the University of Cincinnati. He has organized excavations and archaeological surveys in both Albania and Greece. His research interests range from Greek prehistory through Ottoman-period patterns of settlement in southern Greece.

STEPHEN DUCKWORTH studied Economics at the University of Cambridge. He first visited Crete in 1959 and has been a frequent traveler there since the 1970s. He made his career in housing finance and lives in London. At present, he is writing a book on Victorian Staffordshire pottery religious figures, but his current project is to ensure that the bicentenary of Edward Lear's 1812 birth is appropriately celebrated, particularly by exhibitions of his drawings and other works of art and humor.

LEONORA NAVARI, a reader at the Gennadius Library for many years, is a specialist on the bibliography of early travel in the Levant and on the carto-bibliography of the eastern Mediterranean. She has produced catalogues of major private collections, including *Greece and the Levant: Catalogue of the Henry Myron Blackmer Collection* (1989), *The Ottoman World: The Collection of Şefik E. Atabey* (1998), *Greek Civilization as seen through the eyes of travellers and scholars, from the collection of Dimitris Contominas* (2003), *Greek Costume, Printed Sources 16th–19th centuries.* (J. D. Koilalous Collection, 2006), and *Manuscripts and Rare Books, 15th-18th century* (Bank of Cyprus Cultural Foundation, 2010).

CRISTINA PALLINI (Ph.D., Istituto Universitario di Architettura, Venice) is senior researcher at the Department of Architectural Design, Politecnico di Milano, where she teaches at the School of Civil Architecture. Since 1995 her main interest has been urban reconstruction in eastern Mediterranean port cities, seeking to uncover the tools for radical interventions when catastrophic events create an urgent need not only to rebuild the physical environment, but also to devise strategies for re-establishing socioeconomic and cultural life. Her research has been funded by the Italian Research Council, the Greek Scholarship Foundation, the Greek Ministry of Education, the Aga Khan Program at MIT, and the Alexander S. Onassis Public Benefit Foundation.

PASQUALE MASSIMO PINTO (Ph.D., Classical Philology), is a researcher and lecturer at the University of Bari, Italy, with particular interests in the textual history of the Attic orators and the history of classical studies in the 19th–20th centuries. One of the editors of the new Oxford Classical Texts edition of Isocrates (in preparation), he was a 2010–2011 Cotsen Traveling Fellow of the American School of Classical Studies at Athens. His most recent publications are "P.Kellis III Gr. 95 and Evagoras I" (*Zeitschrift für Papyrologie und Epigraphik* 168, 2009), "Costantino Simonides in America" (*Quaderni di storia* 72, 2010), "Harold Idris Bell" (*Hermae: Scholars and Scholarship in Papyrology*, II.2, 2010), "Harold Idris Bell" (*Philologus* 154, 2010), and "Men and Books in 4th century BC Athens" (*Ancient Libraries*, 2011).

KONSTANTINOS TERZOPOULOS, theologian and independent scholar, is a Greek Orthodox priest on the island of Aegina. He received his B.A. from Holy Cross Greek Orthodox School of Theology in Brookline, Mass., where he later taught Byzantine Chant. He earned a Ph.D. in Byzantine liturgical musicology from the University of Athens. Executive Director of Psaltiki, Inc., he is also on the advisory boards of the American Society for Byzantine Music and Hymnology and the NEUMES Project. He received a 2011 Music & Letters award for research on Byzantine manuscripts containing chant notation at the Badia Greca, Grottaferrata. His publications include Ὁ Πρωτοψάλτης τῆς Μεγάλης Ἐκκλησίας, Κωνσταντῖνος Βυζάντιος· ἡ συμβολή του στὴ Ψαλτικὴ Τέχνη (2004). An annotated translation with historical introduction of the *Protheoria* of Biolakes' *Typikon* and a critical edition of a 7th-century sermon by Saint Anastasius of Sinai are in preparation.

The New Griffon

Το περιοδικό New Griffon είναι μια ετήσια περιοδική έκδοση της Γενναδείου Βιβλιοθήκης. Περιέχει δοκίμια και μελέτες για ποικιλία θεμάτων, ενώ πρόσφατα τεύχη αφορούν συγκεκριμένα θέματα.

Published annually, the New Griffon is a bilingual Modern Greek-English periodical publication produced by the Gennadius Library. Some issues contain essays on a variety of themes while others focus on particular topics.

8: Mapping Mediterranean Lands - edited by Maria Georgopoulou

9: The Modern Greek Resources Project: Libraries, Collections, and Databases - edited by Maria Georgopoulou

10: The Archaeology of Xenitia: Greek Immigration and Material Culture - edited by Kostis Kourelis

11: Αρχείο Κώστα Βάρναλη. Το εργαστήρι του ποιητή και η ιστορία – επιμέλεια Θεανώ Μιχαηλίδου – Kostas Varnalis's Papers: The Poet's Workshop and History (Modern Greek) - edited by Theano Michailidou

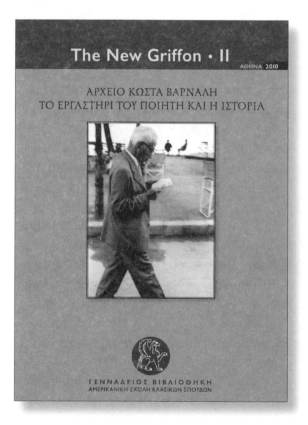

For more information visit the website of the Gennadius Library.
Για περισσότερες πληροφορίες επισκεφθείτε τον ιστότοπο της Γενναδείου Βιβλιοθήκης.
http://www.ascsa.edu.gr/index.php/publications/browse-by-series/the-new-griffon1

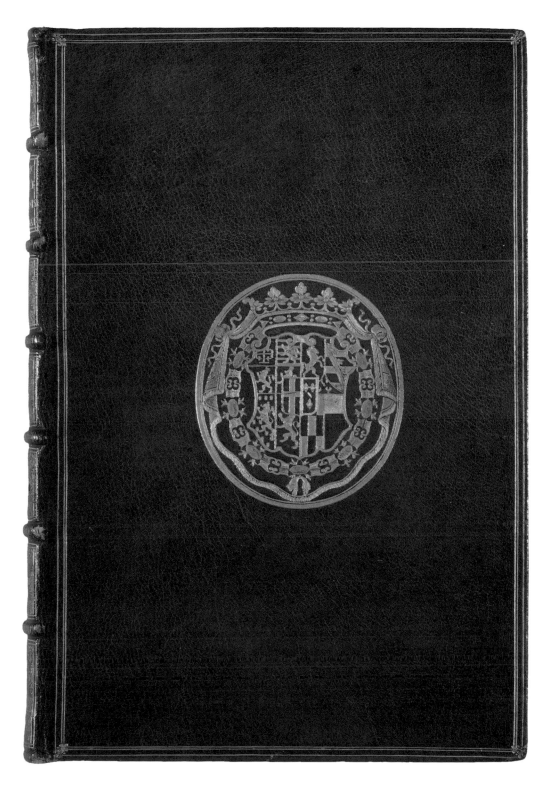

Figure I. Arms of Eugene of Savoy, *In Calumniatorem Platonis libri quatuor*, Venice 1516. Gennadius Library B/GC 3050q.

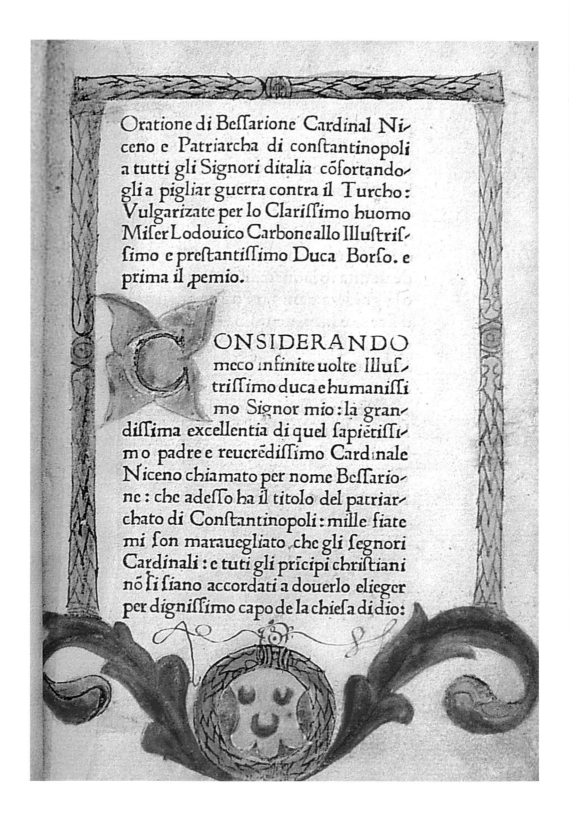

Oratione di Beſſarione Cardinal Niceno e Patriarcha di conſtantinopoli
a tutti gli Signori ditalia cõſortando-
gli a pigliar guerra contra il Turcho:
Vulgarizate per lo Clariſſimo huomo
Miſer Lodouico Carbone allo Illuſtriſ-
ſimo e preſtantiſſimo Duca Borſo. e
prima il pemio.

CONSIDERANDO
meco infinite uolte Illuſ-
triſſimo duca e humaniſſi
mo Signor mio: la gran-
diſſima excellentia di quel ſapiētiſſi-
mo padre e reucrēdiſſimo Cardinale
Niceno chiamato per nome Beſſarione : che adeſſo ha il titolo del patriar-
chato di Conſtantinopoli: mille fiate
mi ſon marauegliato che gli ſegnori
Cardinali : e tuti gli pricipi chriſtiani
nõ ſi ſiano accordati a douerlo elieger
per digniſſimo capo de la chieſa di dio:

Figure 2. Ornamental title page, *Oratione di Bessarione*, Venice 1471. Gennadius Library B/TH 58/B55.

Figure 3. Arms of Michael Wodhull on the upper cover of *Oratione di Bessarione*, Venice 1471. Gennadius Library B/TH 58/B55.

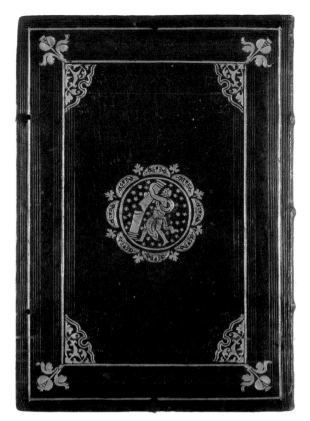

Figure 4. Upper cover, *Orationes de gravissimis periculis*, Rome 1543. Gennadius Library B/TH/B551.

Figure 5. Lower cover, *Orationes de gravissimis periculis*, Rome 1543. Gennadius Library B/TH/B551.

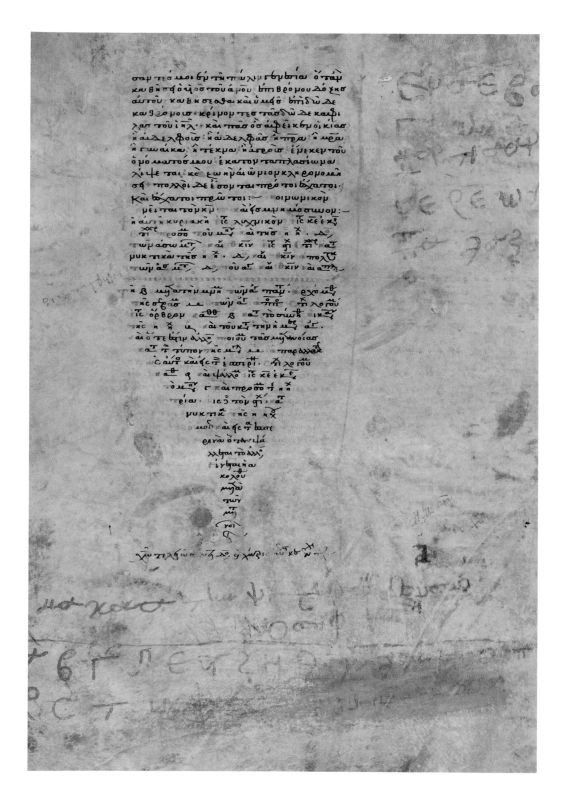

Figure 6. Gennadius MSS 4 (14th century), folio 43v, showing a section of the ekphonetic notation used for scriptural passages. The hypokrisis and teleia signs are in red.

Figure 7. Gennadius MSS 4 (14th century), fol. 32v, showing a section of the notated chants for the feast of the Annunciation of the Theotokos (March 25).

Figure 8. Gennadius MSS 26 (A.D. 1801), folio 12v, with the beginning of the *anastasisma*, resurrectional *kekragaria* of Saint John of Damascus, and *stichera* of the New Chrysaphes, as indicated in the title, mode I.

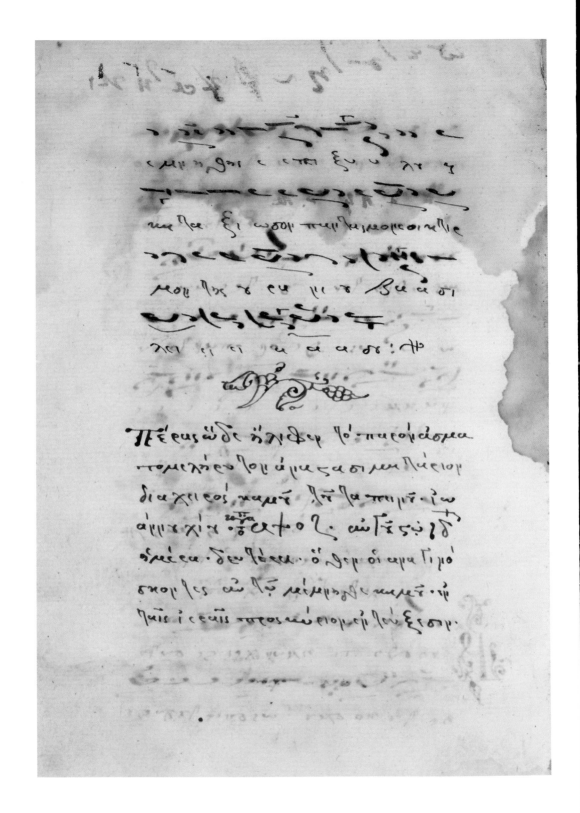

Figure 9. Gennadius MSS Kyriazes 25 (A.D. 1777), folio 106v, written by Joannes of Chios, containing the *Anastasimatarion* of the New Chrysaphes.

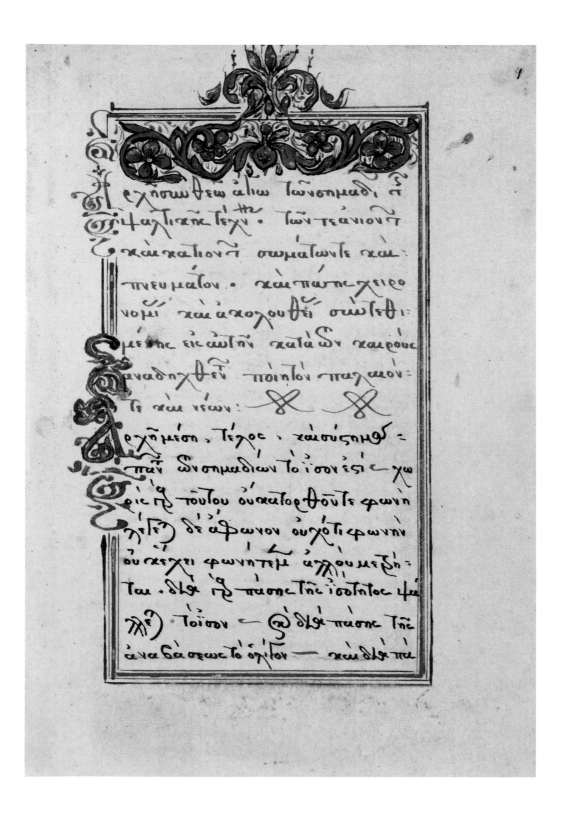

Figure 10. Gennadius MSS 23 (A.D. 1713), folio 1r, and the beginning of the *protheoria*, ἀρχὴ σὺν Θεῷ ἁγίῳ τῶν σημαδίων τῆς ψαλτικῆς τέχνης.

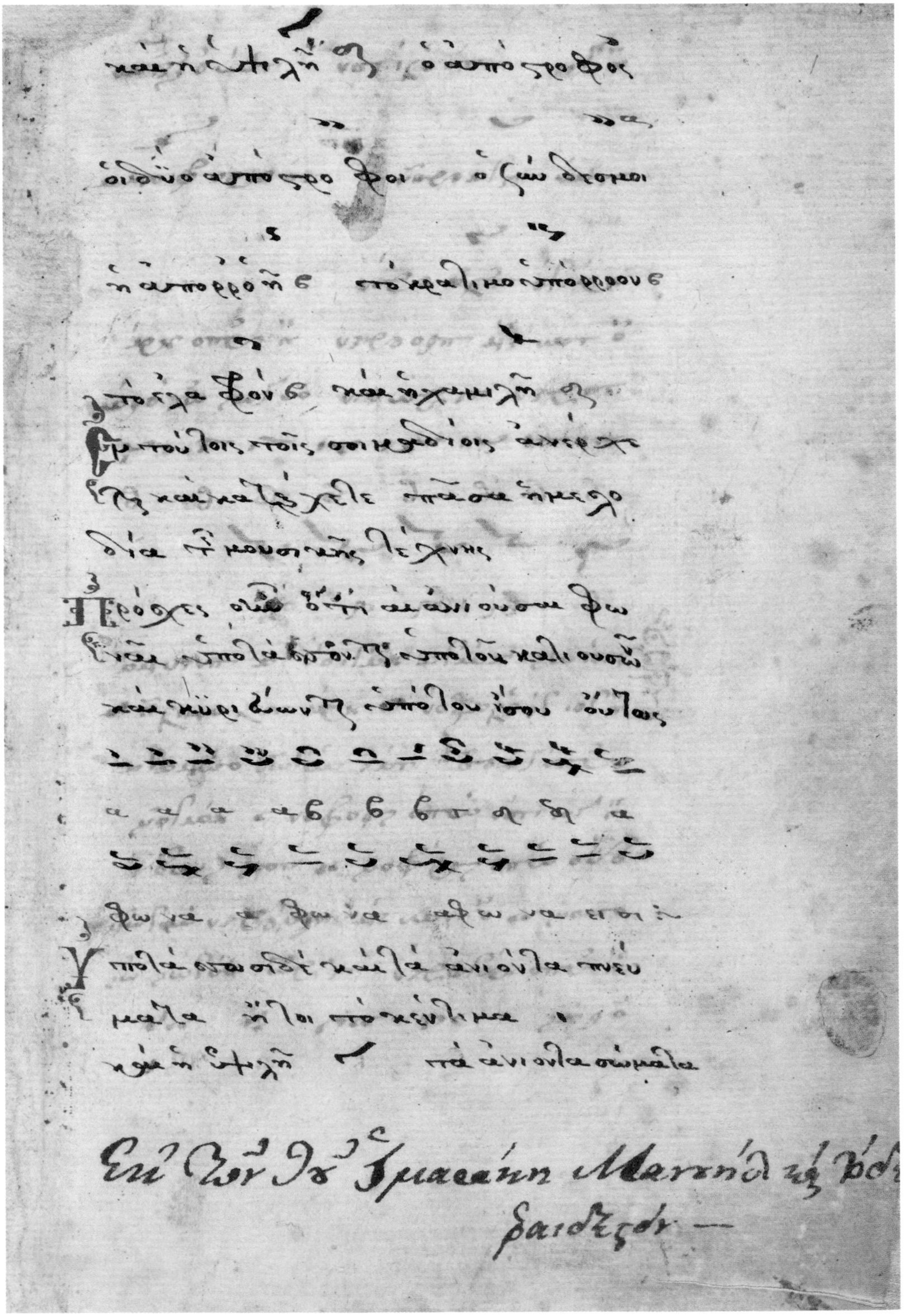

Figure II. Gennadius MSS 24 (A.D. 1734), folio 5r contains a *protheoria* with ktitoric notes about the manuscript's ownership.

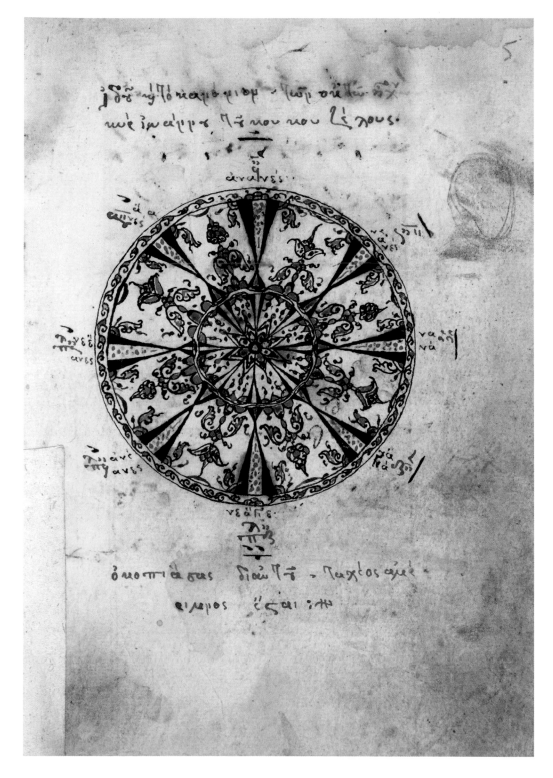

Figure 12. Gennadius MSS Kyriazes 25 (A.D. 1777), folio 25r. Shown here is the wheel-shaped *kanonion* of the eight modes of Joannes Koukouzeles. The inscription reads: ὁ κοπιάσας δι' αὐτοῦ, ταχέος ἀμέριμνος ἔσται (= he who struggles with this will soon be free from care).

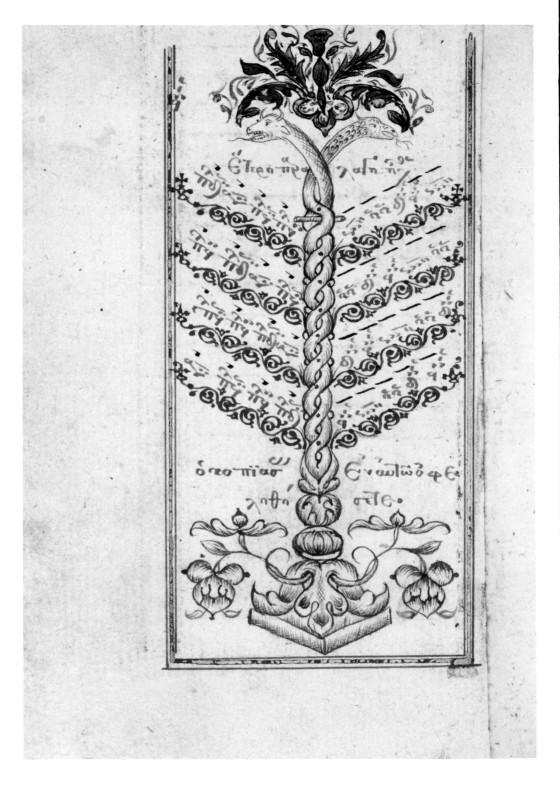

Figure 13. Gennadius MSS 23 (A.D. 1713), folio IIv, another *parallage* diagram, in the form of a tree. The inscription below the branches reads: ὁ κοπιάσας ἐν αὐτῷ ὀφεληθήσετε (= the one who studies this will receive benefit).

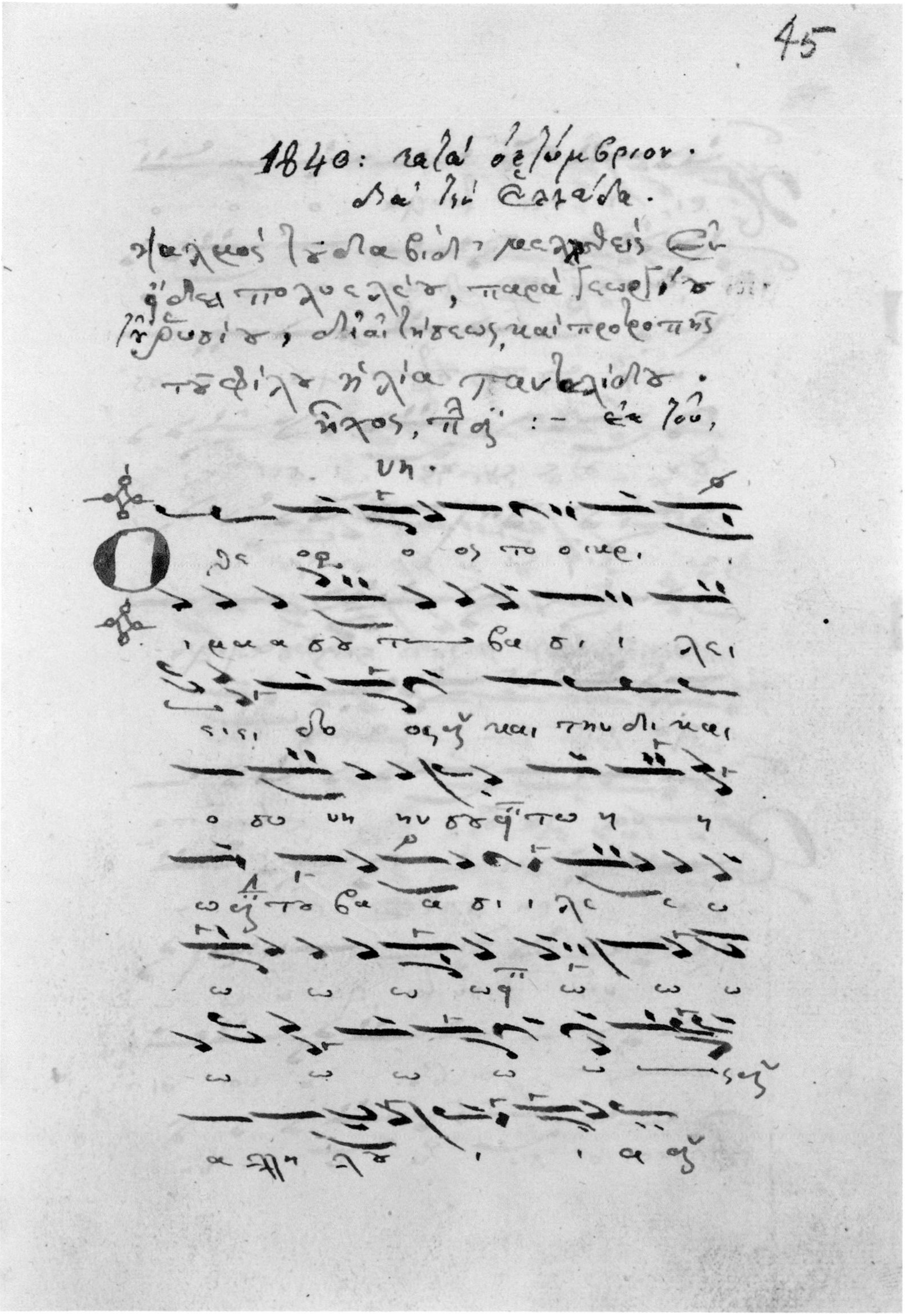

Figure 14. Gennadius MSS 27, folio 45r. This composition by Georgios Rysios, an *ekloge* of the *poly-eleos* using the text of Psalm 71, is dated October 1840 and dedicated "for Hellas" at the request of his friend Elias Tantalides.

Figure 15. Gennadius MSS Kyriazes 31, folio 1r. This collection of doxology compositions and selections for the Divine Liturgy was written before the year 1819.

Figure 16. Gennadius MSS Kyriazes 27, folio 129r. The notation used here is of the exegematic type, the text is from Psalm 118, used in memorial services, and the melody is one still used today.

Figure 17. Gennadius MSS 25, folio 249v, from the year 1777, with a kalophonic heirmos composed by Petros Bereketes.

Figure 18. Gennadius MSS Kyriazes K30. A kalophonic heirmologion written by Athanasios Kalogero-poulos, completed in Constantinople May 23, 1820.

Figure 19. Gennadius MSS Kyriazes K30, folio Ir. A kalophonic heirmologion. The incredibly small yet clear script of the New Method notation is beautifully illustrated in red, gold and black ink.

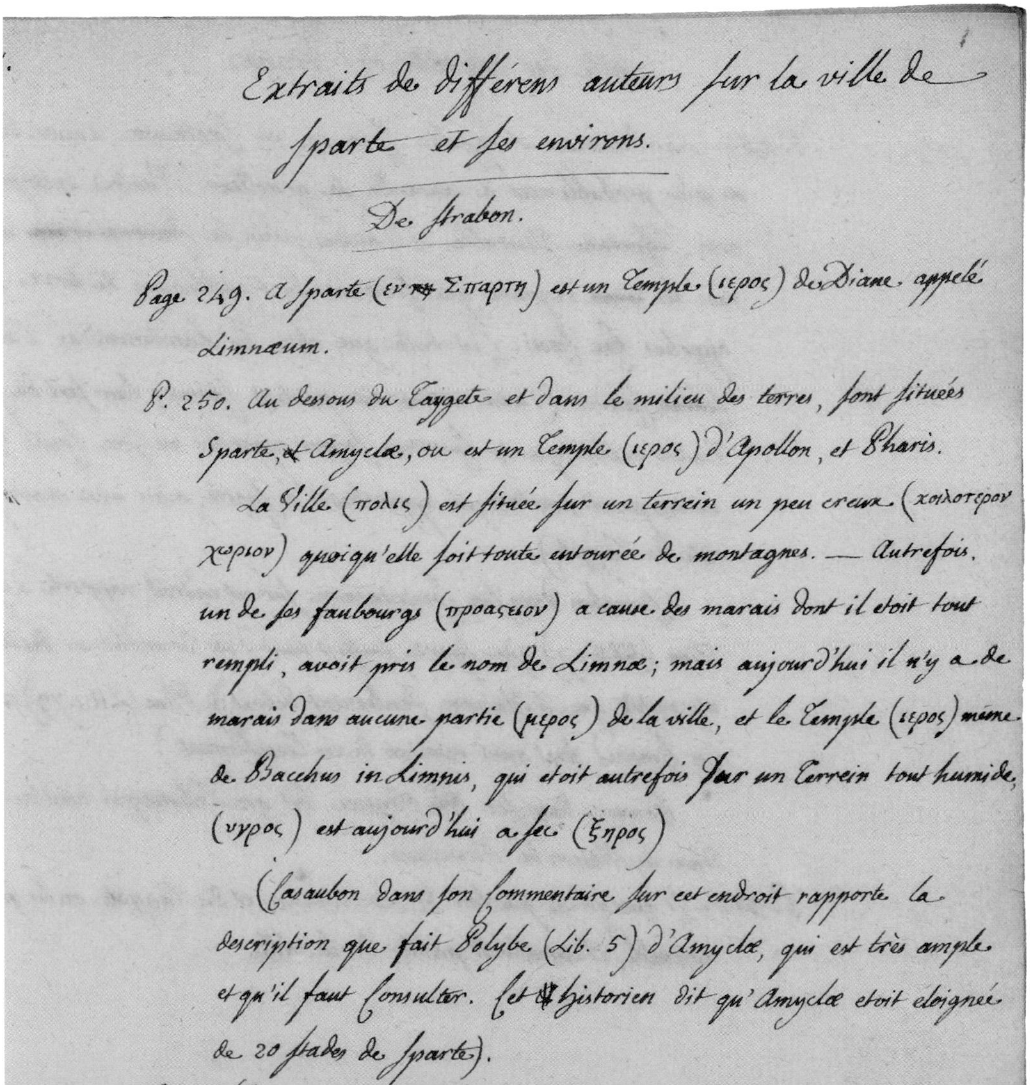

Extraits de différens auteurs sur la ville de
Sparte et ses environs.

De Strabon.

Page 249. A Sparte (εν τη Σπαρτη) est un Temple (ιερος) de Diane appelé
Limnæum.

P. 250. Au dessous du Taygete et dans le milieu des terres, sont situées
Sparte, et Amyclæ, ou est un Temple (ιερος) d'Apollon, et Charis.

La Ville (πολις) est située sur un terrein un peu creux (κοιλοτερον
χωριον) quoiqu'elle soit toute entourée de montagnes. — Autrefois
un de ses faubourgs (προαστειον) à cause des marais dont il étoit tout
rempli, avoit pris le nom de Limnæ; mais aujourd'hui il n'y a de
marais dans aucune partie (μερος) de la ville, et le Temple (ιερος) même
de Bacchus in Limnis, qui étoit autrefois sur un Terrein tout humide,
(υγρος) est aujourd'hui a sec (ξηρος)

(Casaubon dans son Commentaire sur cet endroit rapporte la
description que fait Polybe (Lib. 5) d'Amyclæ, qui est très ample
et qu'il faut Consulter. Cet historien dit qu'Amyclæ étoit éloignée
de 20 stades de Sparte).

P. 251. Casaubon dans son Commentaire sur cette page dit que M

P. 251. Mesoa ainsi que Limnæum, ne sont pas des Contrées (χωραι),
mais des quartiers (μερος) de Sparte. (au sujet de Mesoa Casaubon
renvoye à Etienne de Byzance).

P. 252. Ephorus rapporte que l'on avoit élevé un Temple (ιερος) a Lycurgue
où l'on sacrifioit tous les ans.

Figure 20. Notebook of Barbié du Bocage with notes about excerpts from ancient writers.

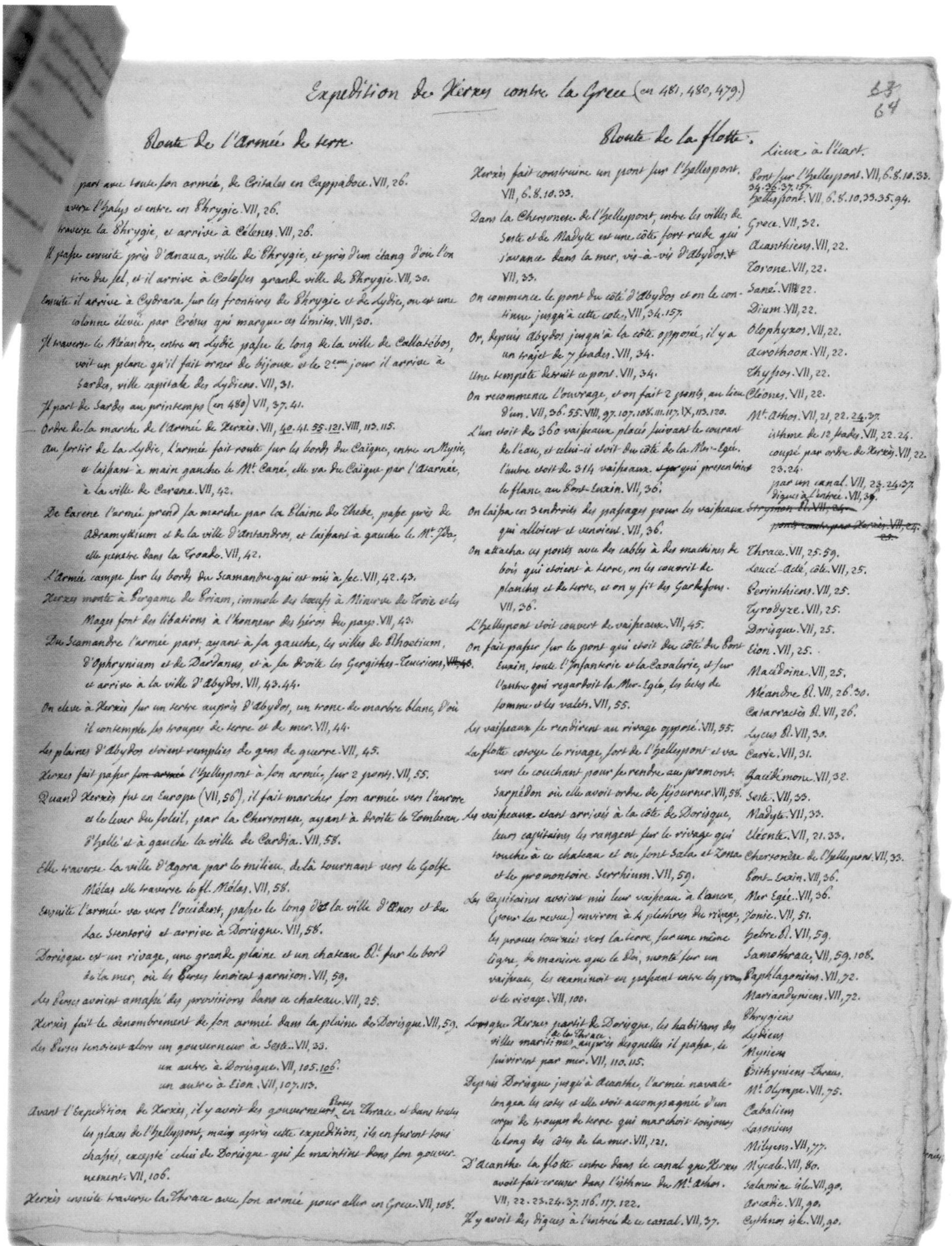
Expedition de Xerxes contre la Grece (en 481, 480, 479.)

63
64

Route de l'Armée de terre

... part avec toute son armée, de Critales en Cappadoce. VII, 26.
... averse l'Halys et entre en Phrygie. VII, 26.
... traverse la Phrygie, et arrive à Célenes. VII, 26.
Il passe ensuite près d'Anaua, ville de Phrygie, et près d'un étang d'où l'on tire du sel, et il arrive à Colosses grande ville de Phrygie. VII, 30.
Ensuite il arrive à Cydrara sur les frontieres de Phrygie et de Lydie, où est une colonne élevée par Crésus qui marque ces limites. VII, 30.
Il traverse le Méandre, entre en Lydie passe le long de la ville de Callatébos, voit un plane qu'il fait orner de bijoux et le 2.eme jour il arrive à Sardes, ville capitale des Lydiens. VII, 31.
Il part de Sardes au printemps (en 480) VII, 37. 41.
Ordre de la marche de l'Armée de Xerxès. VII, 40. 41. 55. 121. VIII, 113. 115.
Au sortir de la Lydie, l'armée fait route sur les bords du Caïque, entre en Mysie, et laissant à main gauche le Mt Cané, elle va du Caïque par l'Atarnée, à la ville de Carane. VII, 42.
De Carene l'armée prend sa marche par la Plaine de Thebe, passe près de Adramyttium et de la ville d'Antandros, et laissant à gauche le Mt Ida, elle penetre dans la Troade. VII, 42.
L'Armée campe sur les bords du Scamandre qui est mis à sec. VII, 42. 43.
Xerxes monte à Pergame de Priam, immole des boeufs à Minerve de Troie et les Mages font des libations à l'honneur des héros du pays. VII, 43.
Du Scamandre l'armée part, ayant à sa gauche, les villes de Rhoetium, d'Ophrynium et de Dardanus, et à sa droite les Gergithes-Teucriens, ~~VII, 43.~~ et arrive à la ville d'Abydos. VII, 43. 44.
On eleve à Xerxès sur un tertre auprès d'Abydos, un trone de marbre blanc, d'où il contemple ses troupes de terre et de mer. VII, 44.
Les plaines d'Abydos étoient remplies de gens de guerre. VII, 45.
Xerxes fait passer ~~son armée~~ l'Hellespont à son armée, sur 2 ponts. VII, 55.
Quand Xerxès fut en Europe (VII, 56), il fait marcher son armée vers l'aurore et le lever du soleil, par la Chersonese, ayant à droite le Tombeau d'Hellé et à gauche la ville de Cardia. VII, 58.
Elle traverse la ville d'Agora par le milieu, de là tournant vers le Golfe Mélas elle traverse le fl. Mélas. VII, 58.
Ensuite l'armée va vers l'occident, passe le long de la ville d'Œnos et du Lac Stentoris et arrive à Dorisque. VII, 58.
Dorisque est un rivage, une grande plaine et un chateau R.^l sur le bord de la mer, où les Perses tenoient garnison. VII, 59.
Les Perses avoient amassé des provisions dans ce chateau. VII, 25.
Xerxès fait le denombrement de son armée dans la plaine de Dorisque. VII, 59.
Les Perses tenoient alors un gouverneur à Seste. VII, 33.
un autre à Dorisque. VII, 105. 106.
un autre à Eion. VII, 107. 113.
Avant l'Expedition de Xerxès, il y avoit des gouverneurs Perses en Thrace et dans toutes les places de l'Hellespont, mais après cette expedition, ils en furent tous chassés, excepté celui de Dorisque qui se maintint dans son gouvernement. VII, 106.
Xerxès ensuite traverse la Thrace avec son armée pour aller en Grece. VII, 108.

Route de la flotte.

Xerxès fait construire un pont sur l'Hellespont. VII, 6. 8. 10. 33.
Dans la Chersonese de l'Hellespont, entre les villes de Seste et de Madyte est une côte fort rude qui s'avance dans la mer, vis-à-vis d'Abydos. VII, 33.
On commence le pont du côté d'Abydos et on le continue jusqu'à cette cote. VII, 34. 157.
Or, depuis Abydos jusqu'à la côte opposée, il y a un trajet de 7 stades. VII, 34.
Une tempete detruit ce pont. VII, 34.
On recommence l'ouvrage, et on fait 2 ponts, au lieu d'un. VII, 36. 55. VIII, 97. 107. 108. 111. 117. IX, 113. 120.
L'un etoit de 360 vaisseaux placés suivant le courant de l'eau, et celui-ci etoit du côté de la Mer-Egée. l'autre etoit de 314 vaisseaux. ~~...~~ qui presentoient le flanc au Pont-Euxin. VII, 36.
On laissa en 3 endroits des passages pour les vaisseaux qui alloient et venoient. VII, 36.
On attacha ces ponts avec des cables à des machines de bois qui etoient à terre, on les couvrit de planches et de terre, et on y fit des garde-fous. VII, 36.
L'Hellespont etoit couvert de vaisseaux. VII, 45.
On fait passer sur le pont qui etoit du côté du Pont-Euxin, toute l'Infanterie et la Cavalerie, et sur l'autre qui regardoit la Mer-Egée, les betes de somme et les valets. VII, 55.
Les vaisseaux se rendirent au rivage opposé. VII, 55.
La flotte cotoye le rivage, sort de l'Hellespont et va vers le couchant pour se rendre au promont. Sarpédon où elle avoit ordre de séjourner. VII, 58.
Les vaisseaux etant arrivés à la côte de Dorisque, leurs capitaines les rangent sur le rivage qui touche à ce chateau et où sont Sala et Zona et le promontoire Serrhium. VII, 59.
Les Capitaines avoient mis leur vaisseau à l'ancre, (pour la revue) environ à 4 plethres du rivage, les proues tournées vers la terre, sur une même ligne, de maniere que le Roi, monté sur un vaisseau, les examinoit en passant entre les proues et le rivage. VII, 100.
Lorsque Xerxes partit de Dorisque, les habitans des villes maritimes de la Thrace auprès desquelles il passa, le suivirent par mer. VII, 110. 115.
Depuis Dorisque jusqu'à Acanthe, l'armée navale longea les cotes et elle etoit accompagnée d'un corps de troupes de terre qui marchoit toujours le long des côtes de la mer. VII, 121.
D'Acanthe la flotte entre dans le canal que Xerxes avoit fait creuser dans l'isthme du Mt Athos. VII, 22. 23. 24. 37. 116. 117. 122.
Il y avoit des digues à l'entrée de ce canal. VII, 37.

Lieux à l'écart.

Pont sur l'Hellespont. VII, 6. 8. 10. 33. 34. 36. 37. 157.
Hellespont. VII, 6. 8. 10. 33. 35. 94.
Grece. VII, 32.
Acanthiens. VII, 22.
Torone. VII, 22.
Sané. VII, 22.
Dium. VII, 22.
Olophyxos. VII, 22.
Acrothoon. VII, 22.
Thyssos. VII, 22.
Cléones. VII, 22.
Mt Athos. VII, 21, 22. 24. 37.
isthme de 12 stades. VII, 22. 24.
coupé par ordre de Xerxès. VII, 22. 23. 24.
par un canal. VII, 23. 24. 37.
digues à l'entrée. VII, 37.
~~Strymon fl. VII, 24.~~
~~ponts construits par Xerxès. VII, 24. 25.~~
Thrace. VII, 25. 59.
Leucé-Acté, côte. VII, 25.
Perinthiens. VII, 25.
Tyrodyze. VII, 25.
Dorisque. VII, 25.
Eion. VII, 25.
Macédoine. VII, 25.
Méandre fl. VII, 26. 30.
Catarractès fl. VII, 26.
Lycus fl. VII, 30.
Carie. VII, 31.
Lacédémone. VII, 32.
Seste. VII, 33.
Madyte. VII, 33.
Eléonte. VII, 21. 33.
Chersonèse de l'Hellespont. VII, 33.
Pont-Euxin. VII, 36.
Mer Egée. VII, 36.
Ionie. VII, 51.
Hebre fl. VII, 59.
Samothrace. VII, 59. 108.
Paphlagoniens. VII, 72.
Mariandyniens. VII, 72.
Phrygiens
Lydiens
Mysiens
Bithyniens-Thraces.
Mt Olympe. VII, 75.
Cabaliens
Lasoniens
Milyens. VII, 77.
Mycale. VII, 80.
Salamine île. VII, 90.
Arcadie. VII, 90.
Cythnos île. VII, 90.

Figure 21. Notebook of Barbié du Bocage with references to passages from Herodotus.

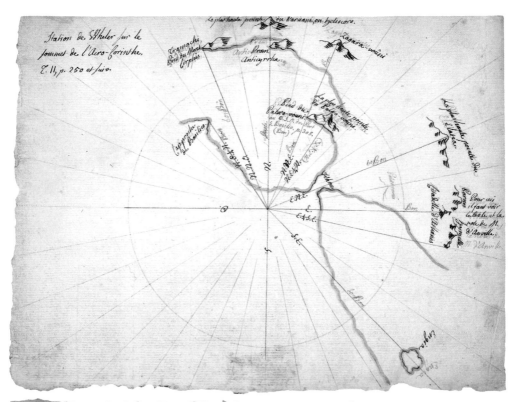

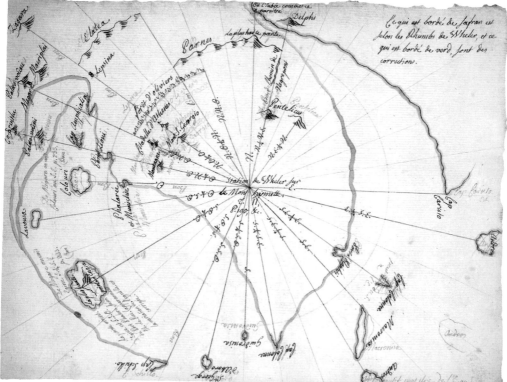

Figure 22. Sketch by Barbié du Bocage used for calculating the latitude of Athens, Acrocorinth, and the Argo-Saronic islands. Gennadius Library MSS 145, p. 59.

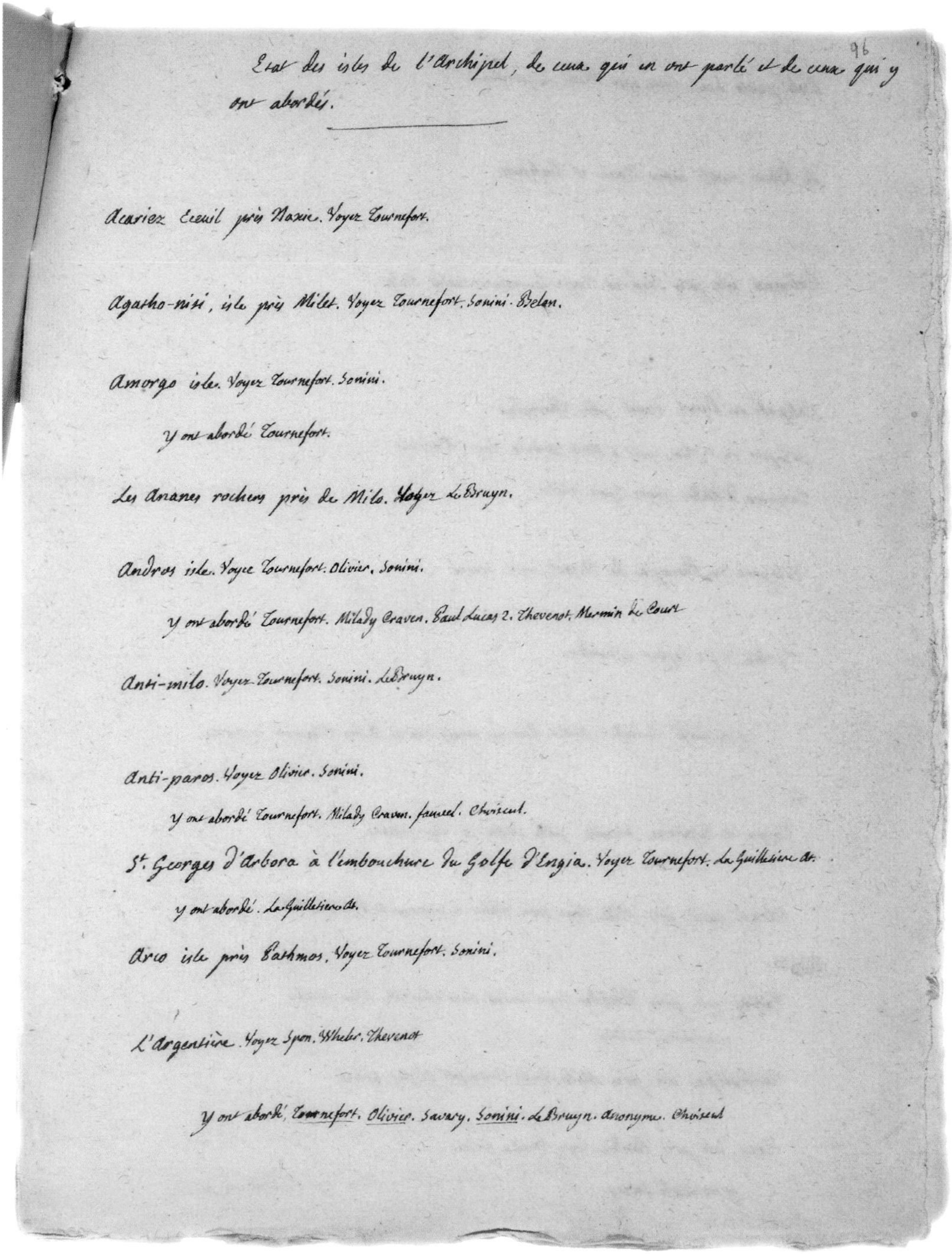

Etat des isles de l'Archipel, de ceux qui en ont parlé et de ceux qui y
ont abordés.

_____

Acariez. Écueil près Naxie. Voyez Tournefort.

Agatho-nisi, isle près Milet. Voyez Tournefort. Sonini. Belon.

Amorgo isle. Voyez Tournefort. Sonini.

　　y ont abordé Tournefort.

Les Ananes rochers près de Milo. Voyez Le Bruyn.

Andros isle. Voyez Tournefort. Olivier. Sonini.

　　y ont abordé Tournefort. Milady Craven. Paul Lucas 2. Thevenot. Mermin de Court

Anti-milo. Voyez Tournefort. Sonini. Le Bruyn.

Anti-paros. Voyez Olivier. Sonini.

　　y ont abordé Tournefort. Milady Craven. fauvel. Choiseul.

St. Georges d'Arbora à l'embouchure du Golfe d'Engia. Voyez Tournefort. La Guillatière &c.

　　y ont abordé. La Guillatière &c.

Arco isle près Bathmos. Voyez Tournefort. Sonini.

L'argentière. Voyez Spon. Wheler. Thevenot

　　y ont abordé. Tournefort. Olivier. Savary. Sonini. Le Bruyn. anonyme. Choiseul

Figure 23. One of Barbié du Bocage's notes, entitled "Extraits des voyages en Orient" (extracts from narratives of travel to the East which describe the Greek Islands). Gennadius Library MSS 140.

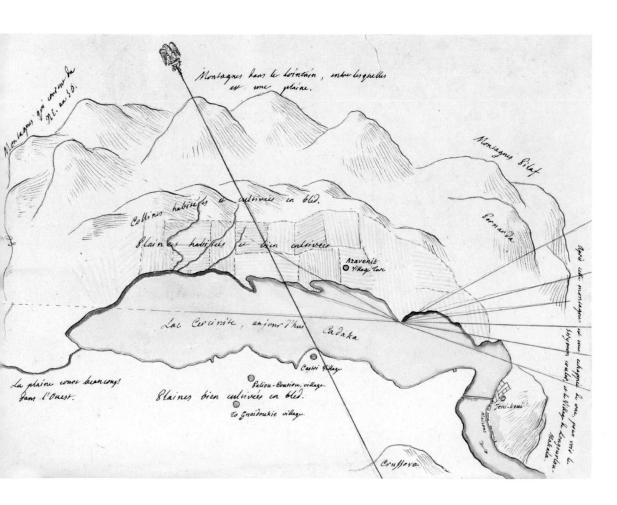

Figure 24. Sketch of the region around Lake Kerkini by Barbié du Bocage. Gennadius Library MSS 140, p. 80.

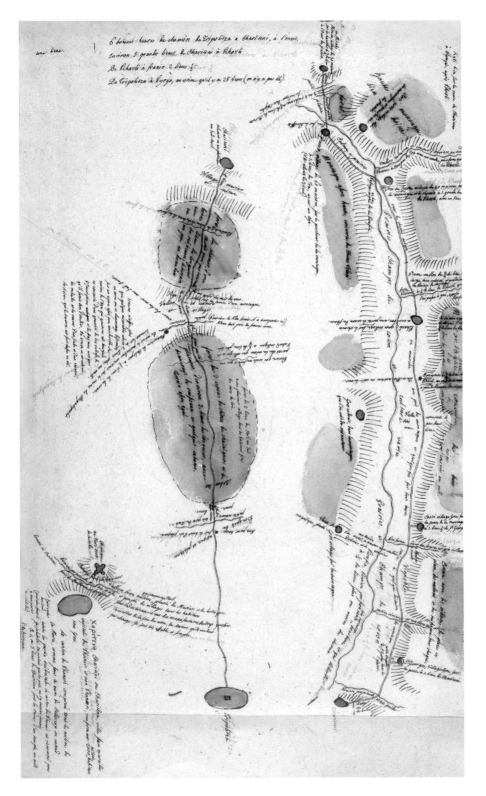

Figure 25. Map by Barbié du Bocage showing the route from Tripolitsa to Karytaina. Gennadius Library MSS 145, p. 78.

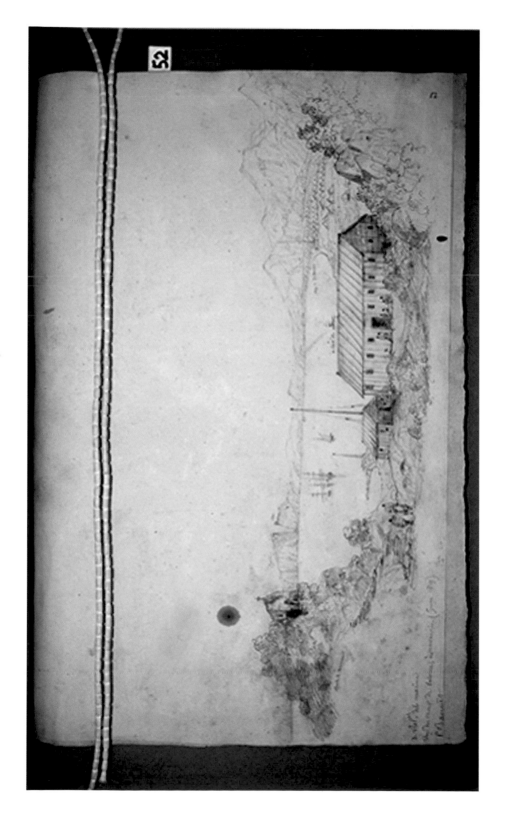

Figure 26. Baccuet drawing no. 52. French military hospital near Yialova. Photo Jennifer Stephens.

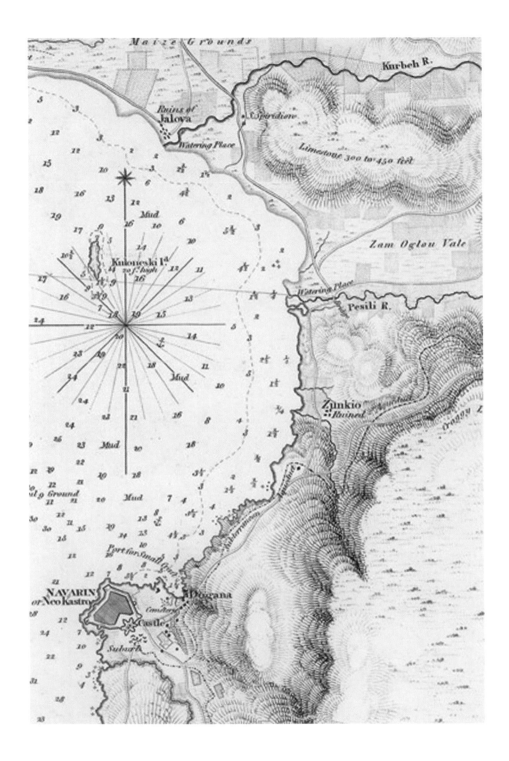

Figure 27. Section of Smyth's map of Navarino (1823). Courtesy National Maritime Museum, London.

Figure 28. View toward Sphacteria and Paleokastro from Ayios Vasilios Ridge. Photo J. L. Davis.

Figure 29. Photograph of Hotel Philip area from "Kuloneski". Photo J. L. Davis.

Figure 30. Bory de St. Vincent, *Atlas*, pl. ix.

Figure 31. Baccuet drawing no. 19. Vignette of woman and child. Photo Jennifer Stephens.

Figure 32. Aqueduct channel beneath road, north of "Hotel Philip." Photo J. L. Davis.

Figure 33. Aqueduct channel next to road, between Vigla and Miden. Photo J. L. Davis.

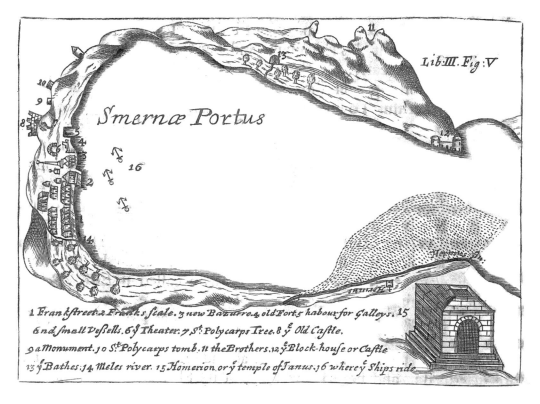

Figure 34. The Bay of Smyrna. Wheler 1682, p. 240.

Figure 35. View of Smyrna from the sea. From the "Album of 18 original drawings in sepia, of views in Phaleron, Sunium, Aegina, Chios, Smyrna, Pergamum" (ca. 1800).

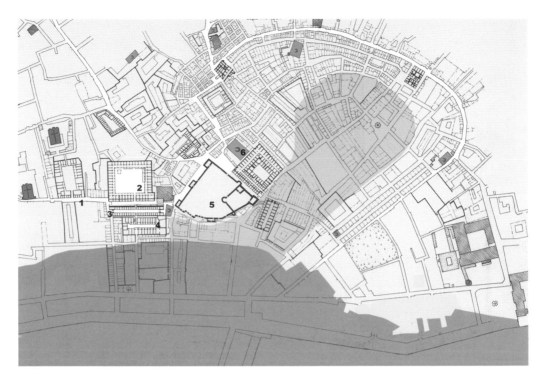

Figure 36. Smyrna, the bazaar and port areas: 1. Frank Street; 2. Vizir Han; 3. Old Bezesten; 4. Han of the Cretans; 5. Crusader Castle; 6. Hissar Mosque. After Müller-Wiener 1980–1981, Plan no. 4

Figure 37. The courtyard of a han. From the "Album of 18 original drawings in sepia, of views in Phaleron, Sunium, Aegina, Chios, Smyrna, Pergamum" (ca. 1800).

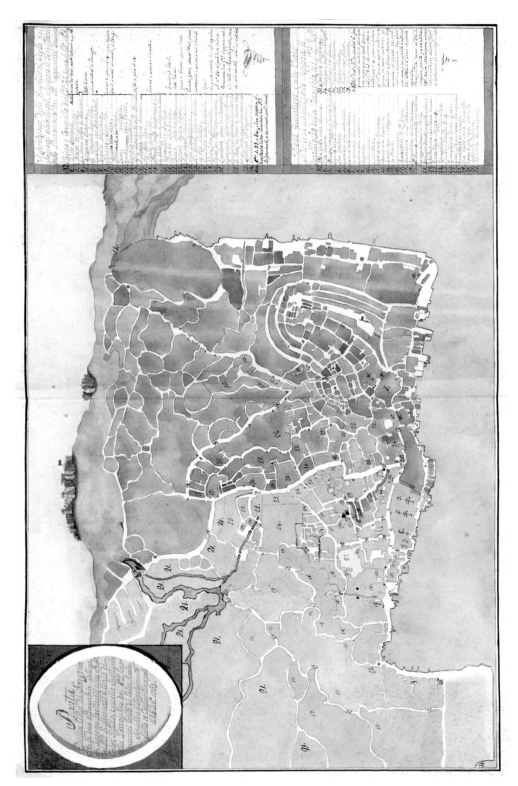

Figure 38. Pianta della Città di Smyrna per le due Parrocchie Latine. . . . Bassi (Bassini?) Piacentiae L'ingegnere Patentato Fecit.

Figure 39. Plan of the City of Smyrna, redrawn by the author; the numbers of the original map's legend have been preserved. After ''Pianta della Città di Smyrna'' (Fig. 38).

Figure 40. Plan of the City of Smyrna, redrawn by the author. After ''Pianta della Città di Smyrna'' (Fig. 38).

CRETE

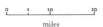

Edward Lear's route in 1864 ------------

0   5   10   20
|----|----|-----------|
         miles

Figure 41. Map of Lear's travels in Crete. After Fowler 1985, pp. 118–119. Courtesy Denise Harvey & Company.

Figure 42. Ruins of Katholiko Monastery, Akrotiri, (drawing 25, April 21). Collection of S. Duckworth.

Figure 43. Mount Psiloritis from Phre (drawing 167, May 25).

Figure 44. Lake Kourna (drawing 77, May 5).

Figure 45. Rethymnon (drawing 90, May 7).

Figure 46. Figures in Hania. Private collection. Courtesy Guy Peppiatt Fine Art Ltd.

142. - AJACCIO (Corse). - Le fond du Golfe

Figure 47: Ajaccio, Corsica : the head of the gulf. Αρχείο Ίωνος Δραγούμη, Ενότητα ΙΒ Αλληλογραφία Οικογενειακή, Εξερχόμενη. Φάκελος 5, Υποφάκελος 3, Καρτ ποστάλ Ίωνος προς την Έφη Καλλέργη, 13 Δεκεμβρίου 1917.

441. - CORSE. - AJACCIO. - Hôtel Continental

Figure 48: Ajaccio, Corsica, Hôtel Continental, Αρχείο Ίωνος Δραγούμη, Ενότητα VI, Φάκελος 45, Αρ. 163.

Figure 49: Dimitrios Gounaris, the Greek priest, Mrs. Pesmazoglou, Ion Dragoumis, and the village's Greek inhabitants, Αρχείο Ίωνος Δραγούμη, Ενότητα VI, Φάκελος 45, Αρ. 187.

Figure 50: The Greek teacher of Cargèse Mr. Peter Ragatsaki Stephanopoli, Ion Dragoumis, Mrs. Pesmazoglou, Dimitrios Gounaris, and Greek inhabitants, Αρχείο Ίωνος Δραγούμη, Ενότητα VI, Φάκελος 45, Αρ. 167.

Figure 51: The Greek priest at Cargèse, Father Kaisaris Kottis, in front of Saint Spyridon, Αρχείο Ίωνος Δραγούμη, Ενότητα VI, Φάκελος 45, Αρ. 193.

Figure 52: The shoe-maker, the old man, Dimitrios Gounaris, Mrs. Pesmazoglou, Ion Dragoumis, the teacher Mr. Peter Ragatsaki Stephanopoli, and some of the village children, Αρχείο Ίωνος Δραγούμη, Ενότητα VI, Φάκελος 45, Αρ. 176.